Market Matters

Applied Rhetoric Studies and Free Market Competition

Research and Teaching in Rhetoric and Composition
Michael M. Williamson and David A. Jolliffe, series editors

Market Matters

Applied Rhetoric Studies and Free Market Competition

edited by

Locke Carter
Texas Tech University

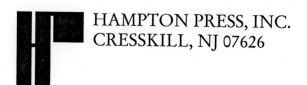
HAMPTON PRESS, INC.
CRESSKILL, NJ 07626

Printed in the United States of America

Library of Congress Cataloging-in-Publication Data

Market matters : applied rhetoric studies and free market competition / edited by Locke Carter.
      p. cm. -- (Research and teaching in rhetoric and composition)
    Includes bibliographical references and indexes.
    ISBN 1-57273-574-0 -- ISBN 1-57273-575-9
    1. English language--Rhetoric--Study and teaching--Economic aspects. 2. Report writing--Study and teaching (Higher)--Economic aspects. 3. Free enterprise. I. Carter, Locke. II. Series.

PE1404.M357 2005
808'.042/0711--dc22
2004060866

Hampton Press, Inc.
23 Broadway
Cresskill, NJ 07626

Contents

Preface

I have long been interested in the way free and efficient markets help organize buyers and sellers, all without the need to have someone planning this activity. *Market* is usually taken to mean only economic activity. But I feel it is useful to expand the term to include not only the mechanisms involving the free exchange of goods and services by people acting in their best interests, but also the processes and mechanisms of the exchange of ideas and arguments, decision-making, and value creation within economic-like, competitive situations. This second sense of *market* captures attitudes and activities that are analogous to economic transactions and which may be described with market terminology and theory. Thus we may speak generally of a *marketplace of ideas* that behaves in many ways like economic markets. And we may also speak specifically of market-like transactions involving assent as the economic currency, as in the statement, "I don't buy his argument."

Free and fair markets function best with a minimum of outside committee guidance, laws, or other sorts of centralized regulation, but this is not to say that free markets seek or require unfettered and opportunistic behavior. Such activity makes markets less efficient and less useful. Truly free markets—those that encourage open competition and respect private property and contracts—not only establish prices, but also formulate policy, decisions, and allocations of resources. In other words, if you imagine any circumstance involving decisions of this sort, there are two opposite approaches to making the decision. One is centralized, planned, legislated, standardized in the form of laws, procedures, central committees, and rules of behavior. The other is decentralized, which means that the interested parties may arrive at a similar, or better quality, decision by submitting the matter to market forces: many people, arguing their interests in a marketplace. In this respect, *laissez-faire* market mechanisms, whether economic or not, serve the interests of democratic principles.

But it is not just capital markets or housing markets that behave this way. Rhetorical activity has many of the same traits. Deliberative rhetoric is activity that helps a group arrive at a decision via argumentation, without having to resort to seeking an authority to make the final decision. In the absence of absolute, knowable truth, judicial rhetoric aims to establish probability of guilt, innocence, liability, and accountability. In both of these discursive situations, the rhetorical activity establishes what amounts to objective decisions and truths without the need for a central authority. Rhetoric is thus a perfect discipline for these relativistic, postmodern times. Truth and certainty may be elusive, but people can arrive at something equally useful through rhetorical activity, through competing arguments in the marketplace of ideas.

Much of the theory underlying composition studies, technical communication, rhetoric, and college English in general comes from a decidedly socialist perspective, one that espouses strong anti-capitalist, anti-competitive sentiments. While members of the academy have learned much about cultural artifacts and practices from these methodologies and critiques, we have also disenfranchised ourselves from the larger world-view—free-market, competitive, and capitalistic. The following book aims to begin filling this gap by asserting a theoretical and practical stance based on free market mechanisms and behaviors.

Through a variety of approaches—from a broad argument to specific examples of market behaviors, from historical criticism to case studies—we make the case that, despite fears expressed by numerous critics of capitalism, technical communication, rhetoric, and composition retain all their force, rationale, and value when theorized and practiced from a free-market perspective. Specifically, we argue that writing disciplines have market value and that socialist approaches to the fields are not capable of recognizing or promoting this value. It follows, then, that participants in these fields need to begin viewing themselves as market participants instead of sidelined observers.

A second general argument we make in the book is that markets are inherently rhetorical, meaning that they create information, are subject to socially constructed trends, and persuade and communicate values and ideas. In other words, the market is not something "out there," belonging to someone else's field, but is a natural and logical domain for rhetorical study and participation.

Finally, a third general argument we promote in the following chapters is that certain activities, distance education foremost among them, create value for these academic fields. If we see our fields as having market value, we do not need to view distance education as a threat to writing disciplines, but rather an opportunity for growth and improvement.

AUDIENCE

This book contains chapters about composition, technical communication, writing programs, distance education, and English studies. This diversity is by design. In selecting essays for this book, I was less interested in particular subsets of rhetoric than I was in the stance communicators take towards competition. Accordingly, the book has been crafted for rhetoricians, communicators, practitioners, teachers, researchers, and writing specialists — theoretical and practical — who are interested in diverse approaches to their fields.

Many in the audience may assume that we humanist academics are supposed to operate under principles different from those for which we argue in the book, principles that involve keeping greedy people honest and pointing out the ways the market exploits its participants. In other words, our mission is to be the watchdogs of society.

But such an approach demands that we stand outside of the system, to function as some kind of external reality check against the "other." This attitude of being outside is precisely the stance I argue against in the first chapter. I do appreciate these voices, however — you can hear them in protests at global economic summits and in conference presentations at the MLA — they provide a constant reminder of Quixotic desires for a balance that will never be. They give us the romantic song of the poet who argues that things *could be different* if we could just change the fabric of reality. These voices are influential and form the basis of much of our postmodernist rhetorical tradition. Indeed, they provide a grounding for what I call in Chapter 1 the critical dimension of rhetoric. It is to complement these voices that I have sought to develop the following collection of essays as a way of augmenting their critical humanism and moving towards a realm of value creation and productivity.

After the page proofs for this book were produced, an article by Marc Bousquet* appeared in *College English* regarding the academic job market. While this preface is not the right place for a full response to the article, it is worth a quick comment since one of the foundations of this book is that markets do matter. Bousquet deserves thanks for his insightful analysis of the academic job market and its historical proponents. His argument that academic job markets are illusory, even though we all pretend that they behave like markets, is dead-on accurate. The system under which we academics operate resides in the gray middle ground of markets because it is neither a truly free market nor a strong central plan. For Bousquet, the

---

*Bousquet, Marc. "The Rhetoric of 'Job Market' and the Reality of the Academic Labor System." *College English* 66.2 (November 2003), pp. 207-28.

solution to the problem of "casualized" labor involves central planning, an approach that invokes old-style collectivist planning, entitlement, protection, less competition, and controlled salaries.

But centralization is not the only way to fix bad systems. We may also look to market mechanisms to provide an alternative solution. Instead of trying to force more centralization into an already broken system, the alternative approach (and probably more successful) would be to encourage a truly free market of academic labor. A free market would identify and quantify the value of teachers, researchers, and administrators through competition for talent and through removing impediments to such information creation in place today.

Free markets require ample information to be efficient, and many things stand in the way of full and free information in the so-called academic job markets. The centralized mentality of the MLA and its "job information list" is one such impediment, for efficient markets should be operating year-round, decentralized. Why should a school or an instructor wait for a "job season" if there is a need to be filled? Another impediment to an efficient market is tenure: the six years assistant professors operate under junior probation are six years where these professor are NOT on the market. Their value is invisible and this invisibility helps keep salaries artificially low.

A free-market system would embrace competition rather than shying away from it; this competition would raise salaries and identify value in ways that central planning cannot. It is true that there would be more availability of, and competition for, academic labor, but a free market would also mean that there are more students available. In such an era of globalization of academics, surplus labor can find opportunities that a protectionist philosophy cannot. The free market I envision would hold no one captive and underpaid.

Technology is already helping to break down these protectionist barriers. Academic departments can advertise a job whenever it becomes available instead of having to list with the MLA. In fact, for the fields of applied rhetoric, we are seeing the end of MLA hegemony regarding our jobs: rhetoric programs are already supplementing the job information list with their own advertising and are increasingly likely to participate in the MLA December job interview process only when it is more efficient to do so. Technology is also creating teaching opportunities off site so that the casualized labor Bousquet champions is free to "go" wherever the jobs are: online, offshore, and outsourced. Nearly universal internet access and innovative restructurings of labor practices are making it look more and more likely that a broad and efficient marketplace of writing labor will emerge with five years, thus enabling the widespread outsourcing of first year composition.

GENERAL ORDER OF CHAPTERS

The book begins with the more theoretical chapters and progresses towards case studies and specific activities. We begin with an introduction to market terms and an argument for why markets matter to rhetoricians. Next we proceed to three chapters that deal with impediments to progress towards a market perspective about applied rhetoric. The book ends with seven examples of the role of the marketplace in applied rhetoric studies.

Acknowledgements

I am indebted to the many people who helped develop the ideas in this book. At the earliest stages of this project, Gerald Pike, Alejandro Zubia, and my University of Texas buddies, the Outliers, acted as critical sounding boards for my ill-formed thoughts. I thank them for listening and for asking tough questions at the right times. I am particularly grateful to Courtland Huber, who introduced me to the intellectual and scholarly side of the market in the form of the economists Arthur Seldon and Fredrick Hayek.

I would also like to acknowledge those who sparred with me in e-mail lists after I had sent out the call for papers, most notably Anthony Chiaviello, John McLaughlin, and John Ronan. These early e-mail arguments helped me recognize the level and nature of discussion and controversy the book would generate and directed me to the early "ah-hah" revelation that we tend to fall back on socialist theories to try to explain the value of communicators. As a result of rethinking my rhetorical strategy and giving specific guidance to my essayists, the book is much stronger.

As I began sifting through chapter submissions and crafting the ideas that appear in Chapter 1, I benefited from steady feedback from visitors to my office and students in my classes. I owe a great debt of thanks to my graduate students at Texas Tech for engaging me and my ideas. They watched me fill white board with Venn diagrams and project deadlines slowly over two years and tolerated my ramblings on the work in progress.

This volume's ideas have evolved through answering their arguments and objections. These ideas have percolated through rationales for graduate courses, conference presentations, grant proposals, and casual conversations. They have been at the very heart of the lengthy process of proposing to offer the Texas Tech doctoral degree in Technical Communication and Rhetoric via distance education, and were one of the keys to winning approval for that program. I have tried to incorporate all those conversations and processes into this book. After the first draft of the manuscript was complete, the conversation got ratcheted up a notch with the publisher's anonymous reviewers, who deserve thanks for not only recommending that the book be published, but also giving me and my writers excellent suggestions about scope, tone, and argumentation. The shape of the book is due in no small part to their thoughtful criticism.

David Jolliffe and Michael Williamson, the series editors, deserve special thanks for taking a chance with this project and for encouraging me to continue developing the manuscript. And I am especially happy to have worked with Hampton's Barbara Bernstein, who has been helpful, prodding, and informative (at different times, always in the right measure and timing).

I must also thank the English Department at Texas Tech University for its steady support and its occasional leave of absence, both of which have helped me to develop and finish this project. My Rhetoric and Technical Communication colleagues at Texas Tech—Ken Baake, Craig Baehr, Thomas Barker, Sam Dragga, Angela Eaton, Fred Kemp, Miles Kimball, Amy Koerber, Susan Lang, Rich Rice, Rebecca Rickly, Kirk St. Amant, and Sean Zdenek—embody an entrepreneurial faculty, and I have had the lucky opportunity to be a part of its innovative and progressive actions. They are living proof that you do not have to go to industry to find superb examples of value creation.

I owe a special debt of thanks to Carolyn Rude and Fred Kemp, who encouraged me to pursue this project and who returned my first complete draft to me filled with editorial, stylistic, and argumentative recommendations. They have been, and will continue to be, my most valued mentors and friends in the academy.

Finally, I must thank my wife and colleague, Rebecca Rickly, who read many drafts of my introduction, my prospectus, and the essays as I was editing them. While I am sure she grew sick of my talk about value and markets and applied rhetoric, she added immeasurable value to my work in the form of friendly arguments, forwarded e-mails of interest, and at least one of the essays that was developed in her graduate seminar. My two boys, Landon and Ellis, are far too young to have helped directly, but I have learned a lot about markets by watching with great interest their inclinations and communication strategies in negotiating trades.

Locke Carter
Lubbock, Texas, 2005

Notes on Contributors

Locke Carter is an assistant professor of rhetoric and technical communication at Texas Tech University, where he teaches undergraduate and graduate courses in argumentation, hypertext, usability research, publication management, and rhetoric and technology. His work appears in *Computers and Composition, Technical Communication*, and the forthcoming Baywood books edited by Cook and Grant-Davie on distance education, and Thatcher and Evia on outsourcing issues in technical writing. As director of usability research, he is currently investigating the role of video in reporting usability test findings to clients in a 2005 article in *Technical Communication*. He received both his MBA and his PhD in rhetoric from the University of Texas at Austin.

Kristine Hansen is Professor of English at Brigham Young University, where she has directed both the English composition and the writing-across-the-curriculum programs. She frequently teaches undergraduate and graduate courses in writing, rhetorical history, and theory and research methods in composition and rhetoric. Her recent publications include an essay on AP credit in the *WPA Journal* and a chapter on religious freedom in *Religious Faith in the Writing Classroom* (vander Lei & Kyburz, editors). With Joseph Janangelo, she co-edited a collection of essays by and about WPAs, *Resituating Writing: Constructing and Administering Writing Programs*. Her textbook, *Writing in the Social Sciences: A Rhetoric with Readings*, is now in its second edition. She is a member of the Council of Writing Program Administrators, NCTE, and CCCC. She served as a member of the Executive Committee of WPA from 1994-97 and currently serves on the editorial board of the *WPA Journal*.

H. Brooke Hessler is Eleanor Lou Carrithers Chair of Writing and Composition at Oklahoma City University. In addition to teaching undergraduate and graduate courses in rhetoric, composition, and organizational culture and communication, she serves as Director of the Graduate

Certificate in Professional and Technical Writing. Her writing on institutional rhetoric and writing program trends has appeared in the *Journal of Language and Learning Across the Disciplines* and in several edited collections. She is currently researching the intersections between academic capitalism, plagiarism, and distance learning.

Fred Kemp is an associate professor of English at Texas Tech University and has written and presented extensively on computer-based writing instruction and innovation in university composition programs. He has also written award-winning software for peer-interactive writing instruction and administrative processes and is one of the chief designers and implementors of Texas Tech's unique but controversial first-year composition program, ICON.

Susan Lang is an associate professor of rhetoric and composition at Texas Tech University, where she is co-director of composition. She teaches undergraduate and graduate courses in computer-based instruction in composition and literature, intellectual property issues, hypertext, and textual theory. Her articles on intellectual property and electronic dissertations have appeared in *College English* and *Computers and Composition*. Her most recent essay appears in Cook and Grant-Davie's forthcoming collection *Online Education: Global Questions, Local Answers*.

Barry Maid is Professor and Head of Faculty of Technical Communication at Arizona State University East where he recently helped to develop their new program in Multimedia Writing and Technical Communication. Until January 2000, he taught writing at the University of Arkansas at Little Rock, where he had been WPA of the first-year composition program as well as English department chair over the course of nearly 20 years at the university. He is currently the co-editor of the *WPA Journal* and is a frequent presenter at conferences like Computers and Writing, the Association of Teachers of Technical Writing, the National Council of Teachers of English, and the Conference on College Composition and Communication. His most recent essay appears in Hardin and Wallace's 2004 collection *The Twenty-First Century English Department: A Delicate Balance* (Mellen Press).

Yvonne Merrill, PhD in rhetoric and composition, teaches writing, first-year composition to graduate and professional business and technical writing, at the University of Arizona, Tucson, AZ. She has been in the English Department for eighteen years, following twenty years as a high school English, French, and political science teacher. Her research and writing focus on how perceptual reality is socially constructed through language, determining what we can know, and especially what historic women have been able to know. Her work combines her specialization in rhetoric with philosophy, psychology, history, sociology, and linguistics.

Patrick Moore received his PhD in English from the University of Minnesota. He teaches English at the University of Arkansas at Little Rock, where he studies how cultural capitalists dominate other workers. He has been president of the Arkansas chapter of the Society for Technical Communication four times, and has received the STC's Distinguished Chapter Service Award. His most recent essay, "Questioning the Motives of Technical Communication and Rhetoric: Steven Katz's 'Ethic of Expediency'," was published in *JTWC* early in 2004. His essay on Carolyn Miller's "Humanistic Rationale for Technical Writing" is forthcoming in 2005 in the same journal.

Keith Rhodes moved from commercial litigation into composition and rhetoric and then back to practicing law. During his stay in academe, he earned a masters and doctorate focusing on composition, coordinated composition at Northwest Missouri State University, and directed Developmental Writing at Missouri Western State College. His publications focused on tempering theoretical excess and negotiating the practical complexities of academic management. The highlight of his career, however, was playing bass in the Composition Blues Band.

Michael J. Salvo is assistant professor of professional and technical writing in the Rhetoric and Composition program at Purdue University, where he teaches undergraduate and graduate classes in rhetorical theory, workplace writing, and information architecture and design. His articles have appeared in *Journal of Business and Technical Communication, Technical Communication Quarterly, Computers and Composition,* and *Kairos,* for which he was managing editor during the journal's first two years of publication. His work positions technical and professional communicators as leaders in the postindustrial workplace. He is currently at work on a book exploring hypermedia databases and the role that technology plays in remediating historical narrative.

Donna Spehar is a doctoral candidate in the technical communication and rhetoric program at Texas Tech University. While pursuing her graduate education in the Teaching of Writing at Southern Illinois University Edwardsville, she participated in a national collaborative writing project, the *Virtual Classroom,* which linked students in writing classes across the nation. Her dissertation, "Distance Education: Politics of the Interface," examines issues in graduate-level distance education.

Marian G. Stone is an Associate Professor of Multimedia Writing and Technical Communication at Arizona State University East's Polytechnic Campus. She has taught engineering and technical communication, intermediate engineering design, technical editing, multimedia writing, visual communication, proposal writing, writing for technical publication, and business reports. Her expertise is in intergroup communication, diversity education in a global world, and Holocaust education. She was recently invited to present at the Conference on Intergroup Communication, Conflict and Hate Crime: Implications for Research, Education Training and Public Policy. She is a founding faculty member at ASU East and a founding Commissioner on the Town of Gilbert's Commission on Human Relations.

1

Rhetoric, Markets, and Value Creation

An Introduction and Argument for a Productive Rhetoric

Locke Carter

Texas Tech University

We live in a new era, a time of virtual companies, distance education, a distributed workforce, and communication technologies that continue to evolve. Called by various writers postmodern, post-Fordist, post- or late-capitalist, this era is characterized by abundant technology, speed and fluidity of information, self-reflexive study of processes, and a shift from industrial to information-based economies. Such a society is also, as Peter Drucker points out, ever more competitive:

> The knowledge society will inevitably become *far more competitive* than any society we have yet known—for the simple reason that with knowledge being universally accessible, there are no excuses for non-performance. There will be no "poor" countries. There will only be ignorant countries. And the same will be true for individual companies, individual industries, and individual organizations of any kind. It will be true for the individual, too. In fact, developed societies have already become infinitely more competitive for the individual than were the societies of the early twentieth century—let alone earlier societies, those of the nineteenth or eighteenth centuries. (308)

This increased level of competition also affects higher education, perhaps even more so than society in general. Education has undergone tremendous changes in the past 20 years in response to shifts in funding, society, and internal operations. Academic programs are no longer insulated from these societal changes and find that they must compete for money, students, space, time, and other resources necessary to stay in operation.

It is appropriate that academic communicators should be interested in these topics. The mindset needed to navigate this transformation and to create value in the new economy involves critical understanding of the means of production, the dissemination and reception of information, and the way organizations and project groups use information intelligently. It involves massaging, presenting, tweaking, delivering, revising, critiquing, and customizing information. The field of rhetoric is ideally suited for these tasks by virtue of its insistence on analytical skills, its productive focus, and its orientation to the concept of audience.

Rhetoric is fundamentally about two things: analysis and production. Analytically, rhetoric is about applying the razor-sharp theories to existing sign systems: advertising, speeches, sermons, social systems, and gender relations. On the production side, rhetoric is about making speeches, constructing solid arguments, making brochures and manuals, crafting all sorts of rhetorical artifacts, and persuading audiences. Rhetoric is also fundamentally sensitive to the marketplace. Practitioners of rhetoric know that the goods and services they produce for rhetorical audiences are implicitly in competition with other messages. We know how effective the message is by whether it achieves its goals in the marketplace of ideas. In other words, an idea does not have intrinsic value, but gains cultural capital based on how effectively it matches a particular community's values. Unlike many technical fields, success for the rhetorical disciplines is not gauged by the quality of the material, but by its reception and its use. In this fundamental way, markets for goods and services are very similar to rhetorical markets. In fact, this new society and new economy should be the age of rhetoric. In the information age, where communication is at the core of almost all new-era activities like teambuilding, knowledge management, customer relations, rapid development, supply chain management, and just-in-time purchasing, benefits should accrue to those who theorize, practice, and teach effective communication.

But instead of being at the heart of the knowledge economy, communicators are generally perceived, inside and outside, as tool-wielders, translators, or critics. I have spent my academic life within academic programs of rhetoric of one form or another, all housed in departments of English. I am concerned that their histories, philosophies of language, and their general theoretical and ideological bent not only fails to equip them with what is needed to adapt to the changing society but also actually hampers our understanding of competition in communication.

In English studies, we do not generally incorporate any sense of value or value-creation into our theories of language, thereby making it very difficult to teach and comprehend how messages might compete for value in a free market—either the actual economic free market or the more metaphoric concept of a free market of ideas. This attitude comes from a variety of places—from current literary theory, which privileges Marxist, feminist, poststructuralist, and other postmodernist approaches to language, to a general romantic attitude about the past: past literature, past ivy-covered towers, past academic practices. It is telling that James Aune, in lamenting the demise of the study of Marxism, finds only one bright spot, our departments: "Virtually the only place where Marxism today possesses unquestioned prestige is in the literature departments of universities in the Western democracies" (144). As I argue here, these critical and humanistic approaches to literature and language have been highly beneficial to rhetoric, but in and of themselves, they are not enough to serve our fields' expansion into this new era. Our pedagogical, critical, and curricular stance is outside the economy, looking in to criticize any one of a hundred faults in the system, rather than being already inside the economy, creating value.

Not only do our theories in the isolation of our departments adapt poorly to this new era, but we—practitioners, teachers, writers—do not do much better. In general, we do not really understand market and market-like activities very well, making it difficult to design our academic programs strategically. Academic programs that focus on applied rhetoric[1]—technical communication and rhetoric and composition, primarily—have begun adjusting in varying degrees to these changes with varying degrees of success.

Following this logic, the main argument I develop in this chapter is that rhetoric programs, involving the study of persuasive messages and how to

---

[1] I use the term *applied rhetoric*, which conflates various communication disciplines, primarily technical communication, rhetoric, and composition, fields that teach and study writing as well as general skills like argumentation and analysis used in generating documents. Although each field has its own methods, its own journals, and its own academic programs, each is a form of rhetoric. For our purposes, they are communication disciplines involving primarily written language. Because the focus of this chapter—and, indeed, the entire book—is on exploring the intersection of market mechanisms with communication fields, I feel that there would be little benefit in attempting to distinguish specific disciplines. A great deal of scholarship on writing, writing theory, and teaching does take place in rhetoric and composition programs and in technical communication programs. But this fact does not diminish the huge amount of communication research that also takes place in programs that emphasize business communication, speech communication, or mass communication, and I do not want to suggest that my focus on English department-related programs is intended to ignore the larger body of communication research. My arguments about value, markets, and competition can be translated easily into these other fields, but I confine the following chapter to applied rhetoric as it generally appears in English departments today. In a similar vein, I call members of these collective fields communicators or rhetors. In an era when we practice and teach information design, information architecture, content management, spoken presentations, web page authoring—all in addition to writing, style, and editing—the label "writer" does not seem up to the task.

create them, are ideally suited to study, teach, and practice competitive, free-market mechanisms. First, these competitive markets are inherently rhetorical, involving complex communications, persuasion, decision making, and knowledge creation. The competitive landscape thus presents us with a rich field to study.

Second (and this claim is the flip side of the first claim), rhetorical communications themselves behave in market-like ways. Thus, competition, markets, resource allocation decisions can provide us with new ways of examining what we do as communicators.

The third claim is normative, that applied rhetoric programs should understand and master markets in order to ensure that we may align our field with society. It may seem like pandering to argue that because the majority of society believes something, our program should believe it, too. But the fact of the matter is that with increased competition for education from online providers, universities, community, and junior colleges, the majority of academic units need to be able to play a good game, and that kind of game does not involve hiding behind esoteric theories that somehow do not need to justify their existence to parents, students, and legislators.

It is true that there has been a great deal of activity in the past decade arguing for new concepts of the communicator. Various writers have argued that this new era calls for refiguring the nature of applied rhetoric. In 2000, Corey Wick argued that knowledge management and the knowledge worker are the new value. Saul Carliner, in 2001, identified information design as the new career path for technical communicators. Bill Hart-Davidson argued in 2001 that the same competencies necessary for the information-technology (IT) revolution are the same ones that applied rhetoric holds dear. And in 1995, in what is probably the most valuable contribution to this discussion, Johndan Johnson-Eilola employed Robert Reich's concept of symbolic-analytic work to identify the new value of rhetoric and argued that such a shift in image allows communicators to "move into a post-industrial model of work that prioritizes information and communication" (1).

In this chapter, I hope to continue and expand this tradition by calling for a re-examination of academic applied rhetoric's stance toward industry, its lineage and pedigree, and role in the new economy's free-market emphasis. Before we begin locating value in any particular re-articulation of rhetoric, composition, or technical communication in this new economy, we must consider both the act of communication and the agents of communication from a free-market, competitive perspective and examine how communicators create value in such a setting. We need to understand how messages compete with each other, to recognize common points of interest at the intersection of the free-market and applied rhetoric from a theoretical, pedagogical, and curricular perspective.

It is a daunting task. So many things need to come first: a definition of markets, an explanation of value and value-creation, a section on the nature of competition. The first half of this chapter identifies and illustrates the relationship between market mechanisms and rhetoric. This theoretical groundwork is designed as an intellectual starting place that can be used to justify existing approaches to new roles for communicators, studies of value creation in communication, and arguments for curricular/pedagogical change in applied rhetoric programs. It is an argument for why the market is an appropriate metaphor by which we achieve an expanded role for communicators and the communication disciplines.

Next, I present my argument for how we can theorize value creation and competitive activity into our self-definitions of rhetoric and rhetorical activities; specifically, viewing applied rhetoric from such a market paradigm leads to an expanded role—a value-creating role—for rhetors. This link is an important part of my argument. One could make the case for an expanded role for communicators without linking such an expansion to the market. Most of the works cited previously make their case by pointing to a different driving force, typically technology, although politics or ethics could serve the purpose equally well. This section argues that humanist, socialist, and literary essentialist foundations to applied rhetoric—although historically and critically essential to the field's growth—are insufficient to provide for full participation in the new economy by communicators. This section ends by proposing a model that accounts for what a free-market viewpoint means for communication practices, theories, pedagogies, and curricula.

Finally, I introduce the chapters that appear in this volume, tying each chapter's thesis to the themes introduced in the current chapter.

The market matters for practitioners, theorists, and students of rhetoric. Applied rhetoric is practiced and taught within a larger context, one that is subject to intense market pressures. Understanding our positions as producers and consumers of resources within that market is critical to formulating strategy and growing into the next century. The new economy's emphasis on communication and knowledge clearly invites rhetoric to a more important role, one at the center of activity. As we examine our own teaching practices, course offerings, and core philosophies, we must bear this invitation in mind. The course of history is not predetermined: If applied rhetoric programs choose to ignore this invitation, focusing instead only on critique or romantic notions of the writer, we may miss the opportunity to help craft this new age, relegated to sitting on the sidelines while other disciplines step in to fill the void. As I argue in this chapter, rhetoric and markets are already remarkably similar endeavors. It remains for us to recognize the similarity in order to capitalize—critically, rigorously—on the opportunities through innovation and entrepreneurship within our fields.

VALUE, COMPETITION, MARKETS, AND RHETORIC

Academic rhetoricians have borrowed methods, techniques, and theories from disciplines as varied as sociology, psychology, linguistics, graphic arts, and philosophy, opening up the field to ethnographic methodology, usability studies, discourse analysis, and approaches to technology, culture, and the relationship between rhetoric and the visual arts. The value of continually triangulating our core approaches to persuasive and informative texts with these other fields is that our teaching, scholarship, and practices are improved as we take the best aspects from these fields and test our field against these other worldviews. At the very least, other fields provide us with metaphors for rhetorical practices, both old and new. A good example is Paul Taylor's 1993 dissertation, which studied "strange attractors" in classroom electronic chat activities, an idea Taylor derived from James Gleick's popular explanation of chaos theory, a new field in physics.

As I began developing the current argument, the field of economics initially seemed to be the best metaphor for the project. The gulf between the "dismal science" of economics and rhetoric is not nearly so large as one would think. One would be advised to read Deirdre McCloskey's excellent work on the role of rhetoric and rhetorical constructs in the field of economics to see how rhetoric may inform other disciplines. If we turn the tables and examine our field(s) through an economic lens, we may use classic economic concepts of equilibrium, supply and demand, and comparative advantage, as well as new concepts like game theory and bioeconomics, in order to examine our own practices—pedagogical, theoretical, and practical.

But economics ultimately seems like a neutral science. True, demand curves and supply/demand equilibrium assume the workings of many participants, but the dynamics of these decisions are all abstracted into lines on a graph. I realized that although economics captures much of what I wanted to argue about applied rhetoric and value, I was more specifically interested in the market mechanisms behind the economics because of the dynamic nature of markets. Marketplaces involve participants making decisions about their resources. As a market participant, one produces and consumes information, interprets signals from other participants, and argues one's case with them in an attempt to arrive at an agreement. These activities also describe rhetoric—rhetors produce information, interpret signals, and create persuasive messages in an attempt to achieve a desired outcome.

One of rhetoric's central concepts is that the audience matters. Speakers adjust their tone and content to the auditor's mood, education level, and motivation. Writers approach their tasks by first conducting an audience analysis. In technical communication, the empirical methodology of usability testing seeks to quantify our users' reactions to the artifacts we produce.

Where the audience meets the rhetor is the marketplace. For this reason, I have gravitated toward the term *markets* to cover a variety of activities in the following chapters. Markets are rhetorical—they are society's rhetorical activity in the economy. They are the manifestation of rhetoric as persuasion in the marketplace. In looking for mainstream rhetoric, we need only to look at markets.

In a competitive environment, units of value (dollars, scholarly articles, units of persuasion) will eventually flow to inevitably to the idea, product, or service that creates the most value for those who adopt the idea, buy the product, or use the service. This inevitability is what Adam Smith described as the "invisible hand" of capitalism—when people make rational choices about how to spend their hard-earned resources, those choices, aggregated in an economy, will reward the most competitive products, services, and ideas. In other words, a marketplace not only helps traders arrive at some kind of agreement, but repeated over many transactions, it also serves as a decision mechanism in which better goods, services, and ideas will be both identified and rewarded.

In order to get into this absolutely key function of communication as determiner of value, we need to first discuss value. The following paragraphs set out to define value as it is used in this chapter and throughout this book, provide a brief review of the literature related to measuring value in communication, and finally offer an explanation of how competition helps to identify value.

Value

In this chapter (and in the rest of the book) *value* means *market value*, which economists define as the most anyone would pay or exchange for a service or a good, given enough information in the marketplace. Thus, value is not something objective or universal, but is located and defined in communities, derived from ample information, ample bidders, and ample competition among them. This market value, or exchange value, gives us a somewhat stable yardstick with which to measure and compare service activities or goods. A thing or an activity may, no doubt, have sentimental value—a photograph or a ride on a train, perhaps—and an economist would certainly not dispute its value. But unless someone would trade something of value for that photograph or train ride, it has no market value. Note that market value does not have to tread over into the realm of monetary policy. I can trade my car for 2-months' rent and there can be little doubt that both the car and the rent had value. In fact, the car has, by virtue of this trade, a value of 2 months' rent, and the rent, by the same reasoning, has the value of half of my car.

Asserting that something has value outside market forces is akin to asserting "my argument is persuasive even though I have not presented it to any auditors."

When something has not been subjected to the market, we do not know its market value. We may know its history, its cost, its budget, or its sentiment, but its economic/market value is unknown. To use an example of salary, if I have always been paid $35,000 to teach, but have not competed in the market with others, then my salary does not necessarily reflect my value. It is somewhat artificial. This is not to say that there is anything "false" or "incorrect" about my salary. In fact, it is historically true that I have earned, and continue to earn, $35,000, and we may further presume that I competed on the market for my job at the time, when $35,000 represented my market value. However, my current market value is the highest amount that someone would be willing to pay for my services today, and that amount cannot be known outside of the marketplace.

If prices are not fixed, then what is the true value of something? Isn't there a solid foundation on which we can determine value? Not really. A key concept in value is that it is subjective and resides in the recipient, not in the seller or provider. As fundamental as this concept is, even economists get confused about the issue, as Peter Drucker chides:

> Every economics book points out that customers do not buy a "product," but what the product does for them. And then, every economics book promptly drops consideration of everything except the "price" for the product, a "price" defined as what the customer pays to take possession or ownership of a thing or a service. What the product does for the customer is never mentioned again. . . . [But value] depends on what the product does for the customer. It depends on what fits his reality. It depends on what the customer sees as "value." (188)

In this regard, the markets should appear very familiar to postmodernists and social constructionists among us. As we know from postmodernism, to seek the fixed is to seek a mirage. In the realm of signs, there is no objective reality, only social constructs. What is good? What is poverty? What is beautiful? All social constructs. It feels like waffling to say "It depends," but that is as close to the truth as we will get. The same applies to the flickering, contingent nature of the value of goods and services. What is this house worth? One could argue that there is $167,000 of materials in the house, but the house's value is not determined by those materials and the labor that went into assembling them. The house's value is determined by the maximum price that someone is willing to pay on the open market, and this price may be $200,000 in our example for a desirable location, or—in a less desirable one—a mere $100,000.

Even in the marketplace of ideas, we see the effects of markets, which we employ to make the best decisions about resources. Textbooks, philosophies, courses, publications, arguments, and students all participate in various academic markets. In fact, any time we talk about scarcity, we can apply market concepts to help us understand how the scarce resources are allocated within a system. As academic units we compete for our inputs (BA, MA, PhD students) both internally (against other colleges and academic departments on campus) and externally (against other universities). We also participate in a competition for our outputs (BA, MA, PhD students) in the form of the job market and the academic job market. In 2004, for example, the job market for technical communication faculty was very strong. There were new programs, and they all needed professors. But there were few producers of those professors. So there might have been 40 jobs available in 2004, but perhaps there were only 10 new PhDs on the market. This situation communicates a great deal to graduate students, to faculty thinking about switching locales, and to programs trying to acquire faculty.

Tenure is a good example of something that participates in this communication process in complicated ways. On the one hand, tenure provides institutions with a probationary period during which they can determine if the new (or apprentice) faculty member will actually live up to their academic and community standards. The process is designed to identify and ensure quality. On the other hand, tenure holds back market forces by keeping the market for professors inefficient. In other words, the job market for PhDs tells us the value of a given professor, but this market comprises only a handful of professors and potential professors. It is only when someone earns tenure that his or her quality is signaled to the marketplace. During one's untenured time, one does not produce salary information in the marketplace. Not only is he or she on probation in the sense of hiring, tenure, and promotion, but also in the sense of being free to capture his or her true economic value. A free-market perspective on this issue would argue for abolishing tenure and encouraging free agents. When everyone in a given job market was a free agent, salary levels would reflect true market values. All of the value that had been previously locked up in artificially low salaries for assistant professors would be freed. And at the same time, salaries for associate and full professors would be free to float with the market.

This subjective nature of value can help explain how noneconomic considerations may be accounted for. After all, there are other kinds of value: emotional, social, ethical, and moral. These values are difficult to quantify and discuss because of their subjective nature. However, when people make decisions about what is valuable to them, these subjective values manifest themselves in those economic decisions. One may assume that these issues are already subsumed in one's decisions. For example, when shopping for a new house, my ultimate decision about the value of a property is based not simply on quantifiable measures like age, quality of roof, insurability, square footage, and proximity to parks and other amenities. I also consider emotional, aesthetic, and social factors like curb appeal, how much the house reminds me of my childhood home, the social makeup of the neighborhood, and so on. These subjective considerations filter into my assessment of the value of the house. Thus, even though market value is "amoral," it does take into consideration various moral, ethical, emotional, and social values.

If value seems rather slippery, then cost is perhaps more concrete. Our discussion of value must also include a discussion of cost, for part of the subjective assessment of value involves cost. All services and goods involve costs, even if they are not monetary. And it is similarly important to distinguish value from cost: they are not equivalent. At the broadest, we can conceive of value as an equation:

$$\text{Value} = \text{potential benefits} - \text{drawbacks or opportunity costs}$$

The cost of a good or service is simply the sum of all its inputs, such as materials, labor, and advertising. Although the concept is simple, determining precise costs is notoriously difficult because of indirect costs like building heating, grounds keeping, and other shared costs. Costs fall into many categories. If I trade my old lawnmower to my neighbor for a bicycle tire, then the direct cost of the tire is my lawnmower. In other words, moneys spent (or items traded) are *direct* costs. Support costs, such as utilities, envelopes, and laser printers are *indirect* costs because these items are generally shared among many projects or activities. But as the equation points out, we also have to consider opportunity costs, which are defined as the value of the next best thing I could be doing. If I know I could utilize my time by teaching classes that would generate $40,000 per year, then that defines my *opportunity* cost of anything else I pursue. In other words, if I choose to use that new bicycle tire to start a bike courier business, I can accurately say that this venture involves not only direct costs like the bicycle, helmet, lock, and saddlebags, but also $40,000 per year in opportunity costs.

Costs are especially difficult to calculate in education. First, budgets are generally dealt with at a higher level than one's classroom, so the data specific to a program or an instructor is unavailable, or worse, often not collected. Second, the infrastructure involved in supporting education is vast, ranging from the physical plant to the university web site that links to your department's web site. Full costs of your classroom or your activities would include not only your time and effort, but also these support components. Although such calculations are extremely difficult, it is important in today's environment to attempt them, for arguments that communicators make about the value we create are moot unless we can also talk intelligently about the costs of our activities. Although it is often the scapegoat of humanist criticism, cost accounting is a critical and integral part of communication activities, academic and workplace, theoretical and practical. Criticism of shortsighted cost accounting is justified, as I discuss later. It is equally shortsighted and illogical, however, for humanist and socialist critics to conflate fiscal accountability with counting paperclips at the cost of losing the future.

In determining value, each individual makes a decision about potential benefits as well as potential costs—direct, indirect, and opportunity. As economist Ramesh Rao puts it, "Every act of choice involves an act of sacrifice" (162). Human, aesthetic, moral, ethical, and social consequences are bound up in the tension between choice and sacrifice. These choices may have nothing to do with money, either. As academic rhetors, we must constantly choose one argument over another, one word over another, one curriculum over another. We make these choices because of scarce resources: scarce funding, scarce students, or scarce time. Chaim Perelman makes it perfectly clear that discourse is subject to scarcity, as well:

> There are psychological, social, and economic limits that prevent a thoughtless amplification of the discourse. If the discourse is presented in manuscript form, the cost of printing can cause the editor to balk, and a too lengthy book risks discouraging its readers. If it is an oral discourse, the patience and attention of the listeners have limits which it is dangerous to go beyond. (139)

Perelman recognizes that because the number of arguments is _a priori_ infinite, speakers or writers must inevitably make a choice, guided by their own evaluation of the respective arguments. This choice and this evaluation belong to the realm of rhetoric and, further, ties rhetoric into discussions of competition and markets. One of the implications of collocating rhetoric and market activities is that we have an opportunity to merge scholarly and academic pursuits with a range of entrepreneurial activities.

Before moving on to a discussion of the value added by communication and rhetoric activities, it is worth noting that value may be created and it may also be destroyed. The value equation above can be negative or positive, depending on the subjective and objective values used. Value is created if benefits outweigh all drawbacks and costs; it is destroyed if those drawbacks or costs outweigh the potential benefits. How does this work? If I spend $5,000 to purchase an old armoire and spend another 12 hours of my time to refinish it, then depending on what my time is worth, the armoire costs between $5,000 and some higher figure (I would use opportunity costs as one way of figuring out the value of my time). My costs include the original purchase, my labor, and whatever products were necessary for the refinishing. Have I created or destroyed value? We do not know until the market speaks. The value of this armoire is the highest amount that someone is willing to pay for it. This amount may be $10,000, in which case, I have created value. But the value may also be $5,000 on the free market, in which case I have destroyed value. In this chapter and throughout the book, the precise sense of the term *creating value* means increasing economic value through activities that add value. It is the goal of value-creators to take their inputs and increase their economic value, and this concept holds for goods and services alike.

But this simple definition does not simplify the task of discovering and affecting value within education or within the workplace. Academic communicators have a doubly difficult task in dealing with the concept of value. First, value in education is quite difficult to measure: The student experience involves not only simple inputs like tuition and time spent on campus, and simple outputs like degrees, but also complex things like friendships, critical thinking, synergies among departments, long-term benefits to society, and so on. Second, communication is difficult to quantify in the workplace and the academy. Composition programs are constantly trying to establish that they create more literate students for the university at large, and for society at large, but proving this "fact" seems to be an ongoing and endless quest. Technical communicators argue that their artifacts save organizations money, but aside from a few excellent seminal studies on the subject, this argument remains assertion only.

The Case for Value

The "value" of communication has been asserted over the years in a variety of forms. The more general field of rhetoric and composition has tended to locate and define value broadly, pointing to students with critical thinking skills, writing abilities, and good trainability as evidence of composition's value. In technical communication, especially since the mid-1990s, the discussion has encompassed both the critical/humanist stance as well as the case for economic value as a rationale for the discipline. Why are economic issues worth pursuing? In a special edition of *Technical Communication* in 1996, Janice Redish gave a solid voice to economic realities of both organizations and of technical communicators, arguing that when communicators act as if they are divorced from issues of economic value, then managers (and society in general) will treat them as having lower value to the organization. Indeed, these economic realities are the cornerstone of pursuing the value question. Redish identifies value as "generating a greater return on investment than the cost of the initial investment" (1). Return on investment (ROI) is another way of describing the "expected benefits" in the value equation given earlier, and comes in many forms, from cost-savings to higher quality, from more loyal customers to faster production. Julie Fisher details a study of roles that technical communicators assume and attempts to quantify the amount of value added by communicators when they are involved in an IT development process. Jay Mead surveys the value literature and focuses on documentation and its costs and benefits. One of the problems he identifies with many of the studies covered in this literature review is that they deal with technical communication as an activity within a given industry, rather than as a well-defined field. He suggests a market approach to revealing value of technical communicators within a firm whereby communicators sell their services to other departments instead of merely "serving" those departments. To determine value added by documents, he looks at quality, data collection, and analysis. Finally, employing Karen Schriver's three-point analysis: (reducing investment on communication, improving ROI, reducing company's after sales costs), he argues that the first and third have received the most research, but that work in direct ROI lags far behind.

Higher status for communicators may come, as several researchers have argued, not from measuring raw ROI, but from recognizing and achieving better alignment with organizational goals and strategy. Using Bourdieu's concept of cultural capital, David Horton points out that communicators are often seen as merely writers, although they traditionally participate in adding value to their organizations in many other ways. What we call ourselves and what other disciplines think of us has everything to do with the value of this cultural capital. In cross-functional teams, he argues, technical communicators should not only be masters of communication, but should also understand their organizations' strategic goals and adapt their vocabulary and activities to reflect those values. Charles Breuninger presents a case study on the use of strategic planning by technical communication teams to show that such teams create more value for their firm because of their "big picture" perspectives. Indeed, this overall view of value is one of the many pieces necessary to demonstrate the value of communicators. Although no researcher has reported a link between communication products and profitability, these newly defined areas may provide the necessary evidence for the argument about value.

These studies represent a critical activity for communicators. The case for value is significant from both a disciplinary perspective and an external perspective. As I argue here, I believe it is possible to conceive of rhetoric as encompassing concepts of value, cost, competition, and markets – not as odd metaphors, but as real components of critical rhetoric-in-use. Externally, others are beginning to do the calculations into the value of all activities, including our academic programs.

Market Forces Acting On Applied Rhetoric Programs

Whether we recognize it or not, academic rhetoricians are both consumers and producers in the economy. The climate for higher education is such that it is harder and harder to justify programs based on their inherent value, but rather on their economic value. One cannot plot strategy in this climate without understanding the nature of the market, one's competitors, one's inputs and processes.

Higher education has changed dramatically in the last 40 years. In the last quarter of the 20th century, higher education was facing many new pressures. Technology was becoming more and more important to society, and society was looking increasingly to universities to provide the research and development and the labor force to drive technological innovation. Education was also increasingly seen as a key competitive advantage in a growing global economy. The nostalgic vision of the university as an ivy-covered sanctuary that was free from the realities of the world was vanishing rapidly, replaced with a vision of the university as partner of both government and business. As community colleges grew, as the number of corporate universities increased, and as the Internet provided learners with many new outlets for learning, the traditional university found itself under unprecedented competition for students and other resources.

In the 1990s, governments around the world responded to these pressures by passing major legislation or initiatives designed to reform higher education. In 1993, the United States started Goals 2000 (the Educate America Act). The United Kingdom enacted the Further and Higher Education Act of 1992, which doubled the number of universities. After the reunification of Germany in 1990, the German government passed the Higher Education Framework Act of 1996, followed by more reforms in 1999. And Japan passed the Lifelong Learning Promotion Law in 1990, followed by the sweeping Programs for Educational Reform in 1997–1999.

At the same time, but coming at the problem from a different direction, private enterprise created unprecedented numbers of relationships, contracts, grants, internships, and other devices—all designed to forge tighter relationships between business and education. Institutions of higher learning were also just learning the mechanics of cost accounting (or so the literature would make it seem), and profit-centered funding rapidly became the norm. Suddenly, in the span of 20 years, higher education was confronted with intense market forces of many sorts. First, it had to justify its existence—not on intrinsic qualities of a discipline, but on profit-and-loss statements. Second, it was encouraged to seek funding in the marketplace in the form of corporate relationships, grants, and so on. Third, it had to get competitive for resources within its own walls. These three types of market pressure are what Slaughter and Leslie called "Academic Capitalism"—

their 1997 study identifies market and entrepreneurial activities as becoming central to institutions of higher education across the globe through the 1980s and into the 1990s. They point out that globalization and conservative politics in the United States and the United Kingdom in the 1980s did much to push this new model. Having far-reaching impacts on higher education, globalization does the following:

1. Constricts the money available for discretionary activities like higher education.
2. Centers "technoscience" and related fields on the markets.
3. Tightens relationships between corporations and state agencies concerned with product development and innovation.
4. Increases focus of multinationals and established industrial countries on global intellectual property strategies.

These political trends provided the governments of the United States and the United Kingdom with an ideology that placed higher education into a milieu of supply-side economics, reduced expenditures for education, lost a sense of entitlement for education, and increased a sense of urgency for technology innovation. Slaughter and Leslie sum up this shift thusly: "Higher education in the UK and US was directed toward national wealth creation and away from its traditional concern with the liberal education of undergraduates" (37). Overall in the 1980s and 1990s, federal policy shifted so that colleges and universities were able to engage in academic capitalism. Federal science and technology policies promoted science and engineering that encouraged academic capitalism and rewarded universities that pursued these initiatives. Professors were discouraged from pursuing curiosity-driven research and were urged to engage in more commercial research (48). Basing their work on Resource Dependence Theory, they argue that those who provide resources to organizations such as universities have the capability of exercising great power over those organizations.

Slaughter and Leslie distinguish between market activities and market-like activities, although the behavior of educators is the same in both cases. Universities engage in market activities by producing goods and services for profit in the larger, nonacademic marketplace. Good examples of this sort of behavior include selling patents in engineering and biology, applying more rigorously for external grants, and engaging in profit-based service learning. In contrast, market-like activities involve academic units competing internally with each other for resources from a university. If a unit is more "profitable" in market-like situations, it does not necessarily realize more funds, but it contributes to the university's bottom line and presumably ensures a continuing stream of support for its activities.

This market-like approach to education is set against a view of education as a common good, one that should be centralized, protected by and subsidized by the government. The arguments on both sides have been made (and continue to be made) in the same way as arguments about the environment, the Internet, and any other "common" good are made. Because the category "higher education" encompasses state-sponsored institutions as well as private ones, brick-and-mortar institutions as well as virtual ones, and full research institutions as well as community colleges, this tension between central planning and market forces is present in virtually all the literature on higher education strategy. And the modern view of higher education, no matter how progressive or conservative, embodies this theoretical line between a government paradigm of planning and a market paradigm of decentralized competition. The question is no longer a matter of *which* paradigm to embrace, but in *what proportions* the two paradigms should be mixed.

In *Market Values in American Higher Education*, Charles Smith offers several ideas that may bridge this gulf. He argues that universities are, in fact, much more market-oriented than the stereotypes portray. He points to distributed faculty governance as one of the ways that universities remain low-cost and competitive, arguing that the best university systems on earth employ faculty governance, whereas the less competitive systems employ central planning. The other reason he finds for a more market-oriented higher education system involves the marketplace of ideas:

> The traditional antihierarchical character of American higher education has historically embodied market principles to a greater degree than have most institutions. This market mentality is commonly only recognized insofar as it is revealed in the market of ideas. Yet the broad tendency to allow all participants to have their say and to allow resolutions to emerge through unfettered interaction is essentially how markets function. Admittedly, these same faculty members often appear hostile to such principles when they are applied to the allocation of resources, but there is no reason that this need be the case. (99)

The ultimate solution, he argues, is for universities to engage in a "flexible market" model, one that recognizes the many missions of the university, understands the true cost of university education, and captures the social and economic gains generated by higher education. It is not a completely free-market model, for the cost of education is to be allocated to society and business as a result of the detailed analysis of who benefits. William Massy echoes this sentiment, arguing that as discretionary revenues vanish and competition drives prices down, universities will behave more and more like a business. For Massy, this is not necessarily a good idea:

Governmental and institutional policymakers must find ways to give effective voice to societal demand while avoiding the limiting case where market forces become completely dominant. Universities must commit to reform, to becoming more efficient and to meeting the rising and more varied demands for postsecondary education *before* being forced to do to by extreme market pressure. Governments must find ways to transmit market-signals to institutions without placing them at the mercy of sometimes ill-informed and shortsighted shifts in educational demand. A new system should be designed to give market-derived revenue a significant role in university decision making but still retain enough discretionary revenue to maintain autonomy. The universities, for their part, must demonstrate effective stewardship by taking the external society's priorities into account when exercising their autonomy. (46-7)

Value creation in all markets, academic markets included, involves paying attention to perceived value, competition, and costs in ways that we are not accustomed to. It is easy to find resistance to this paradigm. I argue that the resistance involves two very different camps that are often conflated in arguments against this trend. Separating these categories of argument can help make sense of the roots of resistance and can open up opportunities for growth. On its face, the 2002 collection of chapters, *Beyond English, Inc.* appears to be against academic capitalism. Indeed, the chapters manage to incorporate all sorts of jabs at markets, globalization, capitalism, and accountability. But behind this veneer of attack, the editors and essayists are actually quite progressive. For example, after raising a huge red flag about the term *globalization*, editors Downing, Hurlbert, and Mathieu write the following:

A great challenge facing English educators is how to imagine and work for reformed curricula that provide alternatives to the exploiting forces of the global economy. The power and scope of economic and technological transformations can make effective change seem impossible. Understanding these processes, however, is a first step in making and claiming spaces of agency within a framework of institutional and economic constraint. (4)

The constraints put on English studies are institutional and economic, and although there may or may not be ideological forces at work behind those constraints, the authors recognize that strategic-minded educators must adapt. This adaptation involves understanding local circumstances: "We must negotiate our visions within specific institutions and against specific constraints of powerful corporate-management models commanding our educational system" (4). Here is an example of the two separate arguments being conflated. On the one hand is an argument about globalization, competition, economic and technological change, and on the other hand is an argument about specific institutional practices, specifically, "corporate-management models." It turns out that the collection has relatively little problem with competition or markets, but has a terrific problem with management and cost accounting: "We may need to resist the corporatized university's exclusive use of short-term cost accounting administered by vertical, undemocratic management practices" (12). In equating "vertical" and "undemocratic" with "management," Downing et al.'s fear and anger about management echoes Friere, who identifies various high-visibility components of free markets, including management, as the oppressor: "The struggle begins with men's recognition that they have been destroyed. Propaganda, management, manipulation—all arms of domination—cannot be the instruments of their rehumanization" (55). For Freire, humanizing pedagogy is the only way to save these destroyed. In *Beyond English, Inc.*, editors Downing et al. recognize that their mission involves not just resistance, but creative rethinking, as their book is "intended to foster visions of what the contributors want our field to become, even as managerialism reaches deeply into our academic lives" (15).

Cost accounting is, however, a necessary component for revealing value creation. Without it, we cannot balance the value equation presented earlier. In other words, without a realistic measurement of costs, it is impossible to tell whether the benefits of our labors are worth the effort or not, even if we intuitively feel that they *are* valuable. Cost accounting aims to determine all costs associated with products and services. Direct costs are usually easy to measure because these costs are directly associated with a specific service or product. For example, if my academic program starts a new usability lab, the direct costs are the video cameras, computers, and furniture, as well as labor and other overhead that is easily associated with the new lab. But indirect costs prove to be extremely difficult. For example, how much does this lab cost in terms of utilities or janitorial services? Short of installing electric meters in the lab or using time cards for janitors, these costs cannot be measured directly. Using indirect means, one could allocate a percentage of my department's costs to the usability lab, based on square footage, for example. If the new lab occupies 1% of the department, then under this philosophy, the lab would "cost" 1% of these indirect costs. The lab may actually use more than 1% of the department's electricity, but this square-foot approximation would not capture that extra use. A newer, and far more accurate, approach to costs is activity-based costing (ABC), an approach that aims to measure activity, rather than objects or categories. Instead of a category called "utilities," an ABC auditor would measure activity in our lab, noting when users entered the lab, when they turned on the lights, when they adjusted the thermostat, and so on. These new categories might be called "heating the lab," "cooling the lab," "lighting the lab," and so on. Depending on how detailed one wants to be, the categories can get very, very specific, like "turning on the cameras" or "shutting down the lab." Each of these categories would aim to capture some labor (if labor is involved), some direct costs, and some indirect costs, so that our account might say that turning on the cameras costs $7.33. The reason this level of detail is important becomes clear when the lab conducts a usability test for a client. If we have conducted an ABC analysis, then we need merely to note which activities happened for how long and add them all up to arrive at the cost of the usability test.

High-quality cost accounting is key to progressive management, but it comprises only one part of it. Cost accounting cannot establish long-range strategy, cannot determine what the market wants, nor can it make decisions about hiring or equipment. These activities must involve the concept of value, of which cost is but one part. The issue of local, knowledgeable control set against oppression from uncaring and uninterested powers rightly concerns many communicators—practitioners and academics alike. We want to be able to make intelligent and strategic decisions based on our own interests, informed by our own past, and matched to our long-term goals. Shortsighted management from elsewhere does not recognize local knowledge, whether that knowledge resides in an individual, a small group of people, or a community. In this respect, I agree with Downing et al. that shortsighted cost accounting runs counter to long-term strategy. If we equate their "managerialism" with shortsightedness, then they have a legitimate complaint, one that can, and should, be kept separate from other issues of competition. Unfortunately, Downing et al. seem to revel in conflating "cost accounting" with unrelated terms like "corporatized," "undemocratic," and "management" without explaining their logic. If accountability is oppressive, it is because it identifies value-destroying activities, shining a bright light on actual practices and outcomes instead of relying on hunches and assertions. Contrary to these vague associations, Peter Drucker, someone who has actually studied management, rightly sees management as a liberal art:

> Managers draw on all the knowledge and insights of the humanities and the social sciences—on psychology and philosophy, on economics and history, on ethics—as well as on the physical sciences. But they have to focus this knowledge on effectiveness and results—on healing a sick patient, teaching a student, building a bridge, designing and selling a "user-friendly" software program. . . . For these reasons, management will increasingly be the discipline and the practice through which the "humanities" will again acquire recognition, impact, and relevance. (13)

As for Downing et al.'s equation of management with "vertical" and "undemocratic," I would argue that management is not supposed to be democratic. In the academy, we manage our programs by trying various innovations, by optimizing our course offerings, by hiring qualified teachers for our service courses, among other things. We do not consult the people in these management efforts, nor should we. The point at which our efforts are tested, however, *is* democracy in the form of the marketplace for our academic services. Students and prospective students speak with the voice of the marketplace during the admissions and registration process. After graduation, employers for our students, profit and nonprofit alike, speak with a similar voice. In this respect, I would argue that the market is considerably more democratic than anything a university bureaucrat can dream up. The free market fosters democracy, as Arthur Seldon observes:

> Capitalism is superior to socialism because, by minimizing the writ of politics and maximizing the writ of the market, it creates a more effective form of democracy for enabling all the people, the common people as well as the political people, to decide their lives. (98)

Finally, let us look at the vague term *corporatized*. Downing et al. are certainly not the only writers to pick on some variant of the word *corporation*. In virtually every conference presentation I have attended and in almost every article and Web site I have read on English studies that finds some kind of fault with *corporations*, the term has been used vaguely, sloppily, and inaccurately. Authors use *corporate* when they mean anything from "industrial" to "professional," from "private" to "large." A corporation is an entity that has filed papers with a state. It is an entity separate from its owners and officers, and thus may enter into contracts, loans, and other agreements as if it were an individual. We cannot assign profit motives to this organizational structure, as both the American Red Cross and Microsoft are corporations. We cannot speak of the owners of corporations in vague, third party terminology, for most of this collection's readers are most likely owners of hundreds of corporations through their IRAs, 401Ks and other investments. The two other forms of organization are partnerships and proprietorships, and their numbers dwarf corporations; in 2000, for example, according to the Statistical Abstract (table 731), the United States had 5,045,000 corporations, 2,058,000 partnerships, and 17,905,000 proprietorships. In this volume, I have tried to edit for precision in this regard. When we want to refer generically to groups of people unified for a common mission, we use terms like *organizations*, *firms*, or *companies*. Where the specific organizational structure is significant, we use terms like *college*, *nonprofit corporation*, *corporation*, *sole proprietorship*, or whatever specific term applies.

Remove the reasonable argument about English studies being victimized by narrow-minded university bureaucrats and *Beyond English, Inc.* falls far short of comprehending what the free market can do for English studies. Instead, its authors approach the subject of globalized competition as the condemned prisoner walks toward the gallows, hesitatingly, regretfully, and wistfully. The truth is that English studies benefit from studying, reflecting, and assimilating such competition, for it forces us to innovate and adapt.

Competition

For suppliers, the mechanism that is most critical for sorting out value creation from value destruction is competition. This can be head-to-head competition of multiple products or services, but it can also be the competition of arguments, ideas, people, and innovation. Without competition, a discussion of value makes little sense, at least in a capitalist economy. What distinguishes capitalist from socialist approaches to value can be found in the debate about how best to allocate scarce resources, either through centralized authority or rather through distributed, individualized choices. Proponents of centralized planning may be found under many banners: Marxism, socialism, collectivism, communism, statism, and even Platonism. Proponents of distributed allocation of resources are called by individualism, capitalism, or globalism. In a free-market system consisting largely of private goods and services, competition is a critical mechanism for sorting out priorities, values, choices, availability, competence, and desirability in an environment of scarce resources. The market *is* competition. Without competition, there is no market, for there are no true options and no true decisions by consumers about goods, services, or even innovations. Hamel and Prahalad argue that the most important competition in the new economy is not for goods, services, or capital, but rather for innovation. We compete in a very real sense for the future, and we do so proactively, as economist F. A. Hayek argues:

> The liberal[2] argument is in favor of making the best possible use of the forces of competition as a means of co-ordinating human efforts, not an argument for leaving things just as they are. It is based on the conviction that, where effective competition can be created, it is a better way of guiding individual efforts than any other. (41)

---

[2]*Liberal*, as it is used here, refers to the *laissez-faire* approach to allowing forces to compete. It is a European sense of the word, which must stand in stark contrast to the American sense of "liberal" as socially minded, leftist, and in favor of more government control.

This concept of ubiquitous competition bothers a lot of educators. On the one hand, we feel education is a public good, and therefore not subject to the choices and values of consumers of education. On the other hand, we also tend to define competition very narrowly for ideological purposes as something akin to battle. Because we are altruistic and optimistic and cooperative, we find this definition contrary to our mission. If we broaden the concept, however, this problem goes away.

Instead of viewing competition as something unfair to weaker players, a more useful stance is to see it as a mechanism for identifying value, as a practical implementation of rhetoric, even as a validation of one's mission. In this light, competition is a process that can be counted on in ways that bureaucrats and planners cannot. For example, when we conduct a job search for a new assistant professor, we do not want our provost or dean to say, "I want you to hire person X." Although this person may be excellent, we want to have the option to choose from among the best candidates. Our choice among options is the benefit we get from competition. Or take the example of which courses to expand and which to cut—the students at our campus have already voted on the courses they want through the competition among departments and among professors to fill the seats in their class. Competition sorts them out and provides us all with suggestions for our strategy, all without any oversight or wisdom by an administrator. And it is not just our students who have spoken; the market for courses is more complicated than a student popularity contest. The market includes these students, their parents, state legislators, taxpayers, current and future employers, professional schools, graduate schools, accreditation boards, and coordinating boards, to name a few. Popularity with students, in other words, is only a small part of a free-market perspective.

Activities that "lose" through competition are destroyed, but this is not the destruction of value. When inefficient, outmoded, or nonstrategic activities cease, value is actually created because all the resources that previously flowed into them are freed to be used elsewhere. In explaining globalized competition in *The Lexus and the Olive Tree*, Thomas Friedman makes good use of Schumpeter's idea that the "essence of capitalism is the process of 'creative destruction'—the perpetual cycle of destroying the old and less efficient product or service and replacing it with new, more efficient ones. . . . Those countries that are most willing to let capitalism quickly destroy inefficient companies, so that money can be freed up and directed toward more innovative ones, will thrive in the era of globalization" (11). This creative destruction is key to innovation, whether in manufacturing, services, or education—competition identifies and rewards new and better ideas.

Although individuals do feel the pain of this creative destruction through layoffs, plant closings, and so on, it is inefficient organizations or operations that are the natural and desirable targets of this process. Thomas Friedman sees a valid role for society to protect individuals, but not organizations, from this process:

> A society that welcomes, or at least tolerates, creative destruction has to be in place for revolutionary products to emerge. This is particularly crucial in a world without walls in which it is much harder to protect the old from the new. A country should worry about the loss of jobs, but not the loss of firms. That may seem contradictory, but it is not. If you worry about the loss of firms, you will end up losing a lot more jobs. You should have safety nets for people who lose their jobs, but not for firms that lose their edge. (237)

Even if the concept of *creative destruction* feels odd, we are all familiar with winning and losing in playing games. In fact, another way of thinking of competition is as a game designed to help us locate solutions and allocate resources. When economists Brandenburger and Nalebuff merged their interests in game theory with Michael Porter's work in competitive strategy, they employed the term *co-opetition* to describe a sophisticated strategy in a highly competitive environment. Michael Porter brought enormous insight to strategic management when he clarified the nature of the competitive landscape within which an organization operates. Instead of seeing the whole world as an undifferentiated blob of players, Porter argued that a sophisticated view of the structure of an industry involves identifying not only direct competitors, but also the suppliers, complementors, buyers, and regulators involved in the entire industry. This structural analysis was a break-through, for it allowed organizations to see how they might compete on other bases. For example, not only does an organization compete head-to-head in pricing and service in dealing with consumers, but it also competes on the strength of its relationship to suppliers and regulators.

Brandenburger and Nalebuff took this structural analysis a step higher, merging it with sophisticated game theory. Although a Porter analysis gives us great insight into the structure of an industry, game theory gives us the mechanisms for action within that environment. In their view, competition need not (and should not) be seen as a winner-take-all (or zero sum) game. Instead, competitors may actually win more profits (or students or whatever the stakes are in the game) by not competing head to head, but instead by forming strategic alliances with complementors, suppliers, and slightly different direct competitors. The intuition that an organization cannot share information with a competitor turns out to be correct only in a few circumstances. In communication fields, a good example of co-opetition would be when a 4-year college no longer sees the freshman composition program at the local community college as competition, but rather as a kind of friendly, competitive partnership. Because of the structure of the labor force, the fees, and the curriculum, it may be better for everyone if the community college teaches all freshman composition and the university focuses on more complicated courses. Internal to rhetoric, an example of this strategy is easy to see in current argumentation theory, where dialectic is viewed as a cooperative, rather than combative, way of fleshing out issues and moving toward decisions. The mechanism of debate appears competitive and employs competitive strategies, but the argumentative purpose of debate serves a cooperative purpose: a decision or a course of action.

Within this environment of supplier competition, the mechanism that actually identifies value is self-interest of decision makers, or more generally, the recipients of ideas, goods, and services, aggregated over many thousands or millions of decisions in a given marketplace. In other words, the creators of a new composition graduate program do not create value by designing the best curriculum, hiring the best faculty, and printing the prettiest brochures. Although these activities are no doubt critical to starting a new graduate program, its value will be determined by the caliber and number of students who apply. And they will apply to this program by looking at their options, weighing costs of moving, comparing offers of graduate teaching assistantships, and generally determining how good of a match this new program is for their career interests. Likewise, despite their choices of competing arguments and my careful arrangement of a case, the ultimate test of success or failure for rhetors is whether their audience is persuaded or convinced.

But it is an error to identify self-interest with egotistical greed, as Oliver Stone does when he has his character Gordon Geckko utter his famous mantra, "Greed is good," in the movie *Wall Street*. Opportunism undermines the power and wisdom of free markets, whereas self-interest strengthens them. The reason the market is so important is that there is an efficiency inherent in the aggregated actions of market players. When each player in a free market makes his or her decisions in self-interest, this behavior improves all of society by moving resources where they create the most value for society. Successful capitalism depends on maximizing behavior within a set of formal and informal rules, norms, and structures. Self-interested behavior implies playing by those rules and making rational decisions for oneself and one's family. Opportunism implies deception, unfair business practices, cheating, and exploitation, and these practices undermine the invisible hand of capitalism. In an argument against collectivist regulation, Milton Friedman explains self-interest:

> The central defect of these [centralization] measures is that they seek through government to force people to act against their own immediate interests in order to promote a supposedly general interest. They seek

to resolve what is supposedly a conflict of interest, or a difference in view about interests, not by establishing a framework that will eliminate the conflict, or by persuading people to have different interests, but by forcing people to act against their own interest. They substitute the values of outsiders for the values of participants; either some telling others what is good for them, or the government taking from some to benefit others. These measures are therefore countered by one of the strongest and most creative forces known to man—the attempt by millions of individuals to promote their own interests, to live their lives by their own values. (200)

Every individual parenting decision, every choice of where to live or which job to pursue, falls under this concept of "strongest and creative forces" to which Friedman refers. Arthur Seldon succinctly identifies self-interest as an inherent trait of people, quite outside of theory: "Whatever the intelligentsia may think, people will trade with one another, inside or outside the law, to improve their condition" (370). The concept of improving one's condition applies equally to the suppliers in a market economy. Alan Greenspan points out, "What collectivists refuse to recognize is that it is in the self-interest of every businessman to have a reputation for honest dealings and a quality product. Since the market value of a going business is measured by its money-making potential, reputation or 'good will' is as much an asset as its physical plant and equipment. . . . Reputation, in an unregulated economy, is thus a major competitive tool" (118). The rhetorical concept of *ethos* has received a great deal of study since the 1970s, but this concept of *ethos* as competitive advantage has received little, if any, attention.

Greenspan takes this concept even further, equating capitalism with supremely high morals, precisely because of decentralized mechanisms: "Capitalism is based on self-interest and self-esteem; it holds integrity and trustworthiness as cardinal virtues and makes them pay off in the marketplace, thus demanding that men survive by means of virtues, not of vices. It is this superlatively moral system that the welfare statists propose to improve on by means of preventive law, snooping bureaucrats, and the chronic goad of fear" (121). Milton Friedman takes a similar approach in explaining that self-interest serves society in far greater ways than central planning does:

The interests of which I speak are not simply narrow self-regarding interests. On the contrary, they include the whole range of values that men hold dear and for which they are willing to spend their fortunes and sacrifice their lives. The Germans who lost their lives opposing Adolph Hitler were pursuing their interests as they saw them. So also are the men and women who devote great effort and time to charitable,

educational, and religious activities. Naturally, such interests are the
major ones for few men. It is the virtue of a free society that it nonetheless permits these interests full scope and does not subordinate them to
the narrow materialistic interests that dominate the bulk of mankind.
(200-1)

These concepts of competition, creative destruction, and self-interest
apply directly to the work we do as academic communicators, both
metaphorically and literally. Metaphorically, we communicators invoke
creative destruction when we edit or revise, and we compete when we
assert an argument verbally or submit an article for publication—all in the
spirit of self-interest as defined above. Nonmetaphorically, our courses
compete for resources in the form of student enrollments. The results of
that competition are evident if we observe the competitive process: if we
offer English 4355 every semester, but it never fills up, then we must ask
ourselves (a) why isn't anyone enrolling? and (b) why do we continue to
grant this course special status? Individual faculty members also compete
with each other for course enrollments, dissertation committees, grants,
service activities, and so on. Our programs compete for resources, as well,
in the form of students, funds, articles, and citations. Programs that do not
capture such resources have only two options: They can be supported or
they can be destroyed. In the first case, central planners step into the market process, prop up the program, and declare that this particular program
is too "valuable" to lose, value being equated by such planners with sentiment, tradition, or necessary service. In the second case, creative destruction frees faculty, students, and staff from participating in a losing cause
and allows them to go where their abilities can be better aligned with value
creating activities.

Central Planning

Assuming we do not live in utopia, all resources are scarce, meaning that
there is not an infinity of any one of them. Money, labor, people, water—
none are infinite. The philosophical difference between capitalism and
socialism lies in the preference for allocating these resources to worthy projects. Capitalism employs the free market to get resources where they are
needed the most. When producers compete for resources, when workers
make rational decisions about what to purchase, and when government
stays out of the mix, everyone benefits. Key to a capitalist system are property rights for individuals, who may do anything they want with their
property.
    In contrast to such a self-interested method of deciding value is a cen-
tralized or socialist approach in which one entity decides the cost and avail-

ability of goods and services. Socialism involves managing scarce resources by making central determinations about their best use. This centralization involves not only decisions about asset allocation, but also who can own property. Central planning imbues an individual or a board with wisdom to allocate resources. F. A. Hayek casts these opposites as two approaches to social decision making:

> The dispute between modern planners and their opponents is not a dispute on whether we ought to choose intelligently between the various possible organizations of society; it is not a dispute on whether we ought to employ foresight and systematic thinking in planning out common affairs. It is a dispute about what is the best way of so doing. [It is a question of whether we should] create conditions under which the knowledge and initiative of individuals are given the best scope so that they can plan most successfully; or whether a rational utilization of our resources requires central direction and organization of all our activities according to some consciously constructed "blueprint." (40-1)

Rhetoric has a role to play in either system. James Aune makes centralization and force in rhetoric very clear in explaining Marx's conception of persuasion: "Whereas classical political theory had understood the necessity of myth (Plato) or at least oratory (Aristotle, Cicero), in the founding and maintenance of just regimes, Marxism simply does not find persuasion a problem. The audience *must* see the truth, like it or not." Aune links this force to a statement from the Communist Manifesto, which insists on "Centralization of the means of communication and transport in the hands of the state" (24). In other words, for central planners, rhetoric participates in coercion, even if the audience is *not* persuaded or convinced.

It is tempting to point to a very knowledgeable leader, perhaps a philosopher king, who would allocate resources wisely in the absence of competition and individualism. F. A. Hayek calls the fallacy of the single viewpoint the "illusion of the specialist," the feeling that if only a rhetorician (or engineer or philosopher) were in charge, they could iron out all the troubles once and for all, setting society on a correct and beneficial path. But, says Hayek, very wise individuals or groups, even if they are not deliberately coercive, will not achieve the efficiency and wisdom of a decentralized marketplace. Any single viewpoint, given power, will be less efficient than a marketplace of views:

> The illusion of the specialist that in a planned society he would secure more attention to the objectives for which he cares most is a more general phenomenon than the term "specialist" at first suggests. In our predilections and interests we are all in some measure specialists. And

> we all think that our personal order of values is not merely personal
> but that in a free discussion among rational people we would convince
> the others that ours is the right one. (61)

This bias is one reason that centralized planning is not as effective or efficient as market-based planning. The flip side of that coin is that the marketplace, composed of millions of rational, self-interested decision makers, has
more aggregated wisdom and less bias (by virtue of canceling it out).
Whether the topic is faculty salaries or the price of gasoline, the result is the
same: to be insulated from the market process is to be inherently inefficient.
Insulation appears in many forms, from the iron-fist of totalitarian communism to the relatively innocuous mechanism of government price controls.
As Thomas Friedman observes, the backlash to globalism is not likely to
come from laborers, but from those who had it good before under a non-
competitive situation, as the following list illustrates:

> . . . Industrialists and cronies who were anointed with import or export
> monopolies by their governments, business owners who were protect-
> ed by the government through high import tariffs on the products they
> made, big labor unions who got used to each year winning fewer work
> hours with more pay in constantly protected markets, workers in state-
> owned factories who got paid whether the factory made a profit or not,
> the unemployed in welfare states who enjoyed relatively generous ben-
> efits and health care no matter what, and all those who depended on the
> largesse of the state to protect them from the global market and free
> them from its most demanding aspects. (337)

Friedman's list brings together some odd bedfellows, but each one is somehow outside of the free market, protected in some way through centralization, monopoly, or socialism. Communicators, whether in universities or in
industry, have also traditionally been perceived as being outside the marketplace. In industry, this view means that communicators are seen as assets
that cost the company money, or cost-centers. In higher education, this
attitude casts communicators as supported humanities departments, something "kept" by necessity. In either case, this "protected" view has done
nothing but shield the value of communication from others. In the world of
ideas, for example, we can compare a free competition of ideas with a
"blessed" canon or paradigm that cannot be questioned. In such circumstances, a discussion of value will be virtually equivalent to a discussion of
institutional values.

In many ways, the debate over the best way to distribute scarce
resources (centralized vs. distributed) resembles the question of the best
way to govern (totalitarian vs. democratic). Indeed, Thomas Friedman

equates decentralized globalization with democracy. He identifies three types of democratization that have come about through the cold war and the fall of the Berlin wall: democratization of technology, democratization of finance, and the democratization of information. What this means is that centralization is nearly impossible: "the days when governments could isolate their people from understanding what life was like beyond their borders or even beyond their village are over. Life outside can't be trashed and made to look worse than it is. And life inside can't be propagandized and made to look better than it is" (67).

As highly trained specialists, we academic communicators are caught in between the two paradigms. We see this tension between the well-trained writer or designer and our general belief that rhetoric is about the reader's or user's experience. For the former, the right decision comes from technical training, years of experience, and innate talent and expertise. For the latter, especially when we employ methodologies like usability testing, ethnographies, and case studies, the right decision comes from asking the marketplace what works through observation, analysis, and measurement. In other words, knowledge comes from the specialist in the first paradigm, and it flows downwards to the marketplace; and in the second paradigm, knowledge is generated in the marketplace, where it informs design and production decisions. The two approaches to epistemology differ radically, and we find ourselves caught in between them in applied rhetoric.

Take the issue of document design. How do we decide what a manual, online help system, or web site should look like? Do we pander to our users, imitating other designs they like in order to please them? Or do we give our users what we believe they need? In one model, a market-oriented one, we listen to our readers and our users and try to adjust accordingly. In the other model, we simply "know" what's right and design the documents according to time-honored rules of thumb and personal preference. There is no correct balance between the two paradigms, however. The best definition of knowledge within such a system is perhaps an iterative one that combines the training and opinions of specialists with the unsympathetic voice of the marketplace, one that that recognizes the flexible and constantly changing boundary between the two models as the momentary equilibrium that constitutes the "right" balance at any one time.

Models of Markets and Rhetoric

What is a market except people negotiating among themselves in order to arrive at a meeting point? The literature on markets, whether we are talking about the capital markets or the bric-a-brac markets typical of yard sales and Ebay, is all about information. This is what makes markets matter to communicators: Markets produce and communicate information. They also make decisions, as the following example illustrates. The U.S. Navy recently announced that it would "unleash the power of the free market on its personnel system" (Jaffe) by allowing sailors to bid on jobs that no one wants, such as being stationed at an out-of-the-way base. Instead of using a central coordinator to match job skills with available jobs, the Navy's new system will let market forces do that task and, presumably, do it better than the coordinator.

Markets *are* information, even to those who are not buying or selling. Many years ago, my Uncle David gave me his old Beatles album, *Yesterday and Today,* the rare version that has the "Butcher Cover" that was covered up by an innocuous alternate cover when executives saw the graphic nature of the original cover. At this moment, I have no idea of this album's market value. I do not have to sell my album to find out this value; instead, I can look on Ebay or some other form of exchange established for buyers, sellers, and traders, in order get a pretty good idea. As I write this paragraph, there is an original Butcher Cover album for sale on Ebay with a current bid of $451. I don't know if I could sell my album for that much or perhaps more, but the astonishing thing about this marketplace is that it was able to provide information to me. In my album cover example, as well as the U.S. Navy example, it is not necessary to employ a specialist—a rare record dealer or personnel specialist—to gather authoritative and strategic information. Instead, individuals in the marketplace do the same thing with no coordination, no standards, no centralization.

Although such a mechanism is astounding, it does not work in a vacuum. Market participants rely on communication, persuasion, argumentation, and information in order to arrive at a price point or an exchange point. Market players make use of as much information as is available in order to make decisions. Markets themselves create valuable information, in turn, revealing aggregate price points and suggesting to producers whether to create more of what they make or less. This aggregate price point is what economists call equilibrium, for it represents a balance of all producers' outputs with all consumers' desires. It is the price and output level that maximizes both parties' desires together. It is where supply meets demand. And although we tend to equate money with markets, markets can function perfectly without a monetary system. For example, if you are trading services with other professionals, and there are enough players in the market, then it will not take long to establish how many hours of lawyer work is equivalent to a root canal (for services) or how many coffee mugs are equivalent to one dirt bike.

Free markets rely on rhetoric to work. Rhetoric helps define goods and services, makes the persuasive case for value, and conveys market participants' *ethos, pathos,* and *logos*. With the exception of the actual trade or purchase, markets *are* rhetorical. Of course, the actual transactions in economic markets involve specific trades or money, whereas transactions within markets of ideas involve assent, understanding, or further query. And in the aggregate, economic markets produce information and supply and demand equilibrium, whereas markets of ideas produce public debate involving the clarification of terms, the nature of claims and grounds of arguments, and the broad sentiments of those participating. Both kinds of markets produce information about their own domains, revealing knowledge that was previously hidden or misunderstood. Shoshanna Zuboff explores this concept within the realm information technology in *In the Age of the Smart Machine*, naming this process of self-awareness *informating* as opposed to *automating* processes that optimize without self-knowledge:

> [this informating technology] simultaneously generates information about the underlying productive and administrative processes through which an organization accomplishes its work. It provides a deeper level of transparency to activities that had been either partially or completely opaque. . . . Activities, events, and objects are translated into and made visible by information when a technology informates as well as automates. (9-10)

Free markets, too, are information technologies, not only automating the flow of resources to where they are needed most, but also providing information about the market itself. For both kinds of markets, the individual transaction is less important for this information-creating activity than those transactions repeated many times. It is in this realm in which participants compete for resources through a series of individual transactions (communicative or economic) that we have a market. The following paragraphs involve one way we might try to model this relationship between rhetoric and economic markets, both metaphorically and literally.

In many ways, models for market transactions are the same as models for communication. Fig. 1.1 depicts a rather standard communication triangle that models the transmission or translation of a signal from an encoder to a decoder by means of some sign system: semaphores, English, sign language, and so forth. In more general communication theory, this communication triangle usually describes an utterance, a one-directional blast of a message from one party to one other. The communication triangle often includes a one-directional arrow from the encoder to the decoder in recognition of this model. But complicated communications do not take place in isolation. The decoder requests clarification or demands evidence. Or perhaps a third party overhears the conversation and pipes in with a new utterance. A realistic model of communication has to account not only for simple transmission or translation, but also competition between sender,

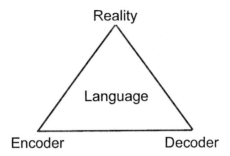

Figure 1.1.   Communication triangle.

receiver, all the other senders and the noise. In the written world, no one says just one utterance or writes just one memo. That memo has a life within the organization, appearing in e-mail lists, being abstracted for use in a proposal or press release, or returning to the sender for more clarification. A complex and dynamic model of communication must also account for the relationship between invention, production, repackaging, and iterative design of communication messages. Such a dynamic model of communication is one that applied rhetoricians live daily. A model of communication that takes into account the competition inherent in market and market-like activities can, I believe, more accurately approximate this reality.

A single economic transaction is similar to the single semiotic transaction in the model above. Fig. 1.2 illustrates the single transmission model of the exchange, changing only the terms from the communication model. Just as the single transmission of a sign produces understanding under the right circumstances, so does the single transmission of an offer to sell produce something: an agreement or a nonagreement.

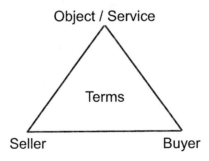

Figure 1.2.   Single transaction triangle.

But aggregate the act of the sale to include hundreds, thousands, or millions of similar acts, and the static model becomes a dynamic model of markets. A market is an aggregation of communication acts, where each act of communication involves a seller, a buyer, a thing to be traded, and the terms of the trade. When all four of these components are present, the market enables trades. More importantly, it produces information. Of course the market is about buying and selling, but behind the act of buying and selling is the much more familiar act of communicating in which we all engage—in our technical communication, rhetoric, and composition classes. If prices are dropping, then we all know that there is too much of the item available and the meeting point of buyer and seller is adjusting downwards until equilibrium is reached. Even offers to sell involve information. In fact, if markets are open enough, competitive enough, and rich enough in information, the market price contains all available information and there is no other better means at determining an object's value—not the government, not a regulator, not past performance, not any given individual. Only market players with special knowledge, such as someone with insider knowledge, can change the price, for they have information that the aggregate does not have. If you know something about a company that no one else knows, and you buy a bunch of this firm's stock, then your act of purchasing reveals information to the marketplace, and you no longer have the information to yourself. You make your quick purchase, and the stock's price rises simultaneously—the stock price now includes your insider knowledge, just as if you had published it on the Internet.

The same process happens in communication. If we aggregate the communication act, as we do in argumentation theory or policy debate, we have a market of communication. Fig. 1.3 shows one way of thinking about how separate communication acts might combine to model such a free market. The simple communication triangle has been augmented in three ways. First, in single transactions, arrows are drawn in both directions from encoder to decoder to suggest the dynamic requirements of debate. Second, separate rhetorical situations are joined to each other to illustrate competition among the many producers of communication. Third, this cluster model incorporates previous clusters of communication through time in order to account for the iterative nature of ongoing discussion. In this expanded model, not every utterance has value, just as a single economic transaction may not represent valuable information for the marketplace. After all, irrational bidders may offer more for an item on Ebay than it sells for in the store; similarly, people utter non-sequiturs and argue irrational propositions. When grouped with many other utterances, all reacting to each other, this din of communication represents something approximating consensus, or at least critical discussion. This mechanism of critical discussion, or market of ideas, determines which information has value.

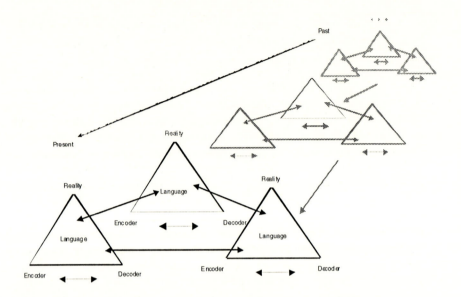

Figure 1.3.   Complex communication market interactions.

An excellent (and much more thorough) discussion of the relationship between theories of communication and the roles and definitions of communicators appears in Slack, Miller, and Doak's 1993 article, "The Technical Communicator as Author." In it, they argue that the field's definition of communicators depends on the theory of communication being embraced. With the simple transmission model of communication, the writer is a facilitator. In the translation model of communication, which seeks to interpret the message, the communicator "works to create symmetry within the negotiation of differential relations of power between the sender and receiver" (14). Their third model of communication is articulation, within which the writer "is complicit in an ongoing articulation and rearticulation of relations of power" (14). This conception of articulation falls short of the market perspective I am arguing, but does provide a theoretical bridge between what I call (in the next section) the critical and productive dimensions of applied rhetoric.

In the same spirit of property ownership, rule of law, contract formation, and other rules that provide free markets with the structure necessary to operate, this model of communication markets needs to make use of rules for critical discussion. Perhaps the most valuable contribution to argumentation theory in the past few decades has been the development of the pragma-dialectical school, which combines elements of logic, speech-act theory, and dialectics. Pragma-dialectical rules for critical discussion include the following:

1. Parties must not prevent each other from advancing stand-points or from casting doubt on standpoints.
2. A party that advances a standpoint is obliged to defend it if asked by the other party to do so.
3. A party's attack on a standpoint must relate to the standpoint that has indeed been advanced by the other party.
4. A party may defend a standpoint only by advancing argumentation relating to that standpoint.
5. A party may not disown a premise that has been left implicit by that party or falsely present something as a premise that has been left unexpressed by the other party.
6. A party may not falsely present a premise as an accepted starting point nor deny a premise representing an accepted starting point.
7. A party may not regard a standpoint as conclusively defended if the defense does not take place by means of an appropriate argumentation scheme that is correctly applied.
8. A party may only use arguments in its argumentation that are logically valid or capable of being validated by making explicit one or more unexpressed premises.
9. A failed defense of a standpoint must result in the party that put forward the standpoint retracting it and a conclusive defense of the standpoint must result in the other party retracting its doubt about the standpoint.
10. A party must not use formulations that are insufficiently clear or confusingly ambiguous and a party must interpret the other party's formulations as carefully and accurately as possible. (Van Eemeren et al., 283-4)

With each individual communication obeying these rules, the marketplace of ideas simultaneously respects each player's right to participate freely and allows for the din of rhetoric to ferret out the key issues at any given moment, to identify main points and their proponents and opponents, and to locate equilibrium in the form of consensus, however fleeting it may be. In other words, this model of communication markets produces information about the society doing the communicating.

THREE DIMENSIONS OF APPLIED RHETORIC

Many scholars, teachers, and practitioners express concern that a free-market examination of communication is surely dangerous, possibly naïve and misguided, probably ineffective, and potentially counterproductive. On the one hand is the argument is that rhetoric studies have come into their own through the advances of critical theory, which supposedly allows humanists to resist the onslaught of capitalist ideology. It follows from this logic, then, that to explore market-based theories and practices is not only to step backward several decades, but also to capitulate to hegemonic forces. On the other hand, and probably more prevalent among teachers and scholars of writing, is a fundamental dislike and suspicion of the terminology and attitude of capitalism, as the following passage from Ira Shor's 1996 book illustrates:

> The free market is not really free. People . . . don't control the job market, the housing market, the money market, the food market, the insurance market, the car market, etc. In reality, they are jockeying for position, couple-by-couple, person-by-person, in a society where wealth and power lie in corporate hands. . . . All the college degree guarantees, economically speaking, is the chance to compete in a job market where corporations are moving North American jobs to cheap-labor havens like Mexico, Poland, and Brazil. . . . Economic "globalization" is ideal for big business but bad news for working people in the United States, who are running faster merely to stay in place or to slow the decline in their standard of living. Thus, the free choice of going to college and the free market are about as fictional as the elective status of my Utopia course. (36)

It is worth noting that after posting a call for papers for this collection in several online e-mail lists, I received many more flames than proposals, portraying this project as a great betrayer, a naïve justification of hegemonic forces. This outcry is ironic given our discipline's pride on openness and a willingness to learn from other paradigms. But I do understand those voices, for they resonate with a training, a humanity, and a caring that is typical of modern rhetors. In fact, those voices are a key component of a modern rhetoric. Without them, rhetoric is stripped of its humanistic agency. After all, modern rhetoric deals with people, with what people want and what people need.

But what the two-dimensional rhetoric that these voices embrace often lacks is productive action, for its stance tends to be to criticize and resist, not to create. A field founded on well-defined fundamentals, coupled with critical agency, but devoid of the possibility of productive action is incomplete. It is a state we might somewhat cynically call *enlightened enfeeblement*. The litmus test for applied rhetoric cannot consist simply of critical resistance. Instead, our fields need a full and realistic view of our missions, curricula, and students, involving not only our skills and abilities, but also theories about how communicators create value in the world.

Corey Wick suggests that communicators are not in the center of economic activity because "we emphasize the products we create instead of the knowledge and competencies we use to create them" (524). And he is partially right. But I think there is more. We cannot move to the center because of broadly held notions inherent in our educational philosophy, notions that often prohibit us from imagining value-creation. We naturally and rightly argue that we create value by bringing an ethical, humanistic perspective to the creation, maintenance, and dissemination of writing and other communication artifacts. But the way we in the field conceive of rhetoric, live it, and teach it, generally does not include a managerial, economic, or market component, thereby erecting a roadblock between humanistic and critical "values" and economic value as defined earlier. This value is not something abstract: It deals with the goals, desires, and behaviors that people seek and benefit from. When we construct a theory of rhetoric that stops short of those natural activities, can we really argue that such critical values are enough?

The model of real-world applied rhetoric for which I am arguing involves three dimensions, each articulated by its own curriculum, worldview, engagement with signs, perspective on tools, and pedagogy. The first dimension is the instrumental, and involves the fundamentals of communication—expression, correctness, style, editing, layout, grammar, and so on. The second dimension is the critical, involving humanism, criticism, observation, analysis, and ethics. The third is what we might call the productive, involving value creation, markets, strategic thinking, and action. This three-dimensional model views communicators as full participants in an economic society.

In 1979, Carolyn Miller made a case for why technical communications should be seen as a humanistic. In making her argument, Miller attacked positivist epistemology and the "clear window" view of language that was typical of science writing at the time. In doing so, she called on concepts of social constructivism, or the idea that hard truths are outside of the realm of communications, and that the more reasonable domain of communication is the probable. Once communications are seen in this light, then it is much more important for the communicator to understand the context in which the communication will take place, and this involves an understanding of the social, scientific, gender, class, race, and organizational influences on these communications. Miller's chapter captured a dynamic shift in the way writers perceived their relationship to their materials, from mere instruments (technical writers) to translators/agents of social change (technical communicators). In my terminology, this shift describes the expansion from the instrumental to the critical dimension.

Since the 1970s, there has been remarkable growth in this critical dimension of rhetoric, composition, and technical communication. As

humanists and critics, communicators acquired agency and developed critical skills that empower us to understand considerably more than the written word. With our new mandate to be able to read and understand the
contexts of communications, rather than on the communications themselves, we have, sponge-like, borrowed concepts from feminist theory,
ethics, philosophy, technology, sociology, and cognitive psychology. This
progress has evolved communicators from mere users of tools to sophisticated readers of texts and situations, able to suggest (but not enact) change
within our organizations. For Slack et al., the new addition of power and
power relations inherent in what they call the articulated theory of communication leads to sophistication in analysis and criticism (but not production) for the communicator, who must "have a superior grasp of the relationship between technology and discourse and between science and
rhetoric" in order to "learn to analyze critically the articulations evoked in
the language of technology and science" (33). Ultimately, this critical stance
will allow us to send out our students well prepared as critics and authors:

> It is impossible for technical communicators to take full responsibility
> for their work until they understand their role from an articulation
> view. Likewise, it is impossible to recognize the real power of technical
> discourse without understanding its role in the articulation and reartic-
> ulation of meaning and power. This understanding would thus empow-
> er the discourse of technical communicators by recognizing their full
> authorial role. (33)

Such a critical dimension has provided communicators with the analytical
breadth, humanistic understanding, and finely tuned ability to examine our
society and own fields meta-critically. This critical dimension of rhetoric
echoes in the work of Paolo Freire, Ira Shor, and James Berlin, but James
Porter may have expressed it better than anyone:

> The central aim of critical rhetoric is clear: It posits as its goal liberation
> of the oppressed; improved communicative relations; the improvement
> of social conditions, including the quality of work life; and, in academic
> contexts, the improvement of learning conditions. For cyberwriters,
> this critical rhetoric translates into an ethic of advocacy for one's elec-
> tronic audiences—users, browsers, electronic readers—that aims to
> improve their conditions of learning and ease their conditions of
> oppression or dominance within institutional settings. (63)

Taking this concept a step further, James Aune links critical rhetoric overtly with ideology: "It is the function of a critical theory of rhetoric to help
formulate strategies to make socialism a desirable and believable end and to
call into being publics who will implement them" (142).

But criticism provides for only one aspect of knowledge-age empower-ment. As critics, communicators are not empowered to act strategically, to manage projects, or to create value. Nothing in the vast humanistic expan-sion of the communication disciplines provides for the entrepreneurial mindset. To be an entrepreneur is to take risks, to produce things, to make deals, and these activities are not found in the vocabulary that describes what we do as communicators. The stance of the critics is to be outside of that realm with their backs to the fence, looking over their shoulders in both snide deprecation of the activities within and jealous longing for the freedom and responsibilities that come from being inside. Disgruntlement over the decades of inward-looking navel-gazing seems to have reached new heights, as a post on the PreText e-mail discussion list by Stephen Bernhardt illustrates: "I worry about a profession too inward looking, too content with the writing of each other for each other, too content to move beyond looking at our students within our institutional contexts" (4/9/00). Peter Drucker, who sees the educated person as the unifying force in the knowledge society, agrees that this humanistic, critical approach to educa-tion is unsuited for the knowledge age:

> Postcapitalist society requires a unifying force. It requires a leadership group, which can focus local, particular, separate traditions onto a common and shared commitment to values, a common concept of excellence, and on mutual respect. The postcapitalist society—the knowledge society—thus needs exactly the opposite of what decon-structionists, radical feminists, or anti-Westerners propose. It needs the very thing they totally reject: a universally educated person. Yet the knowledge society needs a kind of educated person different from the ideal for which the humanists are fighting. They rightly stress the folly of their opponents' demand to repudiate the Great Tradition and the wisdom, beauty, and knowledge that are the heritage of mankind. But a bridge to the past is not enough—and that is all the humanists offer. The educated person needs to be able to bring his or her knowledge to bear on the present, not to mention to have a role in molding the future. There is no provision for such ability in the proposals of the humanists, indeed, no concern for it. But without it, the Great Tradition remains dusty antiquarianism. (289)

Drucker finds humanism's main fault in backward-looking values, but current- or forward-looking activities that lock us into perpetual analysis are similarly problematic in theorizing the value of applied rhetoric. The following quote, admittedly uttered in another time for another occasion, nonetheless captures the enfeebling effects of pure criticism devoid of the possibility of action. Speaking at the Sorbonne in 1910, Theodore Roosevelt said the following:

> It is not the critic who counts; not the man who points out how the strong man stumbles, or where the doer of deeds could have done them better. The credit belongs to the man who is actually in the arena, whose face is marred by dust and sweat and blood; who strives valiantly; who errs, and comes short again and again; because there is not effort without error and shortcoming; but who does actually strive to do the deeds; who knows the great enthusiasms, the great devotions; who spends himself in a worthy cause, who at the best knows in the end the triumphs of high achievement and who at the worst, if he fails, at least fails while daring greatly, so that his place shall never be with those cold and timid souls who know neither victory or defeat. (cited in Nixon, p. 345)

Deferred during the expansion of the humanist critical dimension of the rhetoric, composition, and technical communication since the 1970s is the companion truth about rhetoric—that it is also about production, action, and creation. It is sometimes hard to see this move for a variety of reasons. First, our foundational theories have focused on other things. We do not generally think strategically, nor do we think economically. We think of ourselves as support, either in the generation of documents or in the critique of existing social structures and documents. Second, economy is "other," to be observed and criticized from outside. Deep down, we have this feeling that we simply don't belong inside. We may not even want to be inside because the realm of production is so often the realm of exploitation. But communicators do ultimately produce and distribute their writing, whether it be documentation, correspondence, business plans, organization charts, human resource plans, or any other sort of product. Communicators create and produce value—economic, aesthetic, human— and this value is measurable. When we add production back into the evolution of the discipline, we can move forward from seeing the communicator as critic or analyst to recognizing the communicator as innovator and producer. I call this dimension the *productive*, but its name is less important than the concept that a communicator's activities constitute real value for organizations.

A central aim of this book is to flesh out the implications of this third dimension of communication. As we ponder the communicator's expanded mission, we must figure out how to incorporate our humanist critical stance, which is inherently reactive, into a productive stance. In other words, I am arguing, it is not enough to live, teach, and practice a rhetoric that reacts to the real world as if it is something other than ourselves. Applied rhetoricians must be able to place themselves and their students into the world of value creation, competition, and free markets. As both Table 1.1 and Fig. 1.4 illustrate, this activity does not rely on an either–or dichotomy, but rather on the enfolding of something new. This expanded mission for rhetors reflects a growing sense of value in how we treat and perceive ourselves, how the marketplace sees us, and how we see the marketplace.

Such an expansion is not simply prognostication or wishful thinking: It is already underway. At the end of *User-Centered Technology,* Robert

TABLE 1.1. Three Dimensions of Applied Rhetoric

	Instrumental *(Grammar, Layout, Style, Editing, Logic)*	Critical *(Ethics, Cultural Criticism, Gender, Technology Criticism, Humanism)*	Productive *(Management, Value, Organizational Theory, Project Management)*
Primary engagement	Texts	Audiences	Organizations
Status of practitioner	Tool	Human	Leader
Theory	Language	Culture	Free Markets
Stance	Mastery	Reactive	Competitive/ productive
Mission	Accuracy	Observation	Value creation
Core competency	Skills	Agency	Entrepreneurship
Place in organization	Tool	Cost Center	Revenue center
Pedagogy	Skills	Critique	Synthesis and synergy
Era	Documents	Information	Knowledge
Pay relative to mean	Low	Slightly lower	Slightly higher
Rhetorical theories	Positivism	Relativism	Capitalism
Composition theories	Current-traditional	Epistemic	Professional
Tech. comm. theories	Instructions, description	Ethics, humanism	Knowledge, teams

Johnson points out the severe limitations of what he calls the "critical read-ings" approach to education: "I am unconvinced that merely involving stu-dents with issues through texts is enough to engender a full enough under-standing of how to *act* as technical rhetoricians. Simply put, to *know* does not necessarily translate to *know how*" (160). Johnson calls for communica-tors to "move into the complicated realm of communication in the public and workplace spheres" (160) through a user-centered approach to knowl-edge and text-creation. Although Johnson does not go this far, I argue that recognizing the knowledge and choices of such a body of users constitutes acknowledgment of the inherent market nature of rhetoric. Our increasing love affair with usability as a viable epistemology suggests that we trust the decentralized processes of the market more than the centralized observa-tions that result from critical analysis.

The increased trend in service-learning, or real-world education, along with cross-disciplinary work within rhetoric and technical communication is another indication of these developments. Recent work, especially in dis-sertations and articles, has focused on the role of technical communicators as creators of value within organizations. In 1993, Rachel Spilka recognized the important role technical communicators have within organizations, and suggested that communicators may eventually grow into the role of knowl-edge architect within these organizations. In this view, the rhetorical activi-ties of communicators will make the various organizations within a compa-ny integrate their efforts better. The rapid expansion of technology into society has also created opportunities for communicators. In a 2001 article in *Technical Communication,* William Hart-Davidson argued for an expanded, value-creating role within the information technology sector. And in rhetoric and composition programs around the country, graduate students and professors are increasingly engaging in innovative and entre-preneurial projects. Software products and services have been developed, marketed, and commercialized at Carnegie-Mellon, UCLA, Utah State and University of Texas Rhetoric and Composition programs. Johndan Johnson-Eilola and Stuart Selber argue that this information economy has perhaps been the most important influence on applied rhetoric's continuing expansion:

> Historically, technical communication has served more of a symbolic than communicative function, at least in the eyes of many both inside and outside the field, including technology users. Technical communi-cation was something that was either expected (e.g., support documen-tation) or required (e.g., environmental impact statements), but in nei-ther case was it considered to be at the center of important work. In an information economy, however, technical communication has become a key commodity, a fact the field has exploited in the development of its academic programs. (406)

The model I propose for a fully realized rhetoric brings together the instrumental, critical, and productive components introduced above. The instrumental dimension of rhetoric provides a focus on the text and its presentation. The critical dimension places the text into society, providing analytical and critical views regarding the production of the text, its reception, its history, and power relations around texts and other sign systems. The productive dimension recognizes the texts and the social circumstances around those texts as being part of the competitive arena, providing the means by which we can ask questions like "How do messages compete?" "What is the value added by communication and communicators?" and "To what degree do rhetorical utterances affect decisions involving scarce resources?"

Fig. 1.4 illustrates the relationship among these three dimensions. What this model shows is that these dimensions are not separate; instead, they are overlapping spheres of expertise, skills, and influence. Indeed, each sphere encompasses the text, and by text, I mean any rhetorical product, such as a web site, proposal, verbal presentation, pamphlet, chapter, manual, and so on. The instrumental dimension focuses almost exclusively on the text and its production, so its graphic representation in Fig. 1.4 is that of a circle that remains close to the text. The critical dimension takes the text and its production, style, and norms as a starting point, and augments the model with the analytical and critical perspectives mentioned above. Finally, the productive dimension begins with the analytical and the critical, then engages more activity and takes on more responsibility, while moving further away from the text itself.

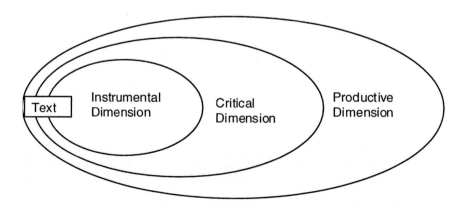

Figure 1.4. Expanding roles, responsibilities, and spheres of influence.

I think many of us in academic rhetoric programs already think like this, perhaps employing different terminology. When I talk with students about the balance we seek in our technical communication and rhetoric and composition programs, I use the terms *on-the-page* and *off-the-page* skills, classes, and theories. These are easy images to convey. Courses that deal with on-the-page issues are traditional writing classes, style, editing, layout, and various genre courses. When we move off the page, we deal with what happens during the creation of those texts, how those texts move around organizations, why certain texts work better in different disciplines, and how the text has a history.

Even without positing the three dimensions that I do, it is easy to see how this shift from on-the-page skills to off-the-page skills impacts what we perceive as their knowledge domain, what we choose to offer in our courses, and how we describe what we do. Table 1.1 expands the figure and fills in terminology for each dimension. I think it helps us recognize that each dimension emphasizes different pedagogies, theories, and core competencies.

IMPLICATIONS

The curricular implications of recognizing this third dimension are large, but we are already seeing such moves within technical communication and rhetoric and compositions programs. The evolution of what constitutes a proper curriculum—teaching, learning, and supporting student's minds and skills—illustrates this point. At their core most rhetoric programs include instrumental dimension skills courses: writing, editing, style, grammar, and history. Add ethics, criticism, and theory to extend this tool-wielding curriculum into the critical dimension. And since the late 1990s, we see entrepreneurial courses focused on information architecture, project management, knowledge management, single-sourcing, and document management, all constituting roles for the communicator as a creator of value in an organization. It is perhaps inevitable that applied rhetoric programs will continue to evolve courses in media, XML, teamwork, and value. Internships will increasingly focus on cross-functional teams and production within organizations.

In our pedagogy, we see productive dimension activities in service-learning, which seeks to contextualize a student's understanding of the discipline not within just the literature, but within the "real world." This move to the real world is an activity that allows for market feedback; it is not simply service to the community, which is a characteristic of the critical dimension, but it is a competitive, market-driven, valued production. In an increasing number of schools, such service-learning is not *pro bono*, but requires payment from the real-world client. A natural evolution of this third dimension is that our programs, our classes, and our students will take a much more entrepreneurial approach to the discipline. In doing so, they will integrate the instrumental and critical dimension aspects of their education with qualities of the productive dimension—in the form of persuasiveness within their organizations, value-based rationale for their activities and activism, and a mentality that will allow them to exploit and create opportunities, not simply observe or critique them.

Theoretically, this third additional perspective involves a broadening of our conceptions of what is appropriate for rhetoric, composition, professional, and technical communications. This volume argues that theories of communication must include concepts of value and value creation. We will continue to engage value in ways we haven't heretofore, using concepts of competition, free markets, entrepreneurship, capital (both human and savings), management, and efficiency. We will see more publications dealing with efficiencies in composition programs. We will see empirical studies on the practical impact on the bottom line of expenditures on communications in the workplace. Research like Saul Carliner's 1997 "Demonstrating Value and Effectiveness" and George Slaughter's 2003 STC presentation "Measuring Value in Technical Communication," points toward methods needed to establish the value that communicators create. In short, all the sacred cows in our fields are fair game in this new paradigm: class sizes, treatment and pay for adjunct faculty, the market for graduate students, the nature and makeup of our curricula.

Another implication of this move involves deeper collaboration between industry and academy, not simply in service-learning projects, but in ongoing studies of organizational communication, knowledge collection and dissemination, and organizational production. In short, our pedagogy and curriculum is already in the midst of a move that allows these trends to flourish so that rhetoric—technical, professional, entrepreneurial—can move into a more central role within organizations and be seen and rewarded as a value-creating discipline. What requires much more investigation is the role of the communicator as chief information officer, where projects, technology, people, language, market share, and other mission-critical activities depend on action—not the blind action characteristic of the instrumental dimension, but critically sophisticated action characteristic of the productive dimension.

Within the workplace, communicators will continue to argue for management roles, merging with marketing, web-mastering, project management, human factors and usability. Rhetors, communicators, and writers have traditionally filled utilitarian (instrumental dimension) roles in their organizations, writing pamphlets, manuals, white papers, reports, and so on for technical products and clients. Innovation in these organizations has traditionally been technically based. Such a model views communication as a form of labor, which, along with other support disciplines (accounting, legal, clerical), provides support for the product-orientation fields like engineering. In this organization, management sits at the top of the pyramid, plotting strategy for technical products.

But in the knowledge age, organizations are rearranging this scheme. Strategy comes from the market, from the user/audience. Von Krogh, Ichijo, and Nonaka observe that knowledge is created close to the marketplace, not "high" in an organization. This marketplace is not some lofty concept that involves stocks, bonds, and advertising; it is where our readers, students, and users live their daily lives. And because rhetors focus on end-users—through task analysis, ethnographic tools, contextual inquiry, usability testing, and audience analysis—it is the communicator who creates new knowledge and the strategies that follow. In this new structure, the organization's strategic focus is on knowledge and on the recipient/customer. The communicator's power is greatly increased and her strategic position is near the top of the organizational pyramid, along with management, giving market-based instructions to a technical and clerical support layer composed of engineers, clerical, and legal disciplines.

As discussed throughout this introduction, value-creation provides an important lens through which we can examine our teaching, research, and practical activities. Depending on how carefully one has calculated costs (direct, indirect, and opportunity), one's activity may either create or destroy value. This observation is obviously not a call to abandon the tools and experiences of either the instrumental or critical dimension, but to integrate them with a productive dimension worldview. As long as the productive dimension is the "other," something that belongs to the realm of job seekers and the "real world," or the object of almost alien observation, then the instrumental and critical dimensions (which characterize our current position) will be oddities—devalued, undervalued. In such a world, it is natural—necessary, in fact—to resist the other, to problematize it. But when communicators have moved inside the productive dimension, they are now value-creators, aware of market values, of competition, of free ideas. Such evolution argues for a promotion of technical communications and rhetoric in organizational hierarchy—for rhetoric is marketing, usability, consumer, production, and technical communication encompasses the market and market activities. The vital skills we acquire in the instrumental and critical dimensions—all the reasons for clarity, precision, expression, and so on that we learned in the instrumental dimension, along with the reasons for empowerment, for human rights, for ethics within technical communications, for understanding organizations, for resisting technical determinism, and so on, that we learned within the critical dimension—all of these lessons remain valid. Indeed, they give the actor inside the productive dimension the agency needed to create value and influence production.

ABOUT THE CHAPTERS

The collection of chapters presented in this volume aims at exploring the possibilities of the expanded academic worldview of communicators, studying the shift in communication stances and roles between analysis and production, positioning the communicator as more than tool user, more than critic, but as entrepreneur and creator of value. These chapters serve as an initial effort at exploring an unexplored knowledge domain: the theoretical and practical stance based on the cultural and intellectual centrality of the free market at the intersection of academic disciplines of applied rhetoric. In doing so, the following authors do not advance the argument that academic communicators should not engage in analysis or criticism. But they do argue that exploring our academic fields from a market perspective will achieve the following:

- Add balance in what counts for knowledge in the rhetorical fields.
- Lead to expanded roles for communicators, especially in arenas that value off-the-page activities like knowledge creation and management, project management.
- Give voice to innovative ideas about pedagogies and curricula in technical communication, rhetoric, and composition programs.
- Suggest strategies for these programs and our students.

In short, this book focuses on market orientation, or a rhetorical concern for what people themselves feel they want and need as a theoretical foundation for rhetoric and applied rhetoric, especially in the way we design our academic programs and teach our students. The following chapters take a variety of approaches in tackling this task, and the order of these chapters mirrors these broad approaches. The volume begins with the more theoretical and ends with the more empirical and practical.

Naturally, these authors refer to their composition program, their rhetoric program, or their technical communication program, and this specificity is both inevitable and desirable. We all work within organizational realities and most of us study and teach within a definable field. Therefore, it makes sense that the following contributors employ examples that come from their own experiences. Where an author uses a term like *technical communication*, the reader is encouraged to both appreciate the specific issues raised by the author and consider the broader context encompassing all communicators.

The first few chapters take on the really difficult questions related to paradigms that either enable us or hold us back. Patrick Moore examines the nature of critical theory as one of the major influences on our current approach to applied rhetoric, one that defines what I call the second dimension earlier in this introduction. Moore turns the tools of critical theory against the method itself, arguing that the ideology of criticism that pervades communications theory has misrepresented capitalism, that it does not permit action in the modern capitalistic milieu, and that a capitalistic approach to the humanities would serve as a suitable antidote to some of the most obvious limitations of critical theory. Another paradigm that informs applied rhetoric involves the "truth" inherent in literary studies. In the next chapter, Fred Kemp deconstructs this typical humanities department's mission as an archaic throwback to Arnoldian literary essentialism, and argues that entrepreneurial communicators must jettison this mindset in order to make progress. Yet another paradigm that never fails to get a knee-jerk reaction from educators is business management, especially quality programs. Lore about Total Quality Management (TQM) on campuses is that it is foisted on us by administrators who do not understand the nature of our crafts, or that it kills innovation because it is antithetical to teaching. Keith Rhodes counters these complaints by pointing out that modern theories of composition overlap with TQM literature. Furthermore, both camps intersect in the common ground of Piercean pragmatics.

The next group of chapters considers various claims about existing markets for applied rhetoric. Mike Salvo argues that the social goal of maintaining a clean environment opens up opportunities for market mechanisms in the form of markets for pollution. Communicators have a critical role to play in this discussion, for the key components of the debate lie in the realm of the rhetorical. One of the most visible and talked-about markets involves commercial providers of online education, and the University of Phoenix is at the forefront of this market. Although it is easy to talk about value, marketing, and entrepreneurship in the abstract, it is common to hear scholars and students complain about private education providers. They are only in it for the money, some say. Or they have no quality control. "Shouldn't we do something about the U of P?" we hear our colleagues say. It must be a low-quality threat to our own programs, we conclude. Brook Hessler points out that while the University of Phoenix is widely cited as a scapegoat, it is in fact a smart competitor to brick-and-mortar education. Its role as scapegoat is based more on emotion than on fact, she concludes. Instead of reacting with fear to its operations, brick-and-mortar providers must learn to analyze U of P's business, curricular, and pedagogical models and adapt accordingly. In a similar vein, Donna Spehar examines the competitive landscape of distance education providers of technical communication courses and analyzes various sector strategies. One of her conclusions is that higher education providers must clearly understand the entire industry in order to formulate strategy, and that it is likely that for-profit provider are less-direct competitors than we may think. How we react to these online competitors says a great deal about the way our own minds work.

After reading this introduction, a reader may be thinking, "What would a market-based approach look like?" The final chapters provide very specific data, narratives, methods, and outcomes of just such market-based approaches to applied rhetoric. The first chapter in this group relates the difficulty of retooling a large writing program in the context of complex micro- and macro-market factors. In this chapter, Susan Lang applies the concepts of innovation to the Texas Tech Freshman Composition program and presents a compelling case study of a program responding to market forces, radically rethinking the nature of the composition labor force, and reinventing the nature of the first-year writing course. Some programs do not have to adapt existing protocols to the market because they are starting from scratch. Barry Maid and Marian Stone discuss the steps they took in developing a new Multimedia Writing and Technical Communication program at Arizona State University East (ASU). In starting with a clean slate, they chose to focus on delivering a service that their intended market needed. This approach required them to survey students and business leaders in the area, to examine similar programs around the country in order to see how market-responsive they were, and to analyze the nature of existing students at ASU East to determine their interests and needs. Writing programs have to argue their cases not only to potential college students, but also to other units on campus in the form of initiatives with names like Writing Across the Curriculum (WAC) or Writing in the Disciplines (WID). Yvonne Merrill takes us through the process of her writing program's WAC initiative as it learns to listen to the market for its services. Ultimately, she describes a compromise between writing experts' know-how and their clients' expectations. Kristine Hansen ends the collection with a hard look at the forces that feed the Freshman Composition machine and that constitute a major part of the competitive environment in which we work. Through this analysis, she exposes the symbiotic relationship between university writing programs and both the advanced placement tests and dual credit system in high schools. Is this a bad thing? Not necessarily, but what it means, as Hansen points out, is that the market perceives value in these activities. If composition programs believe that these activities are harmful, then a market approach is not to seek a central authority's law or regulation to stop them, but for writing programs to make their value proposition more clear to parents, teachers, and students.

REFERENCES

Aune, James Arnt. *Rhetoric and Marxism*. Boston: Westview Press, 1994.

Brandenburger, Adam M., and Barry Nalebuff. *Co-opetition*. New York: Doubleday, 1997.

Breuninger, Charles L. "The DuPont Experience: Strategic Planning for Information Design and Development Organizations." *Technical Communication* 44.4 (1997): 394-401.

Carliner, Saul. "Demonstrating Effectiveness and Value: A Process for Evaluating Technical Communication Products and Services." *Technical Communication* 44.3 (1997): 252-65.

_____ . "Emerging Skills in Technical Communication: The Information Designer's Place in a New Career Path for Technical Communicators." *Technical Communication* 48.2 (2001): 156-75.

Downing, David B., Claude Mark Hurlbert, and Paula Mathieu, Eds. *Beyond English, Inc.: Curricular Reform in a Global Economy*. Portsmouth, NH: Boynton/Cook, 2002.

Drucker, Peter F. *The Essential Drucker*. New York: Harper, 2001.

Fisher, Julie. "The Value of the Technical Communicator's Role in the Development of Information Systems." *IEEE Transactions on Professional Communication* 42, no. 3 (Sept. 1999): 145-55.

Friedman, Milton. *Capitalism and Freedom*. Chicago: U of Chicago P, 1982.

Friedman, Thomas L. *The Lexus and the Olive Tree*. New York: Anchor Books, 2000.

Greenspan, Alan. "The Assault on Integrity." In Ayn Rand, *Capitalism: The Unknown Ideal*. New York: Signet, 1967, 188-21.

Hamel, Gary, and C.K. Prahalad. *Competing for the Future*. Boston: Harvard Business School Press, 1994.

Hart-Davidson, William. "On Writing, Technical Communication, and Information Technology: The Core Competencies of Technical Communication." *Technical Communication* 48.2 (2001): 145-55.

Hayek, F.A. *The Road to Serfdom*. Chicago: U of Chicago P, 1944.

Horton, David. "Technical Communication As Business Strategy: How Changes In Discursive Patterns Affect the Value of Technical Communication in Cross-Functional Team Settings." *Technical Communication*, 47.1 (2000): 77.

Jaffe, Greg. "Navy Turns Auctioneer, Lets Sailors Bid for Unpopular Posts." *Wall Street Journal*, August 11, 2003: B1+.

Johnson, Robert. *User Centered Technology: A Rhetorical Theory for Computers and Other Mundane Artifacts*. Albany: SUNY UP, 1998.

Johnson-Eilola, Johndan. "Relocating The Value Of Work: Technical Communication In A Post-Industrial Age." *TCQ* 5.3 (1995): 245-70.

Johnson-Eilola, Johndan, and Stuart A. Selber. "Sketching a Framework for Graduate Education in Technical Communication." *TCQ* 10.4 (2001): 406-37.

Massy, William F. "Reengineering Resource Allocation Systems." In *Resource Allocation in Higher Education.* Ed. William Massy. Ann Arbor: U of Michigan P, 1996, 15-47.

McCloskey, Deirdre. *The Rhetoric of Economics,* 2nd ed. Madison: Wisconsin UP, 1998.

Mead, Jay. "Measuring the Value Added by Technical Communication." *Technical Communication* 45.3 (1998): 353-79.

Miller, Carolyn R. "A Humanistic Rationale for Technical Writing." *College English* 40.6 (1979): 610-17.

Nixon, Richard. *Leaders.* Warner Books, 1982, 345.

Perelman, Chaim. *The Realm of Rhetoric.* Notre Dame: U of Notre Dame P, 1982.

Porter, James E. "Legal Realities and Ethical Hyperrealities: A Critical Approach Toward Cyberwriting." In *Computers and Technical Communication: Pedagogical and Programmatic Perspectives.* Ed. Stuart Selber. Greenwood, 1997, 45-73.

Porter, Michael. *Competitive Strategy: Techniques for Analyzing Industries and Competitors.* New York: Free Press, 1980.

Rao, Ramesh. *Financial Management: Concepts and Applications.* 3rd ed. Cincinnati: South-Western, 1995.

Redish, Janice. "Adding Value as a Professional Technical Communicator." *Technical Communication* 42.1 (1995): 26-39.

Seldon, Arthur. *Capitalism.* Cambridge, MA: Basil Blackwell, 1990.

Shor, Ira. *When Students Have Power: Negotiating Authority in a Critical Pedagogy.* Chicago: U of Chicago P, 1996.

Slack, Jennifer, David J. Miller, and Jeffrey Doak. "The Technical Communicator as Author: Meaning, Power, Authority." *Journal of Business and Technical Communication* 7.1 (1993): 12–36.

Slaughter, George. "Measuring Value in Technical Communication: A Research Review and Critique." Paper presented at the STC annual conference, Dallas, May 2003.

Slaughter, Sheila, and Larry L. Leslie. *Academic Capitalism: Politics, Policies, and the Entrepreneurial University.* Baltimore: Johns Hopkins UP, 1997.

Smith, Adam. *An Inquiry into the Nature and Causes of the Wealth of Nations.* Ed. Kathryn Sutherland. New York: Oxford UP, 1993.

Smith, Charles W. *Market Values in American Higher Education: The Pitfalls and Promises.* New York: Rowman & Littlefield, 2000.

Spilka, Rachel, Ed. *Writing in the Workplace: New Research Perspectives.* Carbondale: Southern Illinois UP, 1993.

Statistical Abstract of the United States. Washington: US Census Bureau, 2003. Also online: http://www.census.gov/prod/www/statistical-abstract-03.html

Taylor, Paul H. *Computer Conferencing and Chaos: A Study in Fractal Discourse.* Doctoral Dissertation, University of Texas, 1993. UMI: 9401009.

Van Eemeren, Frans H., Rob Grootendorst, and Francisca Snoeck Henkemans, eds. *Fundamentals of Argumentation Theory: A Handbook of Historical Backgrounds and Contemporary Developments.* Mahwah, NJ: Erlbaum, 1996.

Von Krogh, Georg, Kazuo Ichijo, and Ikujiro Nonaka. *Enabling Knowledge Creation: How to Unlock the Mystery of Tacit Knowledge and Release the Power of Innovation.* Oxford: Oxford UP, 2000.

Wick, Corey. "Knowledge Management and Leadership Opportunities for Technical Communicators." *Technical Communication* 47.4 (2000): 515-29.

Zuboff, Shoshana. *In the Age of the Smart Machine: The Future of Work and Power.* New York: Basic Books, 1988.

$\mathbb{2}$ From Cultural Capitalism to Entrepreneurial Humanism

Understanding and Reevaluating Critical Theory

Patrick Moore

University of Arkansas
Little Rock

Authors of contemporary academic studies of technical communication frequently attack capitalism as the source of many of the social problems of our time. These critical theorists believe that capitalism is to blame for dehumanization, alienation, tyranny, consumerism, profiteering, an "ethic of expediency," death, and a host of other ills. "In a capitalistic society," says Stephen Katz, "technological expediency often takes precedence over human convenience, and sometimes even human life" ("The Ethic of Expediency" 271). Summarizing Andrew Feenberg's description of the "substantive" approach to technology, Johndan Johnson-Eilola writes, "the instant we decide, for example, to produce automobiles, we are committed to a long, downward path of pollution, injury, and death" (102). Capitalistic corporations are those who typically "decide" to produce automobiles. Critical theorists are also very concerned about technical communication itself, which many of them believe is one of the primary instruments through which capitalism inflicts its damage on the world. As Carolyn Miller wrote:

> To continue to teach [technical communication] as we have, to acquiesce in passing off a version as an absolute, is coercive and tyrannical; it is to wrench ideology from belief. Much of what we call technical writing occurs in the context of government and industry and embodies tacit commitments to bureaucratic hierarchies, corporate capitalism, and high technology. If we pretend for a minute that technical writing

is objective, we have passed off a particular political ideology as privileged truth. (616)

Critical theorists who write about technical communication often believe that all discourse, including scientific and technical communication, is overtly or covertly rhetoric (i.e., persuasion); that discourse is used to plan, develop, manage, implement, sell, and show people how to use technology; that technology is developed and controlled by capitalistic organizations; and that capitalism is bad for the reasons I just cited. These authors are especially concerned by what they believe to be the deviousness of capitalism and its enabling discourse, and they are wary of any theory, practice, discourse, or technology that does not reveal itself openly as being ideological, as having some design on controlling and oppressing us. Once these critics expose the hidden persuasion of capitalism and the false neutrality of its tools (i.e., technology and technical communication), then they believe that people and cultures can avoid the inevitable dehumanization, tyranny, and death that technology promises for human kind.

Although many of these critical theorists attack capitalism, they ignore the fact that the democratic cultures that give them the freedom to make their critiques are all high-tech state-capitalistic cultures. They further ignore the fact that the cultures that have the most freedoms, the most social opportunities, the most democracy, the longer life spans, and the highest standards of living are precisely the cultures in which high-tech state capitalism plays a central role in the economy. Although critical theorists put many questions to the motives and procedures of capitalism, they never ask if their critiques would be possible if they lived in low-tech non-democratic cultures; they do not supply any viable alternatives to high-tech state capitalism or its many national variations; and they never apply their critiques to their own philosophy.

The bias of these critics does the public a disservice, because, after graduation, their students are likely to work for capitalistic organizations or for local, state, and federal governments that derive their resources from capitalistic corporations. With their heads filled with bias and misinformation, these students may not be well prepared for the realities of the workplace. These critics also do the academy and the discipline of technical communication a disservice because they create hostility and misunderstanding between universities and corporations when there could be civility, cooperation, and mutually beneficial exchanges of information. Finally, these critics do scholarship and technical communication theory a disservice because they are aggressively biased, because they are hypocritical, and because they discourage theoretical innovations.

My arguments in this chapter are (a) that some of the assumptions of critical theory are very dubious, (b) that critical theory is enabled by capitalism, (c) that critical theory is capitalistic in its own way, and (d) that critical theory is of limited use in the workplace.

In the sections that follow, I define and outline the historical background of critical theory, I apply the methodology of critical theory to critical theory itself, I explain how critical theory is capitalistic itself, and I discuss some of the limitations of critical theory.

WHAT IS CRITICAL THEORY?

Critical theory is a 20th-century philosophical and sociological movement that began at the University of Frankfurt in 1923 as the Institute for Social Research. The Institute was funded initially by Hermann Weil, a German-Jewish businessman who moved to Argentina in 1890 in his early 20s, made a fortune exporting grain to Germany, and then returned to Frankfurt in 1908, where he speculated in real estate and trading meat (Wiggershaus 12). The Frankfurt Institute's connection to Hermann Weil was through his son, Felix, who was a student, a political activist, and later described himself as a "salon Bolshevik" (Wiggershaus 13). Felix had been a member of the socialist Fabian Society when he lived in England, and "had been briefly arrested for socialist activities in October 1919, and then expelled from Tubingen University and banned from the state of Wurttemberg" (Wiggershaus 11). In 1920, Felix earned a doctorate from the University of Frankfort in political science and soon after suggested creating an Institute for Social Research.

Immersed in the troubles of his time, Felix Weil was deeply concerned with the social upheavals of the early 20th century. As he wrote in his dissertation:

> One thing is certain, things cannot continue as they are today, with businessmen frightened to carry out their tasks with the daring needed, by strikes, high wages, taxes, works councils, mutual distrust and the fear of socialization, with German economic life drying up.
>
> Back to the free market or forwards to socialism? That is the question. (Wiggershaus 11-12)

Like Weil's dissertation, the Frankfurt Institute was a reaction to the social conditions of its time. In the early 1920s, Germany was torn with the aftermath of the devastating World War I, with massive unemployment, with runaway inflation, and with strikes, bad working conditions, and small businessmen trying to compete with the rising cartels and monopolies. Into this time of collapsing monarchies, rising social upheavals, post-war devastation, and clashing ideologies, the Frankfurt Institute was established and funded by a wealthy capitalist eager to do good for Germany and to support his son's ideas. Over the next few years, of course, social and economic conditions would get progressively worse, leading to the collapse of the stock market in 1929 in the United States, the rise of the Nazis, and the destruction of World War II.

Although the Institute was founded in Frankfurt in 1923, it would only stay there for 10 years. On January 30, 1933, the Nazis came to power in Germany, and Max Horkheimer, the second head of the Frankfurt Institute, was fired from his job at the University of Frankfurt on April 13, 1933 (Jay 29). All of the most prominent first-generation critical theorists—Horkheimer, Theodor Adorno, Erich Fromm, Walter Benjamin, Friedrich Pollock, Leo Lowenthal, Herbert Marcuse—were sons of Jewish families, and each had to leave the country when the Nazis took over. Some went to Switzerland, some to Paris, but eventually most went to the United States. Walter Benjamin, unfortunately, did not survive. After leaving Germany, he stayed in Paris, but as the Nazis took over France in 1940, he left for the Spanish border in the Pyrenees. Depressed, suffering from a heart condition, and hearing that the Spanish had just closed the border before he arrived, Benjamin committed suicide on September 27, 1940 (Jay 198). The fate of the other members of the Frankfurt Institute was happier. Most made their way to the United States, where they passed the war. After the fall of the Nazis in 1945, West Germany invited Horkheimer and Adorno back to Frankfurt to pick up where they had left off. Marcuse, Lowenthal, and others continued to live in the United States (Aronowitz xiii).

The goal of critical theory is to enhance human freedom by criticizing the kinds of domination created by intellectual behaviors, artifacts, and institutions in the modern world. The behaviors, artifacts, and institutions that most concerned the members of the Frankfurt School were science, technology, the mass media, corporations, and modern governments, which—according to critical theorists—use reason, rationalization, and objectivity in ways that limit human freedom, expression, and social participation. The result of limited human freedom, expression, and social participation is alienation, oppression, and the loss of meaningful participation in social life.

First-generation critical theorists had little quarrel with what they called "liberal capitalism," which was the capitalism of small businessmen, tradesmen, and others who entered into business to define and create themselves and to emancipate themselves from various social and economic constraints. "Liberal" and "capitalism" may seem like an odd pairing, but only because the historical context has changed. Milton Friedman explains the development of this kind of liberalism as follows:

> As it developed in the late eighteenth and early nineteenth centuries, the intellectual movement that went under the name of liberalism emphasized freedom as the ultimate goal and the individual as the ultimate entity in the society. It supported laissez faire at home as a means of reducing the role of the state in economic affairs and thereby enlarging the role of the individual; it supported free trade abroad as a means of linking the nations of the world together peacefully and democratically. In political matters, it supported the development of representative government and of parliamentary institutions, reduction in the arbitrary power of the state, and protection of the civil freedoms of individuals. (5)

In the United States today, "liberal" has a very different meaning. As Friedman explains, liberalism has come "to be associated with a readiness to rely primarily on the state rather than on private voluntary arrangements to achieve objectives regarded as desirable" (5). In some key respects, liberals of today are the exact opposite of 19th-century liberals: "In the name of welfare and equality, the twentieth-century liberal has come to favor a revival of the very policies of state intervention and paternalism against which classical liberalism fought" (5-6). The German liberal capitalists of the late 19th- and early 20th-centuries were liberals in the first sense that Friedman defines.

Those liberal capitalists included the fathers of several members of the Frankfurt School. Thus, the first-generation critical theorists were not hostile toward liberal capitalism. But they were shaken by what capitalism had evolved into. As Held says, "Horkheimer [in one of his books] notes the demise of competitive, liberal capitalism and the rise of big, organized industry" (45). Felix Weil, as cited previously, believed that "things cannot continue as they are today, with businessmen frightened to carry out their tasks with the daring needed." The socially beneficial, self-liberating, and self-creating aspects of liberal capitalism began to be eroded by the rise of cartels and monopolies in the early part of the twentieth century, and any social and personal benefits of liberal capitalism were completely destroyed when the Nazis took over capitalism in Germany in the early 1930s. By 1939, Horkheimer identified Nazi-controlled state-capitalism so closely with fascism that he wrote, "he who does not wish to speak of capitalism should also be silent about fascism" (cited in Jay, 121). For the first five decades of the 20th century in Germany, the term *capitalism* meant the gradual annihilation of the personal freedoms so dear to the critical theorists of the Frankfurt School. They were harshly—and justifiably—critical of the activities of the monopoly- and state-capitalists whom they saw around them in Germany.

The method of critical theory is to examine the assumptions, origins, ideologies, and value-judgments of science, technology, corporations, and the bureaucratic state to see if those assumptions and value-judgments enhance or detract from human freedom and social participation. One approach of the methodology is to examine the historical origins of some belief or practice to see if it has later been distorted for some political reason. A second approach of the methodology is to see if there are any omissions in the assumptions or ideologies of a belief or practice. One famous omission in industry, which was not dealt with adequately in economic theory until R. H. Coase, is its effect on the environment. A third approach of the methodology is to look for the motivations behind the intellectual behaviors, artifacts, and institutions in the modern world. Financial profits and beating the competition are usually important motivations in corporate behaviors. A fourth aspect of the methodology of critical theory is to examine the bias and limits of the ideas behind science, technology, corporations, and state bureaucracy. One of those ideas is "objectivity," which critical theorists have tried to discredit. This analytical methodology created by the critical theorists is one of their finest achievements.

Because of their methodology and how they applied it, the legacy of critical theory is considerable: First, the philosophers of the Institute for Social Research encouraged intellectuals to ask important questions. Those questions included the following:

- What are your assumptions?
- What does your practice, belief, methodology, or institution include or leave out?
- Who profits from, who pays for your practice, belief, methodology, or institution?
- What historical conditions influenced the development of your practice, belief, methodology, or institution?
- What are the limits of your practice, belief, methodology, or institution?

Second, critical theorists turned philosophy away from creating static, closed systems of belief and applied philosophy to the dynamic world. They are primarily critics, and for that reason, their contributions are frequently regarded as negative. Third, critical theorists have influenced many academic humanists in their teaching. They shifted teaching from studying and applying the ideas of accepted thinkers and writers to criticizing the status quo. Fourth, critical theorists helped cultures become much more skeptical about the assumptions, methodologies, and limits of science and technology. Fifth, critical theorists gave feminists an important set of critical and methodological practices. Sixth, the Frankfurt School analyzed the distorting effects of the mass media (i.e., radio and cinema) because those media and many of their techniques were developed and exploited during the rise of the Nazis. Today, schools of communication in universities still analyze the distorting effects of the mass media because of the critical theorists, and important areas of contemporary composition theory are based on the insights of critical theorists.

This brief sketch of first-generation critical theorists is obviously incomplete and superficial. For more thorough information, see Held, Jay, Wiggershaus, and the works of Horkheimer, Adorno, and Marcuse.

QUESTIONING CRITICAL THEORY

In this section I ask first-generation German critical theorists three of their own questions:

- What are your assumptions?
- What does your belief include or leave out?
- Who profits from, who pays for your belief?

I have have answered the fourth question at the end of the previous section (i.e., "What historical conditions influenced the development of your practice") in my short history of critical theory, and I discuss the limits of critical theory (Question 5) throughout this chapter. Because critical theory is complicated, my comments are necessarily brief and selective. To do justice to the strengths and limits of critical theory—just American critical theorists alone—would take a lengthy book.

What Are Your Assumptions?

A central assumption of critical theory is that people can be completely free. First-generation critical theorists are fond of calling our attention to our lack of freedom. Marcuse begins *One-Dimensional Man* with this statement: "A comfortable, smooth, reasonable, democratic unfreedom prevails in advanced industrial civilization, a token of technical progress" (1). Humans have finally gained many freedoms in industrialized cultures, but, according to Marcuse, now that those freedoms have become institutionalized, "Such a society may justly demand acceptance of its principles and institutions, and reduce the opposition to the discussion and promotion of alternative policies *within* the status quo" (Marcuse, 1-2). As a result, we have a "comfortable, smooth, reasonable, democratic unfreedom" in industrial cultures. Horkheimer and Marcuse relentlessly emphasize that even with their many freedoms, citizens of democratic, industrial societies are oppressed, enslaved, administered, dominated, and tyrannized. Horkheimer says, "Now that science has helped us to overcome the awe of the unknown in nature, we are the slaves of social pressures of our own making" (187). Marcuse asks, "how can the administered individuals—who have made their mutilation into their own liberties and satisfactions, and thus reproduce it on an enlarged scale—liberate themselves from themselves as well as from their masters?" (250-1) It is not enough that people have many rights and freedoms in democratic, industrial cultures; Horkheimer and Marcuse majestically insist that those very freedoms mutilate us and make us slaves.

When reading Horkheimer, Marcuse, and other first-generation critical theorists, we must never forget that they were utopians. Horkheimer writes in 1946: "Today, progress toward utopia is blocked primarily by the complete disproportion between the weight of the overwhelming machinery of social power and that of the atomized masses" (186). Marcuse says, "The philosophic quest proceeds from the finite world to the construction of a reality which is not subject to the painful difference between potentiality and actuality, which has mastered its negativity and is complete and independent in itself—free" (127). And Marcuse says that negative or critical thinking has a "utopian character" (168). Third-generation American critical theorists like Carolyn Miller do not specifically refer to utopias, but they share the belief of earlier critical theorists that people can be completely free. Thus, in "A Humanistic Rationale for Technical Writing," Miller refers to the "tyranny" (616) and "coercion" (613) of conventional science, the very science that has helped many people reduce and sometimes eliminate the pain, misery, and diseases of the natural world. People, however, can never be completely free. If you have a body, it is exposed to trauma, disease, and the ravages of time. If you have an ego, you are exposed to the controls, manipulations, and egos of other people. If you live in the physical world, you are exposed to the seasons, the physical laws, and the dangers of the natural world. If you live in a culture, you are exposed to the hierarchies, values, and norms of that culture. Science, technology, and state capitalism try to solve some of the problems associated with these kinds of unfreedoms, but in the end, people cannot be completely free. Critical theorists, however, assume otherwise.

A second, related, assumption is that all humans and nature are "dominated." Marcuse defined domination as follows:

> Domination is in effect whenever the individual's goals and purposes and the means of striving for and attaining them are prescribed to him and performed by him as something prescribed. Domination can be exercised by men, by nature, by things—it can also be internal, exer-

cised by the individual on himself, and appear in the form of autonomy. (Marcuse, Five Lectures, cited in Held, 149)

According to the negative theories of critical theorists, even when we try to
liberate ourselves from the natural elements, from diseases, from hunger,
and from the destructive impulses of other individuals, we only create more
domination. Horkheimer says,

> The human being, in the process of his emancipation, shares the fate of
> the rest of his world. Domination of nature involves domination of
> man. Each subject not only has to take part in the subjugation of exter-
> nal nature, human and nonhuman, but in order to do so must subjugate
> nature in himself. Domination becomes "internalized" for domina-
> tion's sake. (93)

As we become more effective at gaining freedoms for ourselves, we only
insinuate our web of domination more thoroughly into all aspects of life.
Marcuse says,

> domination now generates a higher rationality—that of a society which
> sustains its hierarchic structure while exploiting ever more efficiently
> the natural and mental resources, and distributing the benefits of this
> exploitation on an ever-larger scale. The limits of this rationality, and
> its sinister force, appear in the progressive enslavement of man by a
> productive apparatus which perpetuates the struggle for existence and
> extends it to a total international struggle which ruins the lives of those
> who build and use this apparatus. (144)

What many people call liberation and a higher standard of living, critical
theorists call domination and enslavement. First generation critical theorists
magisterially describe the longer life spans, greater freedoms, and increased
social and physical resources of industrial cultures as our ruination. Behind
these accusations of Horkheimer and Marcuse is the assumption that
humans can possess total control over nature, our bodies, our fellow
humans, and our own egos. That is not what I see in the world. I wrote part
of this chapter during an ice storm in Arkansas which shut down many
local institutions (including my university) and large portions of the state's
electrical power network. I see many attempts to control nature, destructive individuals, our bodies, and our egos, but few seem entirely successful,
and some (e.g., curing cancer, predicting the weather, getting some of my
students to attend class regularly) seem quite impossible.

A third assumption of critical theorists, related to their belief in utopias,
is that individuals are perfect or perfectable. There are no bad individuals in

critical theory—only bad societies, bad cultures, bad philosophies, bad methodologies, bad institutions, bad technologies, and bad economic systems. At the end of *Eclipse of Reason*, Horkheimer writes,

> The method of negation, the denunciation of everything that mutilates mankind and impedes its free development, rests on confidence in man. The so-called constructive philosophies may be shown truly to lack this conviction and thus to be unable to face the cultural debacle. (187)

Horkheimer can afford to be confident in man because his assumptions prevent him from acknowledging that humans are imperfect. He never blames individual people for anything and never assumes that individuals can fight and prevail against the all-powerful philosophies, societies, technologies, institutions, and capitalists who, he claims, dominate the world. Although he claims he is confident in people, Horkheimer sees individuals almost exclusively as victims of larger forces. Although he is a utopian, he has little faith that individuals can ever win against the forces of domination massed against them. Thus, his later work is very gloomy. Similarly, Marcuse ends his *One-Dimensional Man* in gloom and victimhood. He believes that there is a "substratum of the outcasts and outsiders, the exploited and persecuted of other races and other colors, the unemployed and the unemployable" (256) who can march in the streets to gain rights: "Their force is behind every political demonstration for the victims of law and order. The fact that they start refusing to play the game may be the fact which marks the beginning of the end of a period" (257). But, as Marcuse adds next, "Nothing indicates that it will be a good end." According to Marcuse, this substratum of outcasts, outsiders, unemployed, and other victims will have little power. And Marcuse holds little hope for critical theory either:

> The critical theory of society possesses no concepts which could bridge the gap between the present and its future; holding no promise and showing no success, it remains negative. Thus it wants to remain loyal to those who, without hope, have given and give their life to the Great Refusal. (257)

Marcuse ends his book with a line from Walter Benjamin, who had killed himself with a drug overdose by the Spanish border in the south of France in September 1940: "It is only for the sake of those without hope that hope is given to us." Intentionally or not, the quotation is ironic: The man who speaks eloquently for hope kills himself; the words and the reality do not match. Because first-generation critical theorists like Horkheimer and

Marcuse assume that individuals are perfect or perfectable, and because their experience shows that the world will forever thwart that perfection, their later philosophy is full of negativity and victimhood.

A fourth assumption of critical theorists is that everything—the natural world, human identity, social groups, and so on—is process. Everything is constantly changing. In their 1969 Preface to the new edition of *The Dialectic of Enlightenment*, Horkheimer and Adorno said, "We would not now maintain without qualification every statement in the book: that would be irreconcilable with a theory which holds that the core of truth is historical, rather than an unchanging constant to be set against the movement of history" (ix). In many ways, life is changing, but some things do not change, for example, human nature. Humans, according to bioethicist Peter Singer, are evolved animals, and we are hard-wired, as it were, for certain behaviors, including aggression, territoriality, and hierarchical relationships. In *The Darwinian Left*, Singer advocates a non-utopian perspective. Singer believes that we should not "Expect to end all conflict and strife between human beings, whether by political revolution, social change, or better education" (61). Singer's Darwinian Left would not "Assume that all inequalities are due to discrimination, prejudice, oppression or social conditioning. Some will be, but this cannot be assumed in every case" (61). A Darwinian Left would "Expect that, under different social and economic systems, many people will act competitively in order to enhance their own status, gain a position of power, and/or advance their interests and those of their kin" (61). In short, for Singer, there are certain constants in human beings. Cognitive psychologists have suggested that some characteristics of perception are shared by different species. In experiments on apes and humans, Gestalt psychologists discovered similarities in how both species solve problems, and in studies of chickens and humans, they discovered similarities in perceiving visual relationships (Hothersall 166-183; Hunt 280-306). The studies of the Gestaltists suggest that there are some shared traits across species and across human cultures and the passage of time. The assumption that all is process helps critical theorists minimize, ignore, or rationalize away the millennia-old awareness that humans are not perfectable or completely free. The assumption that all is process also helps first-generation critical theorists hold out the hope—however dim it seems in some of their later work—that utopia is possible.

These four assumptions of critical theory are not exhaustive. In addition, critical theorists ignore self-organizing systems like markets, languages, and human DNA, they assume that all meanings are socially constructed, and they ignore individual and universal contributions to creating meaning. Descriptions of these and other limiting assumptions of critical theorists will have to appear in other publications.

What Does Your Belief Include or Leave Out?

Each of the assumptions described in the previous sections implies important omissions in critical theory. That is, because critical theorists assume people can be completely free, they cannot accept the idea that people can be happy while being unfree in some areas; because critical theorists assume that all people and nature are dominated, they cannot believe that accepting standards of behavior liberates people from many problems; because critical theorists believe that all people are perfect or perfectable, they cannot discuss the imperfections of individuals; because critical theorists believe that everything is process, they cannot believe that there are constants in human nature. Because I have already discussed these omissions indirectly, I confine my remarks in this section to the negativity of critical theorists and their disdain for practical solutions to problems.

Because critical theorists focus on the negative, they leave out positive solutions to problems. Critical theorists do not want to solve problems; they want to criticize. They offer no specific practical alternatives to problems, although Marcuse does suggest a "therapeutic" value for critical theory (199). The critical theorist's idea of coping with problems is to call for more criticism, more research, more questioning, and more complications. For theorists, those are very easy—if not automatic—behaviors. Critical theorists shun the time-consuming, ego-bruising, inglorious, and compromising work involved in creating and working in human institutions, and developing the procedures and standards that bring conflicting individuals together and try to form them into productive, cooperating groups, practices, methodologies, and institutions. As Richard Miller has said, "for collective action to occur, intellectuals must become 'disenchanted' with the alluring image of themselves as free-thinking individuals whose mental work escapes the logic of the marketplace" (28). Critical theorists, however, cannot set aside their assumptions and develop cooperative ventures because they believe that institutions, procedures, and standards inevitably result in domination and the loss of human freedom. As a result of their negative approach, critical theory shuns the very things (i.e., capitalism, governments, bureaucracies, technologies, scientific methodology) that keep huge numbers of people alive, that enable freedom, that enable human survival, that enable billions of people to cooperate so they can achieve some of their personal goals and raise their families. Capitalism, governments, institutions, and methodologies invariably work imperfectly to better conditions for large numbers of human beings. But despite their imperfect workings, many people around the world are much better off today than they were a few score or a few hundred years ago.

A second omission in critical theory is that first-generation critics never suggest who implements the few suggestions that they do offer.

Horkheimer, for example, offers this idea about incorporating critical thought, individual spontaneity, and opposition to the status quo into industrialism:

> Under the present form of industrialism, however, the other side of rationality has become manifest through the increasing suppression of it—the role of nonconforming critical thought in the shaping of social life, of the spontaneity of the individual subject, of his opposition to ready-made patterns of behavior. On the one hand, the world is still divided into hostile groups and economic and political blocks. This situation calls for organization and centralization, which represent the element of the general from the standpoint of reason. (147)

But Horkheimer realizes that if workers do apply their nonconforming thought, their spontaneity, and their opposition to the status quo, they will pay a price. After all, how does a state, an institution, a company, or even a committee organize, centralize, and manage itself and its members when its members want to promote "nonconforming critical thought," "spontaneity of the individual subject," and "opposition to ready-made patterns of behavior"? For people to cooperate, for nations and organizations to flourish, some kinds of nonconformity and opposition must be limited (preferably self-limited). Critical theorists never give much thought to management, because they are so busy promoting criticism and negativity. For people to work together, they must, at some point, agree to be positive, agree to cooperate, and agree to create standards, even if the standard is "agreeing to disagree." But critical theorists like Horkheimer and Marcuse are opposed to creating positive systems that would establish principles for guiding cooperation. They believe that such positive systems promote slavery, tyranny, and one-dimensional thinking, and they attack anyone who tries to promote cooperation.

Who Profits from, Who Pays for the Belief?

Few people in industrial and postindustrial cultures can profit from critical theory because it is utopian, negative, and self-validating, and because it adopts an artistic stance toward human culture. Almost everyone in industrial culture—scientists, engineers, business people, and anyone who works for wages—pays for their participation in the culture because critical theorists label them dominators, slaves, oppressors, or one-dimensional men.

For Horkheimer, the critical theorist should not present positive solutions. The critical theorist exposes the defects of existing systems of representation and control. The most positive activity that a critical theorist can engage in is considering things for themselves:

> Less and less is anything done for its own sake. A hike that takes a man
> out of the city to the banks of a river or a mountain top would be irra-
> tional and idiotic, judged by utilitarian standards; he is devoting himself
> to a silly or destructive pastime. In the view of formalized reason, an
> activity is reasonable only if it serves another purpose, e.g., health or
> relaxation, which helps to replenish his working power. In other
> words, the activity is merely a tool, for it derives its meaning only
> through its connection with other ends. (37)

Horkheimer rails against any value other than intrinsic value. He rejects
any pragmatic or utilitarian purpose for nature, humans, or art because he
claims that it results in domination. He objects to engineers because "The
engineer is not interested in understanding things for their own sake or for
the sake of insight, but in accordance with their being fitted into a scheme,
no matter how alien to their own inner structure" (151). He also objects to
philosophers when their work is useful to society. For example, he con-
demns the work of Ortega y Gasset: "The very fact that his philosophy is
slanted for popular availability, i.e., its pedagogical character, nullifies it as
philosophy. Theories embodying critical insight into historical processes,
when used for panaceas, have often turned into repressive doctrines" (164).
For Horkheimer, everything that serves a pragmatic end ends up repressing
people.

The assumptions of critical theorists guarantee that no one can benefit
morally from industrial culture except for critical theorists and artists.
Critical theorists condemn as victims any individuals or social groups who
try to promote social cooperation because they support the negative
assumption of critical theorists (i.e., that people are dominated), and critical
theorists condemn people who cooperate socially as tyrants because they
undermine the positive assumptions of critical theory (e.g., that people can
be completely free). Any system of coordination or cooperation created by
scientists, engineers, and business people inevitably limits a person's freedom, inevitably dominates people or nature, inevitably assumes that people
are imperfect, and inevitably assumes some form of stability in human
experience. First-generation critical theorists rig their philosophy so that
everyone who participates in industrial culture is contaminated by the
oppressiveness that critical theorists project on it, either because the person
is an oppressor or one of the oppressed.

The only people who can profit from critical theory are those who
adopt a critical or an artistic stance toward life. One purpose of the artist in
culture is to detect and vividly dramatize the gaps between reality and any
human attempts to represent and control reality for utilitarian purposes.
For centuries people have tried to represent and control reality in order to
cooperate socially, to minimize the ravages of nature, to protect ourselves
from destructive individuals, and to guarantee that we have enough food,

water, clothing, and shelter to survive. These human systems of representation and control include languages, reason, laws, governments, sciences, engineering, and businesses. Invariably, these systems of representation and control are defective because the individuals who use them are fallible, because individuals must give up some of their freedoms to participate in them, and because reality changes, creating discontinuities between the systems of representation and control and the reality itself. Artists are one of the groups (critics are another) who describe or dramatize the gaps between these systems of representation and control and the reality that eludes them. The role of the artist for Marcuse is to present "the unhappy consciousness of the divided world, the defeated possibilities, the hopes unfulfilled, and the promises betrayed" (61). But artists, like critical theorists, often have few workable solutions to the problems of the world because they typically emphasize the negative.

First-generation critical theorists like Horkheimer and Marcuse rig their philosophical system so that critical theorists can appear morally superior to everyone else in industrial cultures. They hold up an impossible ideal—that is, they want us to feed, clothe, and shelter ourselves, to cooperate with others in a variety of ways, to avoid harming nature, and to do all of this without participating in any system that limits any human freedom and without assuming that individuals have any imperfections. When we fail to achieve this ideal because we live in industrial and postindustrial societies and have to work for a living, then critical theorists disparage us as slaves, oppressors, or one-dimensional people.

The attitudes of the first-generation critical theorists are echoed in the writings of third-generation American theorists like Katz, Johnson-Eilola, and Carolyn Miller, among others. These American theorists are never explicitly utopian, and their concerns are often more muted than the first-generation critics who had to face Nazism in the flesh. Nevertheless, the work of the third-generation Americans still expresses a deep concern about technology and capitalism, and their theorizing has the same limitations of the first-generation critical theorists.

THE CULTURAL CAPITALISM OF CRITICAL THEORISTS

First-generation critical theorists were very sympathetic to liberal capitalism, but one of the blind spots of second- and third-generation critical theorists is that they do not recognize the many similarities between the beliefs of economic capitalism and the beliefs of their own cultural capitalism. For example, one of the most important purposes of capitalism is criticism. Marcuse himself points out that "Freedom of thought, speech, and conscience were—just as free enterprise, which they served to promote and protect—essentially *critical* ideas, designed to replace an obsolescent material and intellectual culture by a more productive and rational one" (Marcuse 1). The success of competitive state capitalism depends in part on people and organizations being critical of their competition, their markets, and themselves to bring better products and services to their markets at lower cost and at minimal impact to the environment. Petroski makes the same point about developing the technology of the pencil:

> With growing competition, criticism of pencils was easier not only among competitors but also among consumers, for there were now examples of different styles of pencils to contrast and compare. As artists and draftsmen who would use pencils became more discriminating, their criticisms especially had to be answered or, if the expense was not too great, removed. This dynamic process is essentially self-propagating and self-regulating and results in the development of better pencils, or can at least produce less expensive ones. More or less the same process is followed in all modern engineering development, but in the early days of the pencil it was left largely to artisans and craftsmen to evolve changes in response to forces of imagination and creativity, of art and craft, of supply and demand, of criticism and economy. (52)

Criticism is inherent in almost any human endeavor, whether that endeavor is science, engineering, capitalism, or social philosophy. Being critical is part of the common ground between critical theory and capitalism, science, and technology.

A simple definition will illustrate some of the other values that economic capitalists share with critical theorists. Economic capitalism has at least four characteristics: (a) the belief in private ownership of property (e.g., stocks, bonds, property, cash, jewelry, etc.); (b) the belief that the income from the property belongs to the people who own the property; (c) the belief in free trade; and (d) the belief in the profit motive. Cultural capitalists believe in the same four things: (a) individuals (scholars, critics, artists) privately own their works (books, poems, articles, paintings, musical compositions, etc.); (b) the income (e.g., the social status, royalties, promotions, raises, appointments, scholarships, prizes) from their property belongs to the owners of the property; (c) scholars, critics, and artists should engage in the free dissemination of their works; and (d) their desire to gain social distinction, royalties, promotions, raises, reduced teaching loads, appointments, and so on, is perfectly legitimate. Economic and cultural capitalists also share a common motivation: They want distinction; they want to be socially distant from others. However, cultural capitalists do not want to attain cultural distinction in the same way as economic capitalists—by obtaining money. They want to be morally superior. Cultural capitalists want to earn their distinction through their educations, their taste, and their critical and aesthetic attitudes. For their cultural capital to have distinction, however, it must be rare. As Bourdieu explains,

> Because the appropriation of cultural products presupposed disposi-
> tions and competencies which are not distributed universally (although
> they have the appearance of innateness), these products are subject to
> exclusive appropriation, material or symbolic, and, functioning as cul-
> tural capital (objectified or internalized), they yield a profit in distinc-
> tion, proportionate to the rarity of the means required to appropriate
> them, and a profit in legitimacy, the profit par excellence, which con-
> sists in the fact of feeling justified in being (what one is), being what it
> is right to be. (228)

To gain their distinction, cultural capitalists must have the rarest of degrees: the doctorate; the highest of ethics: the ability to see tyranny or immorality in the slightest nuance or the most trivial artifact; and the best artistic taste: a taste that disdains anything associated with clarity, meaning, or function. As Bourdieu says, "The naïve exhibitionism of 'conspicuous consumption,' which seeks distinction in the crude display of ill-mastered luxury, is noth-ing compared to the unique capacity of the pure gaze, a quasi-creative power which sets the aesthete apart from the common herd." (31). When Horkheimer insists on "understanding things for their own sake or for the sake of insight" (151) he unwittingly proclaims himself a cultural capitalist. For critical theorists, to understand something's meaning, or to use some-thing for a practical purpose is to debase oneself with vulgar instrumentali-ty. To maintain their social distance and their cultural capital, critical theo-rists must despise economic capitalism and anything else—science, technol-ogy, engineering—which sees a practical purpose in nature, society, or arti-facts. What Bourdieu says about the aesthetic disposition applies to the critical disposition:

> The aesthetic disposition, a generalized capacity to neutralize ordinary
> urgencies and to bracket off practical ends, a durable inclination and
> aptitude for practice without a practical function, can only be consti-
> tuted within an experience of the world freed from urgency and
> through the practice of activities which are an end in themselves, such
> as scholastic exercises or the contemplation of works of art. (54)

First-generation critical theorists could formulate their ideas "within an experience of the world freed from urgency" because they were supported by capitalists and because they disdained any instrumental purpose in their own work. Contemporary American critical theorists use their tenure in colleges and universities and their ideology to distance themselves from the practical problems of the workplace.

THE LIMITS OF CRITICAL THEORY

In their grand narratives of intellectual history, the intellectuals—the philosopher, the philosopher-statesman, the artist—are the good guys. Today, critics have elected themselves the good guys, and they are so good that they disdain the genre of grand narratives in order to demonstrate their moral and intellectual superiority. When critical theorists compose their own grand narratives, they invariably masquerade them as un-grand, non-narrative critiques. In their critiques, the bad guys are invariably engineers, scientists, popular artists, and business people. But perhaps we should give some credit to the managers of our complex, dynamic, information cultures—the people who keep a lot of balls in the air simultaneously, who certainly drop one or more of the balls on occasion, and who take all the heat when things go wrong. Many things are now going right in industrial and postindustrial cultures. As Nobel-prize-winning economist Robert William Fogel wrote recently about the United States,

> Food, clothing, and shelter now are abundantly available not only for the typical worker but even for those we designate as poor. Commodities that used to account for 80 percent of household consumption can now be obtained in greater abundance than previously with less than a third of either the market or the household labor once required. Technological change has made the whole range of consumer durables so cheap that even poor households have adequate stocks of appliances that until recently were thought to be luxuries or that were the stuff of science fiction during the first third of the twentieth century. (234-5)

Today in the West, we have many more freedoms, and firmly embedded democracies whose institutions and voters can deal with such aberrations as the recent presidential election of 2000 in the United States in which one candidate had the majority of the popular vote while the other had the majority of the electoral votes. However, we should not take our freedoms, democracy, and standard of living for granted, and we should not demonize the capitalism—or the science and technology—which created some of the conditions for these successes.

It is too early for postindustrial nations to become cultures of critics and artists. We still have to eat, drink, shelter, and clothe ourselves; we still need to maintain our democratic values and social cooperation; we still need to help other nations around the world with the politically touchy problems of building stronger national economies; and we still need to recognize that our freedoms and living standards are recently gained and tenuously held. African Americans, for example, only gained unequivocal access to the voting process in the American South in the mid-1960s with the Voting Rights Acts. Naturally, new times have created new social needs. As Fogel explains, the rise in the material standard of living in postindustrial nations has shown that our spiritual resources are unequally distributed. Fogel cites 15 such spiritual resources:

1. a sense of purpose
2. a vision of opportunity
3. a sense of the mainstream of work and life
4. a strong family ethic
5. a sense of community
6. a capacity to engage with diverse groups
7. an ethic of benevolence
8. a work ethic
9. a sense of discipline
10. the capacity to focus and concentrate one's efforts
11. a capacity to resist the lure of hedonism
12. a capacity for self-education
13. a thirst for knowledge
14. an appreciation for quality
15. self-esteem (204-7)

Although the instrumentality of some of these spiritual resources would offend some first-generation German critical theorists, third-generation American critical theorists might readily support many of them. Based on Carolyn Miller's writings, she would support developing "a sense of community." But other critical theorists in the United States are hostile toward any communication purpose that suggests instrumentality. Capitalism, science, and technology, of course, are driven by such purposes.

In light of all the gains that capitalism, science, and technology have brought to the world, and because of the assumptions and limitations of critical theory, I think it is time to re-evaluate critical theory. I certainly do not advocate abandoning it. This chapter is, in part, an exercise in critical theory. But I believe that we need to better understand the assumptions and limits of critical theory and moderate some of its excesses, and we need a more positive outlook on life—one that includes a more favorable (but not uncritical) outlook on capitalism, technology, and science. We need to understand the following limits of critical theory:

1. It is negative and oppositional: it tries to tear down, complicate, question, and politicize at a point in human history when people have a better chance to cooperate across gender, national, racial, religious, and other kinds of boundaries. We have the chance for a world with fewer destructive boundaries, but critical theorists want to enforce conflict.

2. Critical theory attacks standards, including language and communication standards, at a time when such standards might make it easier for diverse groups to communicate more effectively with each other in order to develop more cooperative ventures that would create and disseminate products and services that would reduce starvation, disease, suffering, and oppression around the world.

3. Critical theory is non-holistic because it focuses on cultural influences on human behavior to the exclusion of human universals and personal responsibility. As a result, it does not respond adequately to the complexity of the contemporary world. Critical theory is intentionally biased in a complex world that needs to analyze behaviors and problems from many perspectives—including universalist and individualist perspectives.

4. Critical theory is too logocentric. There are other systems of signs besides languages (e.g., markets, profits, social customs, mathematics, scientific visualization, computer programs and operating systems).

5. Critical theory is utopian. People are not perfect or perfectable, and so long as we have bodies and egos, so long as we live in cultures and the physical world, we shall never be completely free.

6. Critical theory is too rhetorical, too oppositional, which means that it ignores instrumental purposes that emphasize coordination, cooperation, consistency, economy, safety, ethical conduct, and social cohesion.

7. Critical theory distorts history. It arose during the worst time in German history, and it has analyzed those times as though Nazism and Hitler were the inevitable outcome of capitalism, science, and technology.

Inspired by the analysis, the methodology, the passionate good intentions, and some of the assumptions and distortions of first-generation German critical theorists, younger American critical theorists have developed their own critiques of American culture and technical communication. Although they use the same kinds of analysis and methodology, and though they have the same passionate good intentions, some American critical theorists have also engaged in important distortions. Because of its timing, its analysis, and its good intentions, Carolyn Miller's "Humanistic Rationale for Technical Writing" is probably the most influential of all works by American critical theorists writing about technical communication. It is also the most distorted. What Miller calls "humanism" in her essay is really critical theory, and it has little to do with the humanism that arose in the early Renaissance.

Science, technology, and capitalism played important roles in Renaissance humanism. Humanism arose in the Renaissance as a way to free human attention and salvation from the tyranny of religion and superstition and refocus human interest on the liberal arts, arts which included mathematics and science. In short, science and technology have been humanistic for centuries. Lisa Jardine has shown in her history of the Renaissance that early humanists worked hand in hand with capitalism, especially bankers. The famous merchant bankers of Florence, the Medicis, funded a Platonic Academy which was "devoted to the recovery and study of Platonism in the West" (60), and they funded the work of Marsilio Ficino on Plato (61, 213). For their own social status and hopes for financial gain, bankers and merchants from Germany supported the printing presses in Venice that specialized in humanist works (223). Renaissance humanism was not opposed to capitalism, but cooperated with it for the benefit of many.

In the centuries after the Renaissance, science, engineering, technology, and capitalism helped to bring more and more benefits to humanity. The development of capitalism in the nineteenth and twentieth centuries also played a significant role in the rise of political freedom. As Friedman said,

> Because we live in a largely free society, we tend to forget how limited is the span of time and the part of the globe for which there has ever been anything like political freedom: the typical state of mankind is tyranny, servitude, and misery. The nineteenth century and early twentieth century in the Western world stand out as striking exceptions to the general trend of historical development. Political freedom in this instance clearly came along with the free market and the development of capitalist institutions. So also did political freedom in the golden age of Greece and in the early days of the Roman era. (9-10)

Friedman, however, is careful to avoid the one-sided analysis of capitalism that the critical theorists promote. He recognizes that the connection between the rise of political freedoms in the West and the rise of capitalism is complicated and cannot be reduced to a single cause–effect relationship:

> History suggests only that capitalism is a necessary condition for political freedom. Clearly it is not a sufficient condition. Fascist Italy and Fascist Spain, Germany at various times in the last seventy years, Japan

before World Wars I and II, tsarist Russia in the decades before World War I—are all societies that cannot conceivably be described as politically free. Yet, in each, private enterprise was the dominant form of economic organization. It is therefore clearly possible to have economic arrangements that are fundamentally capitalist and political arrangements that are not free. (9-10)

By the end of World War II, Hitler had used science, technology, and capitalism to create the most destructive regime in Western history. Because intellectuals strongly implicated science, technology, and capitalism in the tyranny and destruction of the second world war, those endeavors became stained with the violence and immorality of war. The first generation of critical humanists (i.e., the Frankfurt School of the late 1920s and 1930s) were reacting—among other things—to the Nazi control of German businesses and science, and so they attacked instrumental reason, capitalism, science, and technology. Many American critics have been influenced by the Frankfurt School's well-earned hostility toward the abuses of the Third Reich. Unfortunately, using a variety of dubious assumptions and the fallacy of guilt by association, the Frankfurt school invented a philosophy that made Hitler and Nazism appear to be the inevitable outcome of science, technology, and capitalism, and not an aberration. In doing so, the first-generation German critical theorists biased Western thinking for two generations.

CONCLUSION

After a half century of increasing freedoms and standards of living the world, it is time to see that Hitler, Nazism, and Fascism were not the inevitable outcomes of science, technology, and capitalism. The Third Reich was created by a variety of conditions—certainly the social conditions that the Frankfurt School was formed to study—but it was also the result of human nature, individual upbringing, and bad decisions of individual politicians and citizens. The situation in Germany in the first half of the 20th century is more complicated than the critical theorists want to admit. Few things are necessarily inevitable from science, technology, and capitalism. Good can also come from laboratories, the workshops of technicians, and factories. We now need to set the Frankfurt School and critical theory in their historical context and see that the philosophy of the first generation critical theorists—well intentioned and well earned although it may seem—is founded on equal parts of bias, overreaction, and insight.

We also need a theory of discourse—especially a theory of composition and technical communication—that does not oppose humanism to capitalism, or humanism to science, or humanism to technology. We need to return to the more embracing Renaissance conception of humanism and not confuse the polarizing sensibility of contemporary critical utopians with humanism. Contemporary American critical theorists are not humanists in the Renaissance sense. They are cultural capitalists. More accurately, they are laissez-faire cultural capitalists masquerading as humanists. By "laissez-faire" I mean that they value individual freedom above all else, including social and governmental standards; by "cultural capitalist" I mean that they use their educations, their taste, their philosophies, and their zeal for social distinction to elevate themselves over people who are just as moral and often more socially useful than they are.

Rhetorical, composition, and technical communication theories need to appreciate the limits of critical theory, and move away from laissez-faire cultural capitalism to entrepreneurial humanism. Entrepreneurial humanism is a combination of state capitalism and Renaissance humanism. Entrepreneurial humanists have the following characteristics, among others:

- Like any entrepreneur, they initiate productive activities like businesses, and they take risks. In the academy, the chief risk that entrepreneurial humanists face is aggressive opposition and interference from critical theorists.
- They are capitalists and believe in the private ownership of property, free trade (within the limits of national and international law), and the profit motive.
- They are critics of themselves, their competition, and their markets in order to create more value for themselves and their customers.
- They are optimists and respect positive systems with the awareness that those systems will change as society, markets, and a variety of environments (e.g., legal, political, natural) evolve.
- They embrace the advances of science, engineering, mathematics, engineering, and all varieties of research, and they try to create value from them.

Entrepreneurial humanism has existed in the West for several hundred years, but many cultural capitalists have disdained it, because entrepreneurial humanists make too much money, think too much about marketing, and try to please too many people. But pleasing people—identifying markets, listening to what they need, and giving them what they want—is not bad when it promotes ethical conduct, enhances human freedom, increases the standard of living, and promotes human cooperation across international boundaries. Moving rhetoric, composition, and technical communication in the direction of entrepreneurial humanism would allow rhetoric, instrumentalism, Renaissance humanism, critical theory, science, capitalism, and technology to work together to create value, to help humans survive, and to increase our freedoms.

REFERENCES

Aronowitz, Stanley. Introduction. In *Critical Theory: Selected Essays*. Max Horkheimer. New York: Continuum, 1999.

Bourdieu, Pierre. *Distinction: A Social Critique of the Judgement of Taste*. Cambridge: Harvard University Press, 1984.

Coase, R. H. *The Firm, the Market, and the Law*. Chicago: U of Chicago P, 1990.

Fogel, Robert William. *The Fourth Great Awakening & the Future of Egalitarianism*. Chicago: U of Chicago P, 2000.

Friedman, Milton. *Capitalism and Freedom*. Chicago: U of Chicago P, 1982.

Held, David. *Introduction to Critical Theory: Horkheimer to Habermas*. Berkeley: U of California P, 1980.

Horkheimer, Max. *Eclipse of Reason*. New York: Continuum, 1999.

Horkheimer, Max, and Theodor Adorno. *Dialectic of Enlightenment*. New York: Continuum, 2000.

Hothersall, David. *History of Psychology*. Philadelphia: Temple UP, 1984.

Hunt, Morton. *The Story of Psychology*. New York: Doubleday, 1993.

Jardine, Lisa. *Worldly Goods: A New History of the Renaissance*. New York: W.W. Norton, 1996.

Jay, Martin. *The Dialectical Imagination: A History of the Frankfurt School and the Institute of Social Research, 1923-1950*. Berkeley: U of California P, 1973.

Johnson-Eilola, Johndan. "Wild Technologies: Computer Use and Social Possibility." In *Computers and Technical Communication: Pedagogical and Programmatic Perspectives*. Ed. Stuart A. Selber. Greenwich, CT: Ablex Publishing, 1997, 97-128.

Katz, Steven B. "The Ethic of Expediency: Classical Rhetoric, Technology, and the Holocaust." *College English* 54.3 (March 1992): 255-75.

Marcuse, Herbert. *One-Dimensional Man*. Boston: Beacon Press, 1964.

Miller, Carolyn. "A Humanistic Rationale for Technical Writing." *College English* 40.6 (Feb. 1979): 610-17.

Miller, Richard E. *As if Learning Mattered: Reforming Higher Education*. Ithaca, NY: Cornell UP, 1998.

Petroski, Henry. *The Pencil: A History of Design and Circumstance*. New York: Alfred A. Knopf, 1990.

Singer, Peter. *A Darwinian Left: Politics, Evolution, and Cooperation*. New Haven, CT: Yale UP, 1999.

Wiggershaus, Rolf. *The Frankfurt School: Its History, Theories, and Political Significance*. Trans. Michael Robertson. Cambridge: MIT Press, 1995.

3 · *The Aesthetic Anvil*

The Foundations of Resistance to Technology and Innovation in English Departments

Fred Kemp
Texas Tech University

The modern English department is largely a creation of the 19th century and that century's struggle with spiritual values and cultural change in light of the decline of organized religion and the rise of industrial society. As such, it is a function of aesthetic assumptions more subtle and potentially more self-destructive in terms of current social and academic disposition than the usual target, the social-justice politics often attacked by conservatives. This chapter is an attempt to describe those assumptions and how they tend to inhibit the modern English department's response to social change, placing it in institutional jeopardy.

The problem lies in the 19-century sanctification of literature and the overt rejection of business, materialism, and the scientific method. Nineteenth century intellectuals, thoroughly indoctrinated by the naturalistic spiritualism of the Romantics and what David DeLaura called the "religious aestheticism" of cultural prognosticators like Matthew Arnold (195), assumed an irreconcilable divide between the world of the arts, literature, and philosophy on the one hand, and the world of science and business on the other, a divide much later made famous by C. P. Snow's term, the "two cultures." Arnold conceives of the distinction in slanted terms.

> The study of letters is the study of the operation of human force, of
> human freedom and activity; the study of nature is the study of the

> operation of non-human forces, of human limitation and passivity. The
> contemplation of human force and activity tends naturally to heighten
> our own force and activity; the contemplation of human limits and pas-
> sivity tends rather to check it. (*Higher Schools* 173-4).

This bifurcation arose in part from the alarming social disruptions caused
by the rapid expansion of industrial and technological processes in the
nineteenth century, and in part from a quasi-deification of an aesthetic elite.
Many writers of that time spoke movingly of the human deprivations of an
essentially immoral, institutional assault on basic human values presumably
implicit in business and science, represented by all the familiar images of
inhumane factory conditions and, in science, by distasteful scientific inves-
tigations requiring vivasection and assaults on a presumably holistic and
inviolable nature. Later in the century, in a largely successful attempt to
retain a transcendental perspective that was at the same time clearly nonthe-
ological, Arnold, Pater, and others engaged in "the persistent merging of
the religious and aesthetic categories; the concern for the transcendence of
human duality at the psychological and ethical levels; and culturally, the
pitting of a 'Greek' ideal of life, derived in large part from the German
Hellenists, against a rejected 'medieval' Christianity" (Delaura 169).
Literature assumed a new transcendence.

> With differing emphases, Arnold and Pater also insisted that, even in
> the absence of faith, a religiously tinged richness of perception is the
> crown of the perfected life; for both, the role of religion thus became
> the crux of a modern literary humanism. The most fertile source of
> confusion in tracing the connection among the three men [Newman,
> Arnold, and Pater] is the fact that Arnold and Pater became the most
> influential advocates of an historic humanist consciousness, while
> rejecting the theological and metaphysical underpinnings of that her-
> itage. (DeLaura 306-7)

Therefore, both an emotional reaction to the clear depredations of early
industrialism and a later, intellectual attempt to assure a transcendental validation to high culture (defined by its "religiously tinged richness of perception"), has led in our time in university English departments to a continuing suspicion of the techniques of business, science, and institutional management. This suspicion is often displayed in the politics of dissent and in
the challenges to institutional processes most dramatically exemplified in
protest works such as Richard Ohmann's *English in America*. Literary criticism has been adopted as a sort of societal and psychological exegesis, tap-
ping into hidden essences beyond the reach of empirical or material
processes. As Robert Scholes puts it,

> Under the influence of romantic thinkers, in Germany and in England,
> the locus of Spirit was extended from Greek to the modern languages,
> with Dante and Shakespeare as the supreme examples of modern litera-
> ture. Enshrined by the aesthetic philosophy of Kant, Schelling, and
> Hegel, literature itself came to be defined as the embodiment in textual
> form of truths superior to those of empirical science. From Schiller to
> Schopenhauer, from Coleridge to Shelley, Caryle, and Mathew Arnold,
> literature was presented as the antidote to science, the place where
> Genius embodied the fruits of pure intuitions in textual form. Even
> within the modernism of Eliot and Pound, this romantic emphasis on
> the spiritual powers of literature persisted. (159)

Matthew Arnold, a focus of this chapter, carried the principle to an extreme, in reverse. In *Literature and Dogma* (1888), Arnold attempted to defend what he saw as a flagging institutional Christianity by presenting the Bible as a work of literature, the proper critical analysis of which could replace, as a societal driving force, a corrupt Christian dogma (institutional Christianity) with a new sense of "righteousness" derived through literary interpretation, or "perception." Religion, in these terms, was not employed to validate literature, but literary criticism was employed to validate religion. Speaking of theologians, with the "we" being readers of literature, he says,

> For while they were born with talents for metaphysical speculation and
> abstruse reasoning, we are so notoriously deficient in everything of that
> kind, that our adversaries often taunt us with it, and have held us up to
> public ridicule as being "without a system of philosophy based on
> principles interdependent, subordinate, and coherent." And so we were
> thrown on letters; thrown on reading this and that—which anybody
> can do—and thus gradually getting a notion of the history of the
> human mind, which enables us (the "Zeit-Geist" favouring) to correct,
> in reading the Bible, some of the mistakes into which men of a more
> metaphysical talents than literary experience have fallen. (350)

Scientists and theologians simply missed the point, according to Arnold: Human conduct ("righteousness") was not a function of physical or meta-physical forces, but of the interpretation of the best thinking that society had produced, and the Bible was the best example of the best thinking, not in itself a sacred artifact or set of foundational principles. The ability of those to "perceive" (those with a special perceptive ability) what the Bible was saying about life and living simply transcended any scientific inquiry into miracles or any metaphysical inquiry into theistic issues of the trinity or whether Jesus was the son of god. It all came down to the ability to "read the history of the human mind," and that history resided in literature.

The Bible, Arnold probably felt himself generous in proclaiming, was the pinnacle of that human thought.

Arnold's attempt to bypass both the scientific and theological problems of Christianity with a *literary solution* clearly indicates the power that he and—because he was a principal thinker of the 19th century—the intellectual community felt that literary criticism engaged. Arnold enshrined "perception," a skill at extricating cultural meaning from the writings of the best and the brightest. Such perception contrasted with the systematic knowing of both the scientists and the metaphysicians (the religious dogmatists) in that it eschewed what Arnold called "machinery" and institutional processes. A heightened sense of culture, supported by literary criticism, would counter the institutional processes that seemed to be dragging humanity into poverty, dehumanization, and – a principal concern – social anarchy.

A major problem with such an anti-institutional fervor, as one can read in *The New York Times'* columnist Thomas Friedman's *The Lexus and the Olive Tree*, a much-praised description of global economics, is that the real progress in humanist consciousness over the last century has occurred not because of progressive ideologies so much as expanding economic forces, led most dramatically by communications technology. One might claim that Ted Turner, who established a global cable news network obviously for profit, had more to do with bringing down the Berlin Wall than a half-century of ideological tracts, political directives, troop deployments, and campus protests. Friedman is saying that the information age, or the largely unfettered flow of information enabled by the near universal distribution of digital media, *as a process* undercuts the brutalities and inhumanity that Romantic literature and Arnoldian high culture has assailed, unproductively, for 200 years in a kind of Wagnerian heroic quest to re-engineer out of existence, not through literature but through *literary sensibilities*, the uglier aspects of human behavior. The free flow of information will undercut those brutalities and inhumanity in what will be, to literary humanists at least, for all the wrong reasons.

Ironically, and contrary to usual assumptions, a university English department is actually a kind of state-run small business implicated in practically every aspect of small business management. This is not to condemn any presumed commodification of English departments, but as a minor celebration of the pervasive and salutary effects of open information and organizational thinking on the human condition. But a serious problem exists in the sometimes desperate attempts of the modern university English department to deny its own nature. By explaining this administrative schizophrenia, I hope to ameliorate some of the anti-business and anti-technology ideological fervor that continues to impede English departments and academic departments in the humanities from maintaining societal validation and administrative support, the decline of which is increasingly bemoaned among English academicians themselves. If we stop thinking we are something other than what we are, we might do a better job of defending our efforts in the eyes of our colleagues, our administrators, our legislators, and in our own often confused minds. I also hope to encourage those who, like me, direct large programs in the university who have for years had to remain muted because of our support of the need for systems thinking along the lines long adopted by the business community, but have been fearful of those who unreflectively reject all management and systems thinking because of a Marxist or aesthetic bias, or both, arising, again, from the historical context I am presenting here.

INNOVATION AND ENGLISH DEPARTMENTS

Innovation requires change, and change is deeply suspect in academic fields such as English that take their primary material exclusively from the past. But I have come to believe that good teaching and the societal rewards that good teaching brings in the 21st century will require innovation as its defining characteristic and change as its principal constant. Innovation and change are the buzzwords of an entrepreneurial vocabulary and deeply, although not expressly, rejected in the typical mission statements of English departments. This disconnect between how English departments would define their mission statements (if they actually defined them) and how the society defines what it wants from English departments will lead to trouble for the departments.

Time and time again, scholars in the humanities and particularly in English studies openly and even self-righteously resist change in what they do, how they do it, and what they themselves understand as their principal teaching and research mission. Especially in the prestigious universities and among the most notable scholars, innovative perspectives are not only not valued, they are resisted. People and departments and schools who have attained a level of success by following one path of behavior are not inclined to challenge that path. The winners have a very human difficulty challenging the same behaviors and perspectives that made them winners. The problem, of course, is that the terms of the overall game are shifting, and what was once considered successful behavior has, by the shifting nature of the game itself, become no longer so considered. One teaches what one knows and came to value during one's formative years, regardless of the current value of such skill. In a society that changes very slowly this is productive and stabilizing behavior, a "venerable wisdom." In a society that changes ever more quickly, as ours does, this behavior can be problematic.

English departments have changed, of course, and rather abrasively in recent years. The notion of an inherent and globally accepted acculturating value in studying (not simply reading) literature has been assaulted by some of the most adventurous literary critics as not so much acculturation as indoctrination. Often the attitudes that such acculturation brings, according to the postmodernist argument, simply mask validation of a dominant power structure. The veneration of dead White males tends to encourage veneration for the live ones. Accordingly, an acid skepticism has grown rapidly within English departments since the 1960s directed against the once unassailable "truths" of a previous literary ethic. But although one cannot deny that some sort of change has occurred between the lionizing of Mark Twain in the early part of the 20th century and the revisionist diminution of Mark Twain in the latter part, real change, change of the entrepreneurial sort, is not being manifested in the shifts of dogma that characterize the movement from modernist to postmodernist literary criticism. Inherent in both is a faith in the transcendent and transforming nature of literary criticism to recode human behavior on a social scale, and its essential opposition to change and the entrepreneurial spirit.

Whether one believes that reading Shakespeare will change one's beliefs and behavior for the betterment of us all, or that reading Shakespeare will further instantiate a cultural hegemony that oppresses some at the expense of others, literary essentialism asserts that Shakespeare is an undeniable force to be reckoned with and English departments will reckon with it in the quasi-mystical process known as "literary criticism." In the 19th century, literary criticism was assumed to be a sort of aesthetic exegesis, an interpretation of the product of genius akin in operation to unraveling the meanings of the Bible. Genius saw things that normal folk did not, and therefore the products of genius require interpretation, translation. Literary criticism is a mediation of genius, a sort of "truth for the rest of us." English departments have traditionally served as the purveyors of such mediation, the expert consultants for those who just cannot get it on their own.

The problem is, of course, that nobody has ever been quite sure what "it" is. We may think we know *it* when we see it, but we have always had a difficult time defining it, hence the professional proliferation of literary theory, often attacking itself in various ways, as Gerald Graff and others have noted. The indefinable, like the ineffable, is a convenient thing. Like the quality of "taste," a talent for "perception," and an appreciation of the sublime that writers like Matthew Arnold posited as a stabilizing cultural quality—encoded in his often repeated phrase "sweetness and light"—characteristics of cultural superiority that require translation by the self-proclaimed culturally attuned neatly allow a circular self-validation. Great literature is not only an aesthetic value, Arnold claimed in *Culture and Anarchy*, but an acculturating one that keeps society stable through a pervasive *zeitgeist* fed by those able to receive the transcendent message of great literature and can therefore experience the Real.

The Real, or as Arnold repeatedly phrases it, "things as they really are," of course, does not change. Although literary critical trends come and go, the vision of literature as an essentially humanizing activity remains unchallenged, even more so outside the intellectual hothouse of university English departments. To challenge the value of teaching Shakespeare all 4 years of a public high school curriculum, for instance, when the student body has trouble reading Hemingway and Vonnegut, is futile. The value of some things, the overwhelming presumption goes, simply cannot be challenged.

But they can. That is the nature of innovation. Nothing is fixed, and "things as they really are" is a fiction of (in Clifford Geertz's terminology) "local knowledge," a manifestation of what Dewey derided as "the quest for certainty." In a society that seems to rearrange its priorities and terms of success daily, assuming that anything is "fixed" is institutionally dangerous, a kind of suicidal determinism in a world in flux. But so many of the presumptions of value and purpose that inform the professional activities of English department faculty go unstated, purposefully so, that articles such as this one almost seem foolhardy and, sadly, futile. There are, however, seismic pressures coming to bear on the university world and on English departments in particular, a kind of tectonic shifting of attitudes and ambitions that are erupting in various "culture wars" in departments that once were monolithic in their mission and purpose but are beginning to fragment into ever more separating "units" or "emphases." In order to clarify (and perhaps oversimplify) these pressures, I distinguish between what might be considered two modes of operating that I see as informing what English departments do. I distinguish these modes by tagging them to two different and highly influential written works, one a seminal work in the 19th century and the other a seminal work in the 20th century. The first is what I consider to be the principal declaration of what has become the operating ethos of the modern English department, Matthew Arnold's *Culture and Anarchy*. The second is a similar manifesto in the world of business, Peter Drucker's *Innovation and Entrepreneurship*. I suggest that someone who understands Arnold understands the modern literary essentialist position on the value of literature and literary criticism. I suggest that somebody who understands Drucker understands what it means to make things work in an entrepreneurial society.

The difference between the two defines the gap between what English departments think they are doing and what they will actually have to do to survive in any recognizable form in the next few decades. English departments think they are supplying a value, based on historical experience, but nobody is really sure what that value is. The interpreters of that value often seem to have their hands around each others' throats. I explore what that value is, assumed and real. I do that by explicating what Arnold's and Drucker's positions are in terms of value added to our society. The first value I call *literary essentialism* and the second I call *innovation and change*.

LITERARY ESSENTIALISM

A presumption that has existed at the heart of the English department's reason to exist at least since its formation in the mid-19th century is that there is a clear and discernable societal value to a critical engagement with literature. There is and has been no such presumption regarding other aesthetic endeavors. Although English and American literature are universally required in high schools and colleges, there is no such widespread requirement for visual art or music or drama. Deep in the instructional tradition in America is a conviction that a formal critical engagement with literature is of value in and of itself, regardless of the professional aspiration of the students.

Reading and writing and arithmetic are unquestioned basic skills in American formal learning, but although mathematics operates on its own terms, much of the reading is tied to the great works of literature and much of the writing concerns itself with writing about literature. This despite the obvious fact that only a miniscule number of American students will ever try to professionally write short stories, poetry, and novels, and only a slightly larger number (English academics and professional literary critics) will ever write *about* short stories, poetry, and novels.

In other words, the number of those who will end up engaging literature in their eventual professional roles is far too tiny to justify the massive public school and college requirement for literature courses. The reason that American assumptions regarding formal learning valorize a study of literature on such a global scale has to arise from a more complex understanding of the societal value of literature than could be explained by any preparation for the work world. There must be something about a study of literature – that is, examining literature *critically* rather than simply reading it – that in and of itself acquires value in the general consciousness.

A basis for such a presumption can be found in Matthew Arnold's *Culture and Anarchy*, a seminal justification for what might be called a general "literary sensibility" and undoubtedly a basis for defining the study of literature as culturally valuable. Arnold was to say, "What is comprised under the word literature is in itself the greatest power available in education" (*Reports* 213). Here the mission of literature is clearly defined as an uplifting of general sensibilities across the population, repeatedly described by Arnold as "sweetness and light." Such a slippery metaphor obviously had considerable power among Arnold's readers, who (one discerns from reading *Culture and Anarchy*) have paranoid doubts about the cultural sensibilities of the great mass of society. Arnold continually returns to a belief, certainly unquestioned by him, that society is on the verge of a social cataclysm in which the mob will run rampant in the streets.

Literature was, therefore, for Arnold a kind of crowd control, a means of engaging more and more of the populace in the civilizing concerns of the educated class. People thoroughly cultivated in the discriminating issues one finds in the best literature, and in the discriminatory skills that one acquires from the best reading, would not engage in the barbaric behavior that appeared, to the class-dominated society of 19-century England, so frighteningly possible. "Through culture seems to lie our way, not only to perfection, but even to *safety*" (*Culture* 180, italics added).

To Arnold, literature was seen as a means of propagating social values that he and his class depended on for their intellectual and even physical survival, although Arnold himself was disdainful of both the merchant class and the aristocracy in favor of a vaguely defined educated class. As societal skills increasingly became separated from cultured sensibilities (a function of increasing societal entrepreneurship in the industrial age and the rise of the middle class), and as the ruling classes became more and more dependant on a self-defined sense of "taste" to validate their superior judgment, the peculiarities of an upper class education came to underpin a special quality of humanness and eventually informed our notion of humanism. Literature is, by its educationally loaded presumptions, a process by which people can come to understand other people, their society, and themselves. It is, so Arnold and others have claimed, a kind of special interrogation of life itself, a means of aesthetically prying open that black box that holds all that we really want to know, the *meaning* of things. As such, it escapes the mundane requirement in science and business to articulate value in objectively defensible terms. The presumption is that if one attempts to pin down definitions and consequences, then one simply demonstrates a lack of that mental or aesthetic equipment necessary to understand the futility of such a project. One has, by the attempt itself, precluded oneself from the possibility of success.

Consider Arnold's assertion about "delicacy," which he compares to a religious sensibility. He is, in this quote, defending a particularly English quality: "This would be more of a reproach to us if in poetry, which requires, no less than religion, a true delicacy of spiritual perception, our race had not done great things" (*Culture* 189-90). The "race" of Englishmen had shown "delicacy of spiritual perception" in its poetry and therefore can claim as a consequence a form of cultural superiority. "Culture is then properly described not as having its origin in curiosity, but as having its origin in the love of perfection; it is *a study of perfection*" (*Culture* 59). "Curiosity" is Arnold's code word for scientific inquiry and experimentation.

Perfection, and the love of perfection, is a dominant theme in *Culture and Anarchy*. "But a lover of perfection, who looks to inward ripeness for the true springs of conduct, will surely think that as Shakespeare has done

more for the inward ripeness of our statesmen than . . ." (*Culture* 194).
Perfection is based on a perception that penetrates materiality, which
Arnold codes as "machinery": "yet perfection can never be reached without
seeing things as they really are; and it is to this, therefore, and to no
machinery in the world, that we stick. We insist that men should not mistake, as they are prone to mistake, their natural taste for the bathos for a
relish for the sublime" (*Culture* 208).

> Culture, however, shows its single-minded love of perfection, its desire
> simply to make reason and the will of God prevail, its freedom from
> fanaticism, by its attitude toward all this machinery, even while it
> insists that it is machinery. Fanatics, seeing the mischief men do to
> themselves by their blind belief in some machinery or other—whether
> it is wealth and industrialism, or whether it is the cultivation of bodily
> strength and activity, or whether it is a political organization—or
> whether it is a religious organization—oppose with might and main the
> tendency to this or that political and religious organization, or to games
> and athletic exercises, or to wealth and industrialism, and try violently
> to stop it. But the flexibility which sweetness and light give, and which
> is one of the rewards of culture pursued in good faith, enables a man to
> see. (*Culture* 71)

One grows weary of this talk of "perfection," "ripeness," "delicacy," and
other terms that are juxtaposed to "machinery," "organization," and
"industrialism" in establishing a binary opposition, an aesthetic line in the
sand that has defined the "who we are" for literary humanists ever since.
The second half of the 19th century roiled in intellectual confusion as technological devices (the telegraph, the telephone, the tickertape) moved from
being quaint discussion pieces to major influences on societal behavior; as
science moved from being a gentleman's *other* pursuit to being a systematic
assault on superstition, magic, and similar idiosyncratic paradigms of reality; and as a larger and larger pool of humanity engaged as contributors to
the general notion of what constitutes their society's dominant belief structure. Arnold's dependence, in a sort of self-assigned validity that borders
on intellectual arrogance, on a vocabulary of key terms that can at best be
described as fuzzy is clearly an attempt to vitalize an emotional presentation in response to the presumed corrupted objective precisions of science
and business.

But terminological excess or not, most English faculty would recognize
that Arnold's argument continues to pop up in the debates centering on the
idea of "change" in what English departments do. Few use words like "perfection," "delicacy," "taste," or "right reason" anymore, but literary essentialism still depends on a validation of that which cannot be expressed.
Ironically, the university department that should most rely on its words far

too often tries to tap into an aesthetic that in fact denies the efficacy of words to tell "things as they are." Much of the argument both orally in departments and in print that seeks to justify literary essentialism relies repeatedly on an "if you have to ask, you will never know" begging of the question.

Any formulation of the value of literature prior to the formation of English departments as literature departments in the mid-19th century was based on entertainment value or as rhetorically valuable lessons for life. But the Romantic justification for literature as a non-theist substitution for religion, the naturalistic spiritualism of Wordsworth, in which artistic sensibilities tap into metaphysical forces without the need of mediating institutions, eventually imbued the study of literature with a kind of life-determining, life-explaining force that moved it into an intellectual currency that religion once held. The convenient advantage that literature had over religion, of course, is that it existed entirely in the abstract. No literary claims faced the same empirical challenge that religious claims did. Even so, the literary elites and especially those who, like Arnold, would presume an acculturating (and stabilizing) power in literary sensibilities and taste, felt threatened by the sheer attractiveness of materiality, of the obvious advantages of scientific and economic progress to people as they lived their everyday lives. In responding to such a threat, the Romantics drew on a traditional Christian disdain for materiality and carnality. While one's salvation may not exist in the heaven of the institutionalized religions, one might find a similarly spiritual salvation through aesthetic engagement, a movement into the *illo tempore* of artistically transcendent experience.

The problem is that Art requires, at least in the minds of those who define and describe Art, the same sort of mediation that religion invests in its exegetical apparatus. Literary criticism attempts, in an admittedly crude formulation, to explain the ways of God to man without worrying about God. Literature, through the mediating genius of the writer and the literary critic, pierces the veil that separates the shadow world of materiality and mortality from the real world of true essences and transcendent values, "things as they are." Literature is not simply an entertainment, a skillful commentary on life, a set of life-lessons, a demonstration of verbal wit, or even a talented manipulation of verbal stylistics. It is a quasi-scriptural interpretation of life itself. As such, by the third quarter of the 19th century, literature (particularly English literature) had assumed a central role in liberal arts education, one once held by Rhetoric and the Greek and Roman classics.

Arnold captures the *social* justification for what might appear to be a largely personal redemption when he says the following:

But the passion is to be found far beyond those manifestations of it to which the world usually gives the name of genius, and in which there

is, for the most part, a *talent* of some kind or other, a special and striking faculty of execution, informed by the heaven-bestowed ardor, or
genius. It is to be found in many manifestations besides these, and may
best be called, as we have called it, the love and pursuit of perfection;
culture being the true nurse of the pursuing love, and sweetness and
light the true character of the pursued perfection. (*Culture* 109-10)

This "sweetness and light" requires discipline.

The very same faults—the want of sensitiveness of intellectual conscience, the disbelief in right reason, the dislike of authority—which
have hindered our having an Academy and have worked injuriously in
our literature, would also hinder us from making our Academy, if we
established it, one which would really correct them. (*Culture* 191-2)

And that discipline must be universal.

But culture, which is the study of perfection, leads us, as we in the following pages have shown, to conceive of true human perfection as a
harmonious perfection, developing all sides of our humanity; and as a
general perfection, developing all parts of our society. For if one member suffer, the other members must suffer with it; and the fewer there
are that follow the true way of salvation, the harder that way is to find.
(*Culture* 192)

The goal of this acculturating effort is suppression of anarchy: "The very
principle of the authority which we are seeking as a defense against anarchy
is right reason, ideas, light" (*Culture* 91).

To be noted in these passages, besides the preponderance of suspect
terms like *perfection, salvation, right reason*, and such, is a growing picture
of a society as mechanically conceived as Plato's *Republic*, despite Arnold's
persistent condemnation of the "mechanical" and the "machine." Arnold's
utopia is not to be disciplined by a priestly elite or a military elite (although
he has no problem, in *Culture and Anarchy*, suggesting that the troops
should occasionally be necessary), but by a *cultural* elite, as defined by
one's ability to perceive and appreciate "the sublime," operating in some
nebulous fashion through the State. "We want an authority, and we find
nothing but jealous classes, checks [*i.e.*, checks and balances], and a dead-
lock; culture suggests the idea of *the State*. We find no basis for a firm
State-power in our ordinary selves; culture suggests one to us in our *best
self* (*Culture* 99). The definition and validation of such a cultural elite arose

in the nineteenth century and led, by mid-century, to the importance of the *study* of literature as a quasi-spiritual endeavor resting on a distinction between the sublime and bathos, a primary quality of judgment for Arnold. But much of that importance relied on the positioning of literature as a counter force to the deprivations of empiricism and the profit motive. Just as the Church had for centuries resisted the emergence of science and capitalism as competing social and explanatory paradigms, literature was to counter the fragmenting, class-threatening, potentially anarchic, eventually *deceiving* forces of science and industry with a clear-seeing, *right-thinking* regimen based on the talent and genius of the best minds of the society, and the interpreters of that regimen were to be men like Arnold.

The point that his program of spreading "sweetness and light" through literature missed is that much of the social progress we must assume that Arnold genuinely wanted has been shown to be more a function of self-structuring, adaptive processes achieved through open communication among our "ordinary selves" than a function of a few, grand, totalizing ideas, whether from men of genius or ideological fanatics. The anarchic forces that Arnold feared, the Darwinian melee of competing ideas arising out of the scientific and economic meritocracies enabled by an open political and economic system, are the result of an entrepreneurial spirit. While Arnold condemned the religious and political organizations of his time as an age-old "machinery" that weakened the stability of a society that should be thoroughly indoctrinated in a single cultural ideal, we see now that political stability and humanitarian growth are best engendered by diversification, that the body politic is best manifested in organic terms allowing for constant expression, experimentation, and revitalization at the margins. Arnold condemned such experimentation arising from competing voices in favor of an homogenizing ethos animated through culture and "right reason."

> Everything, in short, confirms us in the doctrine, *so unpalatable to the believers in action*, that our main business at the present moment is not so much to work away at certain crude reforms of which we have already the scheme in our own mind, as to create, through the help of that culture which at the very outset we began by praising and recommending, a frame of mind out of which the schemes of really fruitful reforms may with time grow. (*Culture* 179, italics added)

The experimentation and revitalization that occurs at the margins of a healthy system by the "believers in action" is best described by Peter Drucker in the terms *innovation* and *entrepreneurship*.

INNOVATION AND CHANGE

The "best ideas" dogma of Arnold presumes an ontologically fixed nature to things. Change in such a fixed system is simply an indication of error, a correcting of what was falsely perceived, properly mediated only by men of special gifts. Arnold would achieve cultural (and social) stability by piercing our veil of ignorance through literary criticism and an instructional emphasis on literary taste and sensibility. The problem, as Arnold believes it, is not how we adjust to the conditions in life but how clearly we see what is Real.

Drucker's take is the opposite, that stable systems must constantly change *in order* to be stable in a life-affirming way.

> Entrepreneurship rests on a theory of economy and society. The theory sees change as normal and indeed as healthy. And it sees the major task in society—and especially in the economy—as doing something different rather than doing better what is already being done. . . . The entrepreneur upsets and disorganizes. As Joseph Schumpeter formulated it, his task is "creative destruction." (24)

The entrepreneur does not, *can* not, assume a closed system in which possibilities are forever trying to catch up to a golden age perfection that is simply hidden from us due to our psychological, mental, or moral imperfections. The entrepreneur, in Drucker's terms, must assume a universe that is open-ended and forever evolving. The goal is not teleological improvement so much as an ever-resolving *difference* that assumes an infinite range of possibilities unbounded by the limitations of perfection. Perfection as a concept relies on a defensive strategy, a constant discharge or whittling away of *imperfection* to reach some ground zero at which imperfection no longer exists. Philosophers have argued whether such a Platonic ideal was ever intended to be more than an abstraction or was actually believed to exist in some transcendent realm, but from the point of the entrepreneur, it doesn't really matter. What does matter to the entrepreneur is that the quest for perfection influences human endeavor in dangerous ways.

The key to understanding the distinction lies in Schumpeter's term, *creative destruction*. One way of conceiving of creative destruction is to apply the tenets of complexity theory, most famously presented by Ilya Prigogine. Stated most simply, complexity theory asserts that although systems constantly seek stability, they evolve only in response to "external perturbations," or influences that disrupt the current stability of the system. As the system attempts to reassert its stability, it evolves to a higher plane in relationship to its environment. In this view, perfectly stable systems are dead systems, and if the system is actually an organic system, then stability is only achieved at literal death.

The tension that exists in life, therefore, is between the very human desire for predictability and stability, for control over the future, and the need to disrupt that predictability and stability so that we can evolve, so we can learn. Intuitively there is nothing surprising about this formulation. What teachers regularly speak of as a facilitating challenge to prejudices and rigid paradigms is, in fact, the external perturbations of dynamic, complex systems. The word *dynamic* here simply means "changing in response to changing conditions." Most teachers (but not all) presume that a major part of their instructional role is to introduce such external perturbations in order to stimulate the world view of their students to broader and more inclusive stages.

The problem with education, as Drucker sees it, is that "public-service institutions" evaluate their efforts in nebulous terms:

> Public-service institutions exist after all to "do good." This means that they tend to see their mission as a moral absolute rather than as economic and subject to a cost/benefit calculus. Economics always seeks a different allocation of the same resources to obtain a higher yield. Everything economic is therefore relative. In the public-service institution, there is no such thing as a higher yield. If one is "doing good," then there is no "better." Indeed, failure to attain objectives in the quest for a "good" only means that efforts need to be redoubled. The forces of evil must be far more powerful than expected and need to be fought even harder. (179-80)

As an example of this tendency, Drucker points to religion.

> For thousands of years the preachers of all sorts of religions have held forth against the "sins of the flesh." Their success has been limited, to say the least. But this is no argument as far as the preachers are concerned. It does not persuade them to devote their considerable talents to pursuits in which results may be more easily attainable. On the contrary, it only proves that their efforts need to be redoubled. Avoiding the "sins of the flesh" is clearly a "moral good," and thus an absolute, which does not admit of any cost/benefit calculation. (180)

Cost/benefit calculation in this context means an empirically validated and clearly expressed understanding of the benefits and liabilities arising from a particular effort. Many argue that education (especially in the humanities) provides students a zone protected from the competitiveness, materialism, greed, and cost/benefit calculations of the society as a whole, but in fact the only ones protected in this zone are ideologues of all persuasions who remain free to articulate, for instance, a problematic 19-century metaphysic (religious aestheticism) or a problematic 19-century social idealism (Marxism). Presuming that clear and empirically derived assessments of a particular instructional emphasis are inherently corrupting will keep English departments, in particular, feeding a "science-art" dichotomy. In particular, the continuing antipathy to computer technology and networks in the humanities reveals the old mistrust of "machinery" and change itself. At the heart of the problem lies the academic humanist's fixation on ideas as opposed to what people actually do (the "believers in action"). Although the 19-century aesthetic humanist's preoccupation with individual transcendence through taste and sensibility has now been shifted to 20th-century theories of social justice or to counterintuitive and self-destructively quiescent concepts of the futility of using language at all, the overall claim that literary criticism is the only truly valid mode of life inquiry remains the same and as troubling. And the precipitating attitude has a built-in, inherent resistance to challenge and change.

As Drucker says, for reasons mentioned previously, it matters not whether a public-service institution succeeds or fails in what it does. "Whether it succeeds or fails, the demand to innovate and to do something else will be resented as an attack on its basic commitment, on the very reason for its existence, and on its benefits and values" (180). As long as the "benefits and values" tagged to English departments remain in Arnoldian terms, as I believe they still largely do, then innovation in response to a changing society will be attacked precisely in the ways that Drucker describes, as an "assault on the very reason for its existence." The assumption behind this defense, however, lies in the usually unstated notion that the reasons why English departments exist are and should be fixed and unyielding, representing what should be an unchallenged stability of purpose.

An entrepreneurial spirit, however, avoids the epistemological argument that what is wrong in life is simply a distorted perception of the Real. The entrepreneurial spirit actually sees nothing as being wrong or in error so much as it sees a continuing opportunity for relating more effectively with one's operating context. This requires, of course, that one's operating context not be a philosophical absolute but a continually shifting and adapting environment. The literary essentialist who seeks to tap into what lies beyond our distorted view of things has no maneuverability in terms of change, for ultimate value cannot be negotiated, only interpreted. Hence, the serious dilemma of English departments that recognize the need to respond to a changing world without depriving themselves of their own reason to exist.

One can see the competing forces staking out turf, albeit sluggishly and with great reluctance. One of the most discernable front lines in this struggle is defined by the use of computers for instruction. It can no longer be denied that computers and the Internet have revolutionized work processes throughout the industrial world and will continue to do so even more dramatically in the future. But in the humanities, and especially in English departments, the pedagogical implementation of computers and computer networks has been strongly resisted for reasons that harkens back to Arnold's condemnation of the "machinery" of systems, organizations, and entrepreneurial activity. A transformation of the instructional encounter between teacher, student, and "content" implied by online processes threatens a direct assault on how formal learning currently delivers whatever it delivers, and even more threatening, it problematizes the character of formal instruction itself. The sheer possibility of various alternative instructional environments, running a wide gamut between the extremes of face-to-face and virtual, challenges the "master-acolyte" nature of the teacher–student relationship and the essentialist nature that relationship implies.

In *Post-Capitalist Society*, Drucker characterizes the 19th century as marked less by industrial and technological change as change in the way that knowledge itself is managed. He sees, from the latter part of the 18th century on, an increasing tendency to apply knowledge to the generation of knowledge itself, a revolutionary, nonepistemological and non-Platonic understanding that knowledge is not a function of *perception* but is a self-reflexive, recursively constructive process of encounter with one's environment, an environment that is itself an evolving product of such knowledge.

> The knowledge we now consider knowledge proves itself in action. What we now mean by knowledge is information effective in action, information focused on results. These results are seen *outside* the person—in society and economy, or in the advancement of knowledge itself. (46)

Drucker italicizes the word *outside* because it emphasizes an important principle: the Socratic quest for internal self-knowledge that has dominated the presumptions of a humanist education and was easily translated from a religious perception (revelation) to a literary perception, and that Arnold assumed could be acculturated to improve societal conduct and stability, is now replaced by *knowledges*, a constantly shifting technology of knowledge itself. Arnold is concerned about what people know. Drucker is concerned about what people know about knowing.

The final question comes down not to *what* we want English departments to be, but *how* we want English departments to be. I see the distinction not in terms of this type of classroom or that type of research so much as between an entrepreneurial and a nonentrepreneurial spirit underlying the activities of the department. An entrepreneurial spirit seeks adventurous accommodation with the forces of society in general in an adaptive relationship. An entrepreneurial English department sees itself as learning from its society and its students and feeding what it has learned back to its students in a dynamic relationship with them and society as a whole. A nonentrepreneurial English department sees itself as an Old Testament prophet crying in an increasingly hostile wilderness, interpreting "truths" that mean less and less to people as once hugely influential 19-century cultural assumptions fade.

REFERENCES

Arnold, Matthew. *Culture and Anarchy and Other Writings*. Stefan Collini, ed. Cambridge: Cambridge, UP, 1993.

_____. *Reports on Elementary Schools, 1852-1882*. F. S. Marvin, ed. H.M.S.O., 1908.

DeLaura, David. *Hebrew and Hellene in Victorian England: Newman, Arnold, and Pater*. Austin: UT Austin, 1969.

Drucker, Peter. *Innovation and Entrepreneurship: Practice and Principles*. New York: Harper & Row, 1985.

_____. *Post-Capitalist Society*. New York: Harperbusiness, 1994.

Friedman, Thomas L. *The Lexus and the Olive Tree: Understanding Globalization*. New York: Farrar, Straus, Giroux, 1999.

Ohmann, Richard. *English in America: A Radical View of the Teaching Profession*. New York: Oxford UP, 1976.

Prigogine, Ilya, and Isabelle Stengers. *Order Out of Chaos: Man's New Dialogue With Nature*. New York: Bantam Doubleday Dell, 1989.

Scholes, Robert. "An End to Hypocriticism." In *Beyond Poststructuralism: The Speculations of Theory and the Experience of Reading*. Ed. Wendell V. Harris. University Park: Pennsylvania State UP, 1996, 157-73.

4 Rhetoric, Pragmatism, Quality Management

Managing Better Writing

Keith Rhodes
Fields & Brown, LLC

WHY RHETORIC, PRAGMATISM, AND QUALITY MANAGEMENT?

Over the last few decades, composition has transformed itself from a simple course into a complex discipline. Mostly, this rapid transformation became possible when composition became the site for the revival of another, more ancient discipline: rhetoric. Rhetoric has offered to composition, above all else, recursive techniques that improve written results by improving writing processes. Furthermore, even the "postprocess" turn mainly just focuses on other processes, bringing social, political, and ideological processes into the realm of "writing processes" that competent composers need to understand and control.

Meanwhile, a seemingly unrelated trend has brought the tenets of quality management[1] into play within the administration and planning of com-

---

[1]To be consistent in style, I do not capitalize academic terms like composition, rhetoric, pragmatism, and so on; and so I also do not normally capitalize the terms for the management theories under discussion, despite the fact that in normal use these management terms usually are capitalized. I find it not only consistent to do this, but instructive. None of these terms are best seen as stable, trademarked "products," but rather—consistently with the principles they describe—should be seen as dynamic processes.

position pedagogy. Starting with total quality management but now moving into more finely nuanced (and variously acronymed) theories, quality management has thus far been a rather haphazard movement in education; but the growth of its influence has been steady. In part, the advance of quality management comes from the worst of reasons. Simplistic calls for "accountability" in education have driven not only the call for increased assessment of learning but also the demand for applying business management approaches to academic work. Quality management theories, generally proceeding mostly from W. Edwards Deming's original theories of the statistical control and team behavior, have the relative virtues among management theories of stressing complex assessment and working well with shared governance models like those used at most universities and colleges.

Such a convenient model for assessment and business management might appeal mostly to our collective cynicism, but a growing number of composition administrators have begun to embrace quality management principles. Drawn by the interesting advantages of bringing a wide array of voices into the making of decisions, of giving relatively greater control to lower level workers, and of systematically analyzing the results of one's efforts, composition's "quality managers" seem poised to bring an increased stability and reflective awareness to some of the more vexing areas of composition work, such as Working Across the Curriculum assessment (Morgan), the preparation of novice composition teachers (Burnham and Nims), and wholesale curricular reform (Roberts-Miller). My first 5 years as a composition administrator were spent at a school that aggressively pursues the application of quality management to education. My experience brought home the problematic value of quality management: Although often poorly understood even by its champions,[2] and hence often poorly implemented, the concepts are useful and even at times inspiring. Furthermore, as I hope to demonstrate here, the coherence of quality management principles with discursive rhetoric and American pragmatism should permit us to forgive quality management the occasionally misplaced zeal and awkward terminology of its business-world advocates.

In what may be simply a fortuitous accident, philosophical pragmatism has also had a growing influence on composition; and as I hope to show, it offers a bridge between what otherwise might seem merely parallel movements in composition and management theories. The case for pragmatism in composition seems clearer than that for quality management because pragmatism is already so strongly present, both in the Deweyan aspects of many composition pedagogies and the Rortyan cast to much of our theo-

---

[2] I can enthusiastically recommend Myron Tribus and David B. Porter as educational leaders who do understand very deeply what they are doing with quality management. I imagine that there are others, but the search has been largely disappointing.

retical work. Yet, older Peircean pragmatism has the reputation of being archaic and "foundationalist," whereas Deweyan pragmatism often looks suspiciously "expressivist." Within composition scholarship, as Berlin predicted, the more postmodern "epistemic" viewpoint—compatible with Rortyan "neo-pragmatism"—has become theoretically dominant; one almost feels the need to say "amen" to our collective, highly Rortyan creed as composition scholars: "Reality is socially constructed by discourse communities." And yet it is much more problematic to make a similar claim for how composition is actually taught. Furthermore, the open relativism of Rortyan pragmatism makes it both intellectually and politically difficult to defend as the basis for any pedagogical plan that one must "sell" to department chairs, deans, provosts, regents, legislatures, and even students and teachers themselves. Although, as West indicates, the many strands of pragmatism are connected in their critical, cultural project, pragmatism can seem a confusing and unstable base for effective pedagogical thinking in particular, then.

Even so, a few prominent composition scholars have braved the perils, mainly by harking back to the central pragmatic notion that the whole purpose of intellectual disciplines has traditionally been to improve on the versions of reality that unregulated discourse communities construct. These contrarians fairly consistently raise pragmatism as the means to think our way past the problems of epistemicism, not as simply an extension of it. Ann E. Berthoff is by far pre-eminent among this group, having spent more than a quarter of a century as a persistent pedagogical critic of all manner of composition theories, using basically the same, coherent message about the pragmatic construction of meaning to trouble a wide variety of trends as they have come and gone. Peirce, the founding American pragmatist, figures prominently in Berthoff's own theoretical work, especially in her landmark *The Making of Meaning*. Although Berlin tried to co-opt Berthoff as just another epistemicist, Berthoff's subsequent "emerita" articles ("Rhetoric as Hermeneutic"; "What Works?"; "Problem-Dissolving By Triadic Means") and writing in semiotics (*Mysterious Barricades*) clarify that she has never bought into the reigning, Rortyan paradigm.

Reed Way Dasenbrock and Thomas Kent have also been fairly successful at publishing critiques of epistimicism. Like Berthoff, Dasenbrock and Kent have grounded their theoretical approach in American pragmatism, although they draw more explicitly on the work of contemporary philosopher Donald Davidson. Although this work with Davidson has not yet made a great deal of progress toward classroom applications, it has put epistemic orthodoxy to some fairly stern challenges that have not yet been met squarely. Hephzibah Roskelly and Kate Ronald have now made much more explicit the pragmatist base for their championing of Berthoff's work, augmenting their earlier, more specifically Berthoffian collection *Farther*

Along with the more full-blown and wide-ranging pragmatism of *Reason to Believe*. As the latter book most completely demonstrates at this point, pragmatism, properly conceived, offers a fully articulated response to epistemicism, in some sense containing epistemicism as a special case of pragmatism. In sum, for reasons that should eventually make a good deal of sense, pragmatism in a sense that almost excludes (or at least contains) Rortyan relativism has come to serve as the officially sanctioned critical opposition to epistemic orthodoxy within the realm of composition scholarship itself. Recent signs, such as Janet Emig's speculations (Phelps and Gale), indicate that this opposition is likely to grow in strength and currency within the field.

These three trends—rhetoric, pragmatism, and quality management—have more in common than simply a shared destiny in composition theory and practice, however. Interestingly, they also appear to share a past convergence. The American pragmatists, most notably Peirce, were vitally concerned with rhetoric, a fact not lost on I. A. Richards in particular, whose work on rhetoric has in turn been championed by Berthoff. Furthermore, Deming, the chief originator of quality management, appears to have constructed his theories on models drawn from pragmatic theories of philosophical inquiry (at least at one remove, as is explained later in this chapter). What we see converging in composition may be nothing more than a harbinger of a very widespread intellectual movement. This movement, strongly catalyzed by Peirce's work in the late 19th century, dispersed by the vagaries of his personal and professional career, converging into a second wave in the 1930s and now coming into its full force, may well position rhetoric as a dominant mode of knowledge-making, and in ways more ambitious and more genuinely potent than current epistemic theories can countenance. Such an historical tide also has very interesting consequences for composition as a discipline.

Most importantly, these three methods share a methodological coherence, one that resolves the unsatisfactory oscillation between the personal and the social with a sense of the systems in which both are involved. Perhaps above all, these movements have the potential to rescue us from postmodern despair. All of them are based on optimism, on a sense that life can be improved in every facet—although never perfected—through the application of better methods to thought and action. Academics caught up in the thrill of postmodern intellectualism have been altogether too ignorant or even dismissive of the human consequences of a loss of belief in grand narratives. Although that in itself is no reason to adopt a grand narrative, the idea that there may be a narrative that meets the postmodern critique and can move beyond it is very good, welcome, and even necessary news for most of us who work to improve and to evaluate student writing according to some sense that there is, in fact, a standard for what we do.

PRAGMATISM AND COMPOSITION: APPLYING THE SPECULATIVE RHETORIC OF CHARLES SANDERS PEIRCE

It is frequently difficult for those who do not study Peirce directly to grasp just what difference his style of pragmatic thinking makes, particularly in distinction from the postmodern thought with which Rorty is more compatible. Trapped in a sometimes unwitting dualism, postmodern thinkers tend to see Peirce as either just like them or just like positivists. Peirce's essentially triadic reasoning opens up a better perspective for resolving this false duality, but it is difficult to see that before one has studied Peirce extensively. From the dualistic viewpoint, when Peirce holds that reality is that with which all communities, after the result of infinite inquiry, would be compelled to agree ("How to Make"), he seems to be inferring that there is a reality "out there" that language simply apprehends. At worst, then, he seems simply unable to make up his mind. Given his incredibly scattered and prolific output, it may be generations before anyone can say definitely just what Peirce himself believed. After all, his chronological collected works, now in progress, are projected to fill more than 30 volumes, a task that at the present rate will not be completed before most currently active scholars have retired.

Even so, a relatively stable group of tenets can be said to contain the essence of a "practical" command of Peirce's brand of pragmatism. Peirce also, for all his complexity, was very much interested in seeing philosophy applied, and hence labored at maxims that might do such work. Some of them he expressed many times, in somewhat different ways. These are somewhat closely paraphrased versions, put in a sequence that attempts to preserve Peirce's underlying logic:

- We know what things and ideas are above all by their effects ("How to").
- We should maintain a persistent provisional hope about the possibility of knowing the real and the true and the good ("Grounds").
- We should nevertheless maintain a contrite fallibilism about our every belief (Philosophical).
- We should not pretend, however, to doubt in our philosophy that which we do not doubt in our hearts ("Some Consequences").
- We should have greater faith in a community of inquiry than in any individual belief ("Some Consequences").
- We should, as a further consequence, seek for better methods of inquiry rather more than for better answers, since the

former can be resolved more reliably and shared by communities of inquiry ("Fixation").
- Above all, we should not block the path of inquiry (sources
are legion).

At first glance, the statements can seem simply to go back and forth, as
in the oscillation between "he who hesitates is lost" and "look before you
leap." But in fact they qualify and limit a particular central attitude, not easily contained in any simpler formula, that joins theory, practice, and evaluation into one system. As Kevelson, reveals, this system became, in Peirce's
mature work, that of "speculative rhetoric"—an art at once inventive, interpretive, and dispositive. The dispositions, as in any good "epistemic"
rhetoric, remain always subject to further argument, further dialogue; and
yet they also presume to be fit for acting on, because produced by good
method, including communal inquiry.

The difference between a Peircean pragmatism and social constructivism is so subtle as to be easily missed, particularly by those who cannot
manage Peirce's negotiation of the way out of dualistic thinking.
Pragmatism, in both Peirce's and Davidson's formulation, offers the hope
of a genuinely mediating third position coordinated with relativism and
positivism, not merely a muddle in the middle. For Peirce, rhetorical
processes are themselves part of the dynamic, simultaneously interpreting
and determining "reality"; but underlying all is a coherence of method
itself, the means by which some dispositions bind us despite our will and
others do not. The Peircean mantra might be: "Reality is constructed of
discourse, interpreted by communities." Discourse communities have constructive power; but they are also fallible, and they are also bound by deeper constructions that they can interpret but not perfectly apprehend; and
more to the point, none of us individually can manage to apprehend what
communities, at least theoretically, have the ability to interpret with great
aptness. Reality is neither "out there" nor "in here" nor even in communal
discourse, but consists of manifest method—and that method is rhetorical,
semiotic, and in all senses coherent with the method of signs. Such a reality
certainly can, and does, act despite the strongest wishes of the most unani-
mous human discourse community. There is little reason to doubt in our
philosophy that if we step before a speeding train we will die—a matter
none of us doubts in our hearts; and there is ample reason to believe that
scientific and logical discourse, whatever its false claims to absolute knowledge, has enormously valuable practical applications. Life is not politics; it
is rhetoric, full featured, where all things are not possible but new inven-
tions manage what was previously thought to be impossible. Toward the
end of his life, then, "the method of justification [was] subordinate in
Peirce to his concern with a method of discovery" (Kevelson 23).

AN HISTORIC CONVERGENCE:
SEEING QUALITY MANAGEMENT AS AN OUTGROWTH
OF PRAGMATISM

In 1938, Walter A. Shewhart, whose theories of statistical control were to become the seed of quality management theories, published a seminal book entitled *Statistical Method From the Viewpoint of Quality Control*. Part of what makes this book a canonical work in quality management is that it was essentially published by W. Edwards Deming, the chief originator of the modern quality management movement as a movement. Shewhart, Deming's greatest influence in terms of actual business operations, is often treated as an admirable but eccentric patriarch in quality management literature. As Lewis writes:

> Walter Shewhart was an engineer, scientist, and philosopher. He was a very deep thinker, and his ideas, although profound and technically perfect, were difficult to fathom. His style of writing followed his style of thinking—very obtuse. Still, he was brilliant. (45)

Shewhart's exact philosophies are not discussed often, but in a prominent and interesting appendix on "symbols and nomenclature," he cites to Charles W. Morris' "Foundations of the Theory of Signs." Morris, in turn, refers to Peirce as "second to none in the history of semiotics" (31). In his appendix, Shewhart adopts a triadic system of symbols that, if not entirely Peircean, is about what Peirce's system would look like if Peirce had been rather more of a pure realist—as one should suspect that an engineer–philosopher like Shewhart would be.

This would be a very thin thread with which to connect pragmatism and quality management if it were not for—very satisfyingly for a pragmatist—the striking similarity in the results of each line of thinking. Van Patten illustrates this connection most fully by demonstrating the similarities between Dewey's theories of education and Deming's theories of management. Van Patten especially highlights the theme of experimentalism that both have in common, and these particular common subthemes:

1. Both stress a commitment to a radically changed culture of organizations.
2. Both Dewey and Total Quality Management adhere to a philosophy of and commitment to change.
3. Dewey would support empowerment of teachers and students [as does quality management]. (110-3)

More fundamentally, both methods use an experimental attitude to explore the effects of whole systems—of institutional *habits* to use a Deweyan term (35) that has relatively close connection to Peirce's thought. Shewhart's great insight was that using statistical analysis to reveal the effects of systemic change was much more effective than the "habitual" tendency to check quality piece by piece and punish supposedly isolated errors. Indeed, in a simple mechanical experiment he could demonstrate that "normal" correction of a simple mechanical device would tend to increase, not decrease, the variance in quality. When Deming applied this insight to systems that included human beings, he realized that empowerment, not punishment, of workers was likely to produce the greater degree of quality. Dewey can seem almost too neatly the "humanizer" of Peirce's insights about habit as Deming was of Shewhart's insights about systems; but in fact the neatness may be simple fact, based on the similarity, even connection, between the underlying ideas and their necessary elaboration into human affairs.

Those who have been exposed to reductive models of quality management in education may be revolted at about this time by any connection between Dewey and Deming (or delighted, if Dewey, too, is on their hit list); but this may have more to do with bad implementation of quality management ideas than with the ideas themselves. For instance, Myron Tribus, one of the most fully informed and experienced translators of quality management principles into actual pedagogical practice, joins most educators in claiming that schools are not factories or stores, and students are neither products nor exclusive, "always right" customers of education (Schultz 111-12). Within the business world, quality management actually distinguishes itself by escaping from reductive "bottom-line" and dehumanizing thinking like that which is so often being done in its name within education. At a deeper level, quality management, like pragmatism, asks us to value the social aspect of human endeavor: to seek after changes in systems, not in personnel; to recognize both the inevitability of human fallibility and more-than-corresponding value of human creativity; and above all, to escape the habitual seeking after getting it right every time to permit a more productive seeking after making it reliably good, then better.

COMPLETING THE TRIANGLE: COMPOSITION AS QUALITY MANAGEMENT

Despite the dubious merits of large-scale applications of quality management to education as a whole (Pallas and Neumann), writing program administrators have applied these ideas successfully to their administrative work (Burnham and Nims; Morgan; Roberts-Miller). Still, to be internally coherent, any application of quality management needs to be pervasive, to infuse the entire system. In education, as is perhaps not readily appreciated by those who harp on the mantra "student as customer," this also should mean that learning itself—the main work of the enterprise—should proceed according to quality management principles. If there has been a dominant blind spot in most visions of quality management in education, it has been an inability to appreciate the unique economic structure of school—one in which students are at once the main producers, the key "customers," and the product itself. Indeed, interestingly, it is as "customers" that students are perhaps least accurately cast, since the majority of the funds that purchase higher education do not come from them (although students do direct them); and just as interestingly, it is as "producers" that they are most accurately cast, since whatever may be the quibbles about who is really buying education and what they are truly buying, there is no question that student effort absolutely must be the main productive activity. Hence, if quality management is really to be applied to education, it is students who ultimately must participate most strongly in the application; and further hence, if quality management truly is applicable to composition, it must be most fully applicable not to writing program administration or even teaching, but to composing—and especially to learning to compose.

In fact, the fit between quality principles and better composition practices is so neat as to be well beyond the need for bringing in practiced conspiracy theorists to make the connections. Let's look at a laundry list of quality management maxims altered only slightly to fit composing:

- Composing must be looked at as a system, with the goal of improving processes rather than nit-picking particular errors.
- To compose well, the needs of customers—usually readers, but also those on whose behalf the composing is done—must be made visible and must be the main criteria for assessment.
- For composing to improve, we must "drive out fear" from the composing process (Aguayo 124).
- For composing to improve, we must "remove barriers that rob [writers] of their right to pride of workmanship" (Aguayo 125).
- "Put everybody in the [classroom] to work to accomplish the transformation. The transformation is everybody's job" (Aguayo 125).
- The best culture for producing quality features collaborative effort and a spirit of teamwork that flattens hierarchies.
- "Cease reliance on mass inspection to achieve quality" (Aguayo 124).

Our conspiracy theorist might, at this point, be off to check Janet Emig's dissertation drafts for later dropped references to Deming. More seriously, what we can gather from the coherence between composition scholars' research into composing and quality management principles is that complex human systems have patterns that occur consistently across activities. Like even a mechanical model, students subjected to error-hunting as their only source of corrective advice will get progressively worse, not progressively better. Like any workers, textual composers needs to seek out the needs of their audiences and maintain a clear sense of their aims. Like any workers, composers do best when they can take pride in workmanship and exercise sensible control over the conditions for their work. Like any human effort, learning to compose becomes more successful when it is a collaborative effort in which experts and novices, leaders, and workers, participate together. Like any activity, composing is best adjusted for quality by means of systemic analysis, not end-of-the-line product inspection.

There are consequences to accepting this view, of course. First, Emig is right (including in her new call that we take seriously the information on the neurological systems that underlie composing processes); "postprocess" advocates are wrong. That is, whatever may be the weakness of a reductive, machine-like approach to composing, to see composing as a process is the most fundamental requirement for actually improving it. Second, Elbow is right and Bartholomae is only half-right. That is, little is accomplished by intimidating students into accepting our alternate "epistemic" authority in place of their previously held notions of positivistic authority. We need to "drive out fear" and enter into more completely collaborative relationships with students. Furthermore, "inspections" along the lines of noting traits and general trends (Elbow) is much superior to the detailed, scatter-shot critique still used by most teachers of any persuasion other than the "Expressivist" kind. Still, we have to consider the system as a whole in which students compose, and in that this is most critically a social system, it is essential to help students see the aspects of the system that compromise both their individuality and their reliance on authority. Of course, this is an area where only Bartholomae and his advocates seem to believe that he and Elbow actually disagree.

And above all, the Alliance for the Teaching of English Grammar is wrong. Whatever else might be going on in composing, grammar is clearly enough not a part of the composing system, but only of part of the end-of-line inspection system that, as a whole, tends rather more to increase error than to avoid it. That some of the most advanced inspectors learn to apply grammar "mid-stream" in their own writing should not fool us into mistaking its actual function. This may also apply more broadly to a whole range of narrow critiques of a kind often used. Rather than criticize mounds of papers, each in turn, for making the usual errors and omissions, we ought to investigate what it is about the system and the processes used that generates those errors, then focus on what changes in processes improve quality.

As almost a postscript, this makes critical the need to know what it is that really does count for quality in composing. As things now stand, students tell us the truth: it is subjective, varying from teacher to teacher, with little visible connection between our standards and "real" ones. If it is true that error correction based even on a fixed standard produces more variance than quality, it might be that error correction based on a floating standard might produce utter chaos—although it may also be that, ultimately, this is how the system eventually corrects itself and students actually learn good composing systems.

BEYOND EPISTEMIC RHETORIC: THE RHETORICAL, PRAGMATIC, QUALITY MANAGEMENT APPROACH TO COMPOSING

Although I do see this grand scheme as an unfolding trend rather than a completed one—and as such subject to many surprises—given the practical bent of all three converging ideas it should be appropriate to imagine a hypothetical program that would apply currently available insights.

First, the main focus is on systems. Holistic systems, with all portions responding to each other interactively, become clearly the main sites of action. Here we must pause to recognize that there are actually four different systems to which any writing teacher must attend, as all affect the results. Most fundamentally, there is the system of communication within which the writer interacts—the system of genres and rhetorical practices within which writing makes meaning. There is little anyone can do to alter this system, but it must be understood well—and understood as a system, not just a collection of parts—by both teachers and students. This is perhaps the central wisdom toward which "postprocess" thinking steers us, but we must be cautious about the temptation to turn this body of testable knowledge into the main part of our teaching purpose. The remaining systems become the focus of action: the system of writing itself (the "writing process"), the system of learning to learn, and the system of institutionalized schooling. Although ideally one would work toward coherence among these latter three, it is important to recognize that for most teachers and most students they are not well aligned.

The writing process, as distinct from these other processes, is the process of generating works that enter the larger, more unyielding rhetorical process. Although writing to learn is a wonderful idea, and although it does improve the quality of writing, it does so indirectly, and only to the extent that learning processes in general are advanced. That is, writers who are not prepared to alter their learning processes will not gain much from exercises like free-writing or dramatizing, which exercise mainly an indirect effect on writing by enhancing globalized learning processes. Rather, the main wisdom already gained in this area is simply that writing is a system, composed of parts that can be separately identified and practiced. What quality management can add to this view is the necessity of seeing an improvement in the system as that which genuinely does produce better results in less time. The idea of doing something just because ordered starts to seem rather silly, as does the notion that change itself is valued for its own sake. Improvements in individual processes must come in small increments, mainly identified by the students themselves, intended to shore up weaknesses in methods so that overall results improve. Despite the focus on results, students and teachers must not use error detection alone as a guide to improvement. One of Deming's most interesting and central experiments demonstrates that systems actually become more unreliable when we consistently react to errors by making immediate corrections. Students would be helped to recognize that merely correcting in response to error disrupts their writing system as a whole, and that improvement of results comes rather from identifying parts of the method that might be generating problems and working on the processes, reviewing the results as a whole to check for improvement.

But perhaps the tidiest answer is simply to turn to the already expressed composing system of our pre-eminent pragmatist rhetorician, Ann Berthoff. Like Peirce and Deming, Berthoff composes her system not of rigid and oversimplified outlines, but of maxims held in tension with each other. Globally, the process of writing is seen as one of *forming*, an act of mind that creates and structures in "allatonceness" by engaging in "seeing and seeing again," while also engaging in the direct experience of both one's subject and one's writing. It is a reflective practice in which one assesses all along the way, but in which a faith in the ability to form meaning out of chaos drives out the fear of being unable to learn (*Making*). Like any good pragmatist, she begins her process with experience and inquiry into experience, moving from there into (she'll hate this, I'm sure, but there's no helping it) continuous quality improvement and the use of structures for ideas that readers find most apprehensible. She aims for a profound understanding of both writing and the subjects of writing, generating the pride of an artisan in the work of the creative, practiced hand and eye (*Forming*). Indeed, it is not hard to imagine Berthoff as being the farthest pioneers of quality management, extending its deepest principles farther into the complex territory of work with symbols and meaning, where it meets up again with the achievements of its pragmatist progenitors.

I certainly understand that this is an unfamiliar way to portray Ann Berthoff, but perhaps it should not be. Perhaps the ivory tower, the world of ideas, has a more interesting relationship with the world of commerce than either scholars or business managers often imagine. Rather than fear being sullied by the dross of commerce, we academics could hope to bring our ways and ethics and insights to bear on the generation of more fully humane modes of production—perhaps even starting with our own. We might benefit from a more conscious experiment with "quality management" approaches to curriculum and even assignments, done on our own terms rather than those of "top–down" managers who barely grasp what we do. At the very least, we can often explain our moves (like not marking every error) in terms that potentially hostile audiences readily accept in other areas. In the end, teaching wrting is also systems management; we should at least explore these most obvious connections.

REFERENCES

Aguayo, Rafael. *Dr. Deming.* New York: Fireside-Simon, 1990.

Berthoff, Ann E., with James Stephens. *Forming/Thinking/Writing: The Composing Imagination.* 2nd ed. Portsmouth, NH: Boynton/Cook, 1982.

———. *The Making of Meaning.* Upper Montclair, NJ: Boynton/Cook, 1981.

———. *The Mysterious Barricades: Language and Its Limits.* Toronto: U of Toronto P, 2000.

———. "Problem-Dissolving by Triadic Means." *College English* 58 (1996), 9-21.

———. "Rhetoric as Hermeneutic." *CCC* 42 (1991): 279-87.

———. "What Works? How Do We Know?" *Journal of Basic Writing* 12.2 (Spring/Summer 1993): 3-17.

Burnham, Christopher C., and Cheryl Nims. "Closing the Circle: Outcomes Assessment, TQM, and the WPA." *WPA: Writing Program Administration* 19.1-2 (1995): 50-65.

Dasenbrock, Reed Way. "The Myths of the Subjective and of the Subject in Composition Studies." *JAC* 13 (1993): 21-32.

Dewey, John. *Experience and Education.* 1938. New York: Collier-Macmillan, 1963.

Elbow, Peter. "Ranking, Evaluating, and Liking." *College English* 55 (1993): 187-206.

Kevelson, Roberta. "C. S. Peirce's Speculative Rhetoric." *Charles S. Peirce's Method of Methods.* [The Hague]: John Benjamins, 1987.

Lewis, Ralph G. and Smith, Douglas H. *Total Quality in Higher Education.* Boca Raton, FL: St. Lucie Press, 1993.

Kent, Thomas. "Language Philosophy, Writing, and Reading: A Conversation with Donald Davidson." Interview. *JAC* 13.1 (1993): 1-32.

Morgan, Meg. "The Crazy Quilt of Writing Across the Curriculum: Achieving WAC Program Assessment." *Assessing Writing Across the Curriculum: Diverse*

Approaches and Practices. Eds. Kathleen Blake Yancey and Brian Huot. Greenwich, CT: Ablex, 1997, pp. 141-57.

Morris, Charles. *Foundations of the Theory of Signs.* Chicago: U of Chicago P, 1938.

Pallas, Aaron M. and Anna Neumann. "Lost in Translation: Applying Total Quality Management to Schools, Colleges, and Universities." In *Restructuring Schools.* Ed. Maureen T. Hallinan. New York: Plenum, 1995, 31-55.

Peirce, C. S. "The Fixation of Belief." 1877. *Popular Science Monthly* 12 (November 1877): 1-15.

————. "Grounds of Validity of the Laws of Logic: Further Consequences of Four Incapacities." *Journal of Speculative Philosophy* 2 (1869): 193-208.

————. "How to Make Our Ideas Clear." *Popular Science Monthly* 12 (January 1878): 286-302.

————. "On a New List of Categories." 1868. *Collected Papers of Charles Saunders Peirce.* Eds. Charles Hartshorne and Paul Weiss. 6 Vols. Cambridge: Harvard UP, 1931-58 1:545-559.

————. "Philosophical Fragment." 1879. *Collected Papers of Charles Saunders Peirce.* Eds. Charles Hartshorne and Paul Weiss. 6 Vols. Cambridge: Harvard UP, 1931-58. 1:8-14.

Peirce, C. S. "Some Consequences of Four Incapacities." *Journal of Speculative Philosophy* 2 (1868): 140-57.

Phelps, Louise, and Fredric Gale. "A Conversation with Janet Emig." *Composition Forum* 8.2 (1997): 1-14.

Roberts-Miller, Trish. *CQI Interim Report.* 28 October 1997. 25 June 2001. <http://web.missouri.edu/~eng20www/cqirep.html>.

Ronald, Kate and Hephzibah Roskelly, eds. *Farther Along.* Portsmouth, NH: Boynton, 1990.

Roskelly, Hephzibah and Kate Ronald. *Reason to Believe.* Albany: SUNY P, 1998.

Schultz, Louis E. *Profiles in Quality: Learning from the Masters.* White Plains, NY: Quality Resources, 1994.

Shewhart, Walter A. *Statistical Method from the Viewpoint of Quality Control.* 1939. Mineola, NY: Dover, 1985.

Van Patten, James. "Total Quality Management, Fall Out from John Dewey's Theories?" In *Understanding the Many Faces of the Culture of Higher Education.* Ed. James Van Patten. Lewiston, NY: Edwin Mellen, 1993, 107-20.

West, Cornel. *The American Evasion of Philosophy.* Madison: U of Wisconsin P, 1989.

5 *There Is No Salvation*

Rhetoricians Working in an Age of Information

Michael J. Salvo
Purdue University

We consider it a sign of flimsy thinking, indeed, to let anti-Communist hysteria bulldoze one into neglect of Marx. (We say "bulldoze," but we are aware that the typical pedagogue today is not "bulldozed" into such speculative crudity; he welcomes it, and even feels positively edified by it. If he cannot grace his country with any bright thoughts of his own, he can at least persuade himself that he is being a patriot in closing his mind to the bright thoughts of his opponents. No wonder the tendency is so widespread. It is a negative kind of accomplishment for which many can qualify.)

Burke (105)

This volume argues that rhetorical study, and in particular the field of technical communication, should seriously study, consider, and incorporate contemporary economic concepts into both research and teaching. Technical communicators, technically trained rhetoricians, are being welcomed into the ranks of highly skilled workers in many industries and, as many authors here implicitly and explicitly argue, it is imperative that students understand both the language and culture of the work world they are joining. Indeed, as Johndan Johnson-Eilola's investigation of symbolic–analytic work described in Robert Reich's *The Work of Nations* demonstrates, economics is important not only to communicate with one's peers in related and contributing fields of study, but it is imperative to surviving in a changing academy. It seems that one's very existence in the university must be justified in terms of economics: in the language of income and costs, of profit and loss, and of the value added to students' degrees when they take technical communication or practical rhetoric courses. It is in this climate of economic and academic flux that I offer a rhetorical perspective of economic language and offer a pragmatic approach aimed at interpreting economic language on the one hand, and constructing representations of rhetorical study that can be understood by an economic audience on the other. Although technical communicators have a responsibility to understand economics and economic theory, this chapter asserts that, in order to be effective technical rhetoricians, we must maintain a clear focus on the rhetoric of economics and how this rhetoric works to empower some and displace others in the marketplace and in culture. We should not strive to become economic thinkers, but to engage economic texts and practices with the critical rhetorical skills that enable technical rhetoricians to make unique contributions.

This chapter offers a rhetorical analysis of economic innovation, specifically in the creation of new markets in the trading of pollution rights. Whereas either Donald's first or Deirdre's second edition of McCloskey's *Rhetoric of Economics* (1985, 1998) offers an *economist's* perspective of rhetoric in the economic field, this chapter offers a *rhetorician's* perspective on economics. As McClosky's work demonstrates, economists have effectively borrowed from rhetoric to explain the processes of the field of economics to students and other economists, yet few rhetoricians have engaged economics as a rhetorical system. Jim Aune's *Selling the Free Market* is an exception. I return to Aune's critique of the free market later in this chapter.

The key to understanding economics as a symbol system is in the constructed nature of the economic market: A market only works as well as its rules can be understood, enforced, and followed. Rules work such that the players understand what can and cannot be done. Rules are important so that those engaged in speculation in the marketplace can be assured that although they are accepting a certain amount of risk, others have no unfair advantage that guarantees someone else's success at the cost of their own failure. At least markets are supposed to work this way.

The market system celebrates individual freedom, personal agency, and democratic access to the system (if not exactly offering a level playing field for all). The market also accepts risk as part of the system. But for the market to work, the risks must be real. As the DOW and NASDAQ continue their "correction" after many solid years of bubble-growth as I write this chapter, people's spending on all kinds of commodities is decreasing, consumer confidence in the short-term economy is down, and people are really losing their jobs. Maintaining real risk requires the threat of consequences, but as Anthony Giddens persuasively argues in *The Third Way* and subsequent books, the consequences of failure in the market need not be cata-strophic to be effective. Intervention in the market is, according to Giddens and others, as old as the market itself and the hope of a "free market" is the hopeful chimera of an economic religion.

But as the risks of the marketplace are real, so are the rules. They are not natural, but have been *naturalized*. I assert that there are opportunities for markets to be manipulated by effective rhetoric. For instance, Alan Greenspan, currently chairman of the Federal Reserve, can encourage a stock market rally by announcing cuts in the prime lending rate. This strat-egy failed to rally investors in the tumultuous market of 2001, but perhaps the Federal Reserve will invent a new strategy or conditions will improve such that rhetorical tactics become effective once again. George Bush has represented his administration's tax cuts and deficit spending as attempts to stimulate the economy, although economists are divided as to whether these actions have inspired recent stock market growth. I cannot inspire such real change in the financial markets through rhetorical means because I do not have the standing in the financial community (the ethos) nor do I understand the context for decision making (the kairos). However, in dif-ferent markets—like that for effective usability testing of documentation—I might have the position and the understanding to create an argument using relevant facts (logos) to appeal to my particular audience.

I use the establishment of pollution trading markets in this chapter to illustrate the cultural moment when rhetoric is most powerful: at the moment of establishing the rules of a new endeavor. This was the appeal of emerging digital and networking technology in the late 1980s and through the 1990s—the appeal of observing and participating in the creation of something different, if not entirely new. Formative years—the time of cul-tural *invention*—offer powerful opportunities for rhetoricians to engage and influence the development of emerging cultural formations. Indeed, as the world works to create a global economy, activists are trying to incorpo-rate environmental values into the economic system in the hopes that assigning monetary value to clean water, unpolluted air and unspoiled habi-tat will inspire new, green economic thinking. New economic thinking, represented in the language of globalized capital as well as the trading of new pollution rights, represent specific opportunities for technical commu-nicators to become knowledge workers, or symbolic–analytic workers in Reich's language. However, the more important lesson is to see economic language as a symbol system, as a rhetorical field. Seen as such, both rhetoric and technical communication can innovate in the definition and establishment of new trading systems and, indeed, intervene in the process of defining value.

This chapter uses Burke's critique of the "monetary psychosis" of both Communism and Capitalism in the first half of the 20th century to first demystify, or *defamiliarize*, the rhetoric of the marketplace. This section concludes with an exploration of the rhetorical dimensions of economic representation. Once defamiliarized, the concept of the market is explored for potential moments of innovation. Of particular rhetorical interest here is the link between American narratives of ingenuity and the canonical concept of invention in rhetoric. The chapter explores the establishment of new markets for pollutants. These markets define economic value in two innovative ways. First, they put economic value on environmental factors such as fresh water and unspoiled habitat that were never included in economic equations before. Second, these new markets assign economic value and define limits for environmental pollution. One such market, for sulfur dioxide, has enjoyed success and both national and international viability, whereas the other newer market for carbon dioxide has experienced some major national and international challenges.

BURKE ON CAPITALISM'S PSYCHOSIS

In the opening citation in this chapter, Kenneth Burke makes a number of distinctions that are important for understanding the chapter as a whole. First is Burke's distinction between Marx and Communism and even Marx*ism*. Burke separates the value of understanding the ideas expressed in text from the orthodox application of these ideas in a political system. It is a distinction made by many of the "new left" of the time who witnessed the rise and fall of socialist activism from the depression through the end of World War II. This passage was first published in *Grammar of Motives* in 1945, after Burke's disillusioned break with socialist thought. However, like Melville, Burke "can neither believe, nor be comfortable in his unbelief; and he is too honest and courageous not to try to do one or the other." In the global postmodern age, rhetoricians should neither accept at face value the narratives spun by economists nor should we ignore them: They must be taken seriously, but disassembled and seen rhetorically. We should neither believe nor be comfortable in our unbelief.

Kenneth Burke has a most interesting history with Marx, Marxism, and capitalism. Coming of age through the depression and living through the darkest times of 20th-century American capitalism when the United States considered both Fascism and Communism, or at least socialism, as alternatives to the boom-and-bust cycles of industrial capitalism, Burke was fascinated by socialism and Communism. The critic found much value in the Marxist critique of capitalism, and is particularly critical of those who would dismiss Marxism because of its affiliation with Soviet Communism and its inconvenient placement on the opposite side of the Cold War. Burke states: "We consider it a sign of flimsy thinking, indeed, to let anti-

Communist hysteria bulldoze one into neglect of Marx" (105). For more regarding Burke's interest in and falling out with Marxism, Jack Selzer's book *Kenneth Burke in Greenwich Village* follows Burke's early career in New York.

Burke finds more commonalities in capitalism and communism, and even fascism, than many of his American, or indeed European or Soviet contemporaries, apparently considered. Drawing on the histories of the United States, Soviet Russia and Nazi Germany, he develops a rhetorical critique of money, or what he calls the "monetary psychosis." All three political economic structures, Burke asserts, suffer from this psychosis in which all value is determined by its monetary valuation. The distinction between each, then, is not in each placing symbolic monetary value on all things but on the way in which these political systems arrive at value. Fascism determines, once and for all, the value of things to the fatherland and to the führer and all others are to obey, whereas Communism depends on the Communist party to assign value based on the party's needs and desires for the betterment of the workers the party represents, and capitalism depends on the magic of the free market to create and assign value:

> There is an ironic possibility that orthodox capitalism, Fascism, and Communism may all three be variants of the "monetary psychosis" insofar as all three are grounded in the occupational diversity (classification) of technology. In any case, Russian communism was the most "idealistic" of the three, since technology was willed there in accordance with Marxist values rather than being the material ground out of which such values arise. (116)

After his statement, Burke tells an anecdote relating to the placement of value in capitalist versus communist economies. In the same week, two economic events take place: first, a hurricane blows through New York and, second, the stock market loses value. The hurricane floods property, drowns crops, washes out roads and train tracks, and does other physical damage worth $3 billion. Similarly, a stock market dip results in the loss of $3 billion of investment. In Burke's analysis, the Marxist and capitalist interpretation of the hurricane is the same: $3 billion in property has been lost. For Communist and capitalist thinkers alike, material wealth has been destroyed by the raging storm.

What has happened to the money that apparently disappeared from the stock market? Burke asserts that the $3 billion is lost from the capitalist economy, although today's economic rhetoric would assert that this money is not lost but only "reallocated" to other investments. Whether lost or reallocated, the capital is nevertheless perceived as real by fund managers and investors. In an open marketplace, such a loss (or adjustment) of revenue can, depending on context, trigger a selling or buying trend and may result in further economic consequences, perhaps rippling out into the economy at large. Whether reallocated or lost, capitalists perceive a significant change, whereas the Communists do not bat an eye. For capitalism, symbolic wealth represented in stock and bond certificates is as real as the physical material of wealth represented in assets such as crops, transportation infrastructure like roads and train tracks, and the potential value of the timber in the forest. (Burke does not offer the perspective of the Fascists.)

> Though Communist industrialism relies on financial accountancy, neither communism nor Fascism will accord to money the primary order of "reality" it possessed for, say, the financial priesthood of capitalism. (116)

Whereas capitalism sees the symbolic increase of wealth in machinations of the stock market and, subsequently, decrease as well, Communism is simply indifferent to this specific symbolic manipulation of wealth. Perception of the ebbs and flows of the stock market as change in wealth with links to local economic conditions is a particular marker of a capitalist culture: It is not *natural* to perceive stock market gyrations as an indicator of one's own status. Rather, as the monetary psychosis becomes naturalized in capitalist culture, the symbolic value of a dip or jump in market valuation is linked to one's own identity and results in an individual's association of the market with personal ill- or well-being. Burke's rhetorical investigation of the "monetary psychosis" opens potentially valuable space for engaging capitalism as a construct rather than as natural.

Writing in the middle 20th century, Burke's critique of capitalism is dated and does not account for the innovations that have enabled markets to flourish through the end of the 20th century. However, Burke's critique helps defamiliarize the accustomed *perception* of the market system, particularly to those without familiarity of contemporary economic theory. By revisiting the monetary psychosis, this chapter hopes to question the limits of economic representation and to comprehend the demands that will be made of the rhetorical elements of any solutions that are offered in the service of humanizing the market system.

Burke's critique and its potential insight into capitalism reveals the continuing value of knowing, applying and studying Marxist ideas even after the so-called end of history. Indeed, in the information age, intellectual capital, a decidedly nonmaterial wealth whose only existence is symbolic, depends on people *accepting* it as valuable. Tyanna Herrington's work on intellectual property and copyright, *Controlling Voices: Intellectual Property, Humanistic Studies, and the Internet,* discusses how control of access to information will be an increasingly potent form of power in the

information age. Brown and Duguid highlight the newness of legal protection for computer code, questioning whether intellectual property rights
strike the proper balance between "public and private good." They continue, "Code now makes it possible to decide in fine degrees of detail not only
who can or cannot use a certain digital text, but also how it can be used. . . .
The 'public domain' and all the public goods connected to it have no part in
the new encoded balance" (249). Indeed, access will define value. We are
already paying for access in the form of monthly fees to internet service
providers and other online content providers: Think about how access to
the Internet itself has become valued as a commodity. Regardless of its rise
or fall in the stock market, it is both *part* of the stock market and has redefined how investors get *timely* access to market information, redefining the
value and understanding of the market itself. How else can things and ideas
be valued, if not in market terms? Can things have value in terms other than
the economic market? How does one define worth if not in economic
terms? One decidedly non-Marxist economist, Robert Heilbronner,
explains it thus: "That is why, despite the changes that time has brought,
Marx's *Capital* is still germane and relevant in a way that Adam Smith's
Wealth of Nations, for all its marvelous discernment, is not" (17).

Heilbroner states that we read Marx "to learn what capitalism *is*" (18).
It is this insight, that reading Marx opens up and defamiliarizes capitalism,
that makes Marxist critique valuable for capitalists and critics of capitalism
alike.

GLOBALIZATION AND/AS/AT THE END OF HISTORY

Technical communication is a recent and timely rhetorical development
that stands to gain considerable prestige in the emerging information age.
Bioinformatics, genomics, personal information management, information
design, online information systems, software and hardware documentation
are all information-based, politically powerful, and popularly celebrated if
not widely understood. These are the growth industries of the "third"
phase of the industrial revolution, the areas offering employment opportunities in the postindustrial, information-based first world. These knowl-
edge-based fields rely on the skills of effective communication: on the ability to construct and share complex information effectively across space and
time.

The information age will employ and reward knowledge workers. As
the third wave of the industrial revolution, however, it becomes unclear
what exactly *work* will come to mean. As mechanization and automation
replaced human muscle and brain power, there is less need for human labor
in the production of goods. Rhetoric re-emerges in technical communica-

tion precisely when humans seem unnecessary to the production of goods and services. But then the question remains: For whose good has the automated production of commodities been created? And if no one is earning wages in the processes of production of goods, then who will consume the products of automated labor? What will the new relationship between capital and wealth look like as physical labor is automated and displaced to cheaper locales? As rhetoricians, we must remind citizens to inquire about such cultural effects of economic innovation.

The market capitalist system has come to dominate the world economy at the dawn of the 21st century. The fall of Soviet-style Communism in eastern Europe demonstrated the failings of central control and demonstrates the faulty logic of communism. Or at least this is what we are supposed to believe. The failure of Soviet Communism is taken as the end of debate between competing economic ideologies, opening the world for a global economic system that sees all as commodity. America, strong in innovation, sells ideas, designs, processes, and techniques in the global market to other nations. Other nations either complete in the production of rival ideas, designs, processes, and techniques in the first-world postindustrial market or apply the designs, processes, and techniques in automated production facilities for consumption in mostly first-world economies. This is the basic practice of economic globalization: competition for the ideas that are applied worldwide to create desirable products and services while taking advantage of opportunities to increase profit. But, as the analysis of markets demonstrates below, even a global marketplace is only as effective as its regulation—the market will only succeed in the long term if the players in the market (from labor to management to capital) are satisfied that their interests are articulated and accommodated in the rules of the market.

As much as I would like to divert my argument and begin an extended critique of global capitalism here, this volume is specifically about taking another path—one of constructive engagement with capitalism rather than a deconstruction of globalization. Those interested in a critique of capitalism will not have difficulty finding texts that accomplish just this. In particular, Ernest LaClau and Chantelle Mouffe's *Hegemony and Socialist Strategy* is a good starting point, particularly with *JAC*'s interviews with the authors foregrounding the relevance of the book for studies in literacy and writing. There are also many texts exploring the possibilities of third-wave industrial society, from Toffler's *Third Wave* that celebrates emerging change while it describes and defines post-industrial or postmodern capitalism to Jeremy Rifkin's *The End of Work,* which critically explores possible definitions of work in an information age. Aune's *Selling the Free Market* critiques globalization and free-market ideology from an unapologetically socialist perspective. Each of these texts anticipate, interrogate, or celebrate globalization without investigating the market system that undergirds it, leading proponents to accept pronouncements and opponents to reject them. I have taken this as an opportunity to examine market capitalism as a symbol system and to understand globalization rhetorically, relying on Burke for guidance. Globalization is, in the philosopher Baudrilliard's terminology, an *orbital* phenomenon: Ideas and values regarding capital and trade revolve around a core of tightly packed cultural constructs. Like an atom, we assume a core binds the cultural construct of capitalism/democracy but, like so many protons and neurons, we can only indirectly infer their existence.

The global economic system for the design, production and distribution of manufactured *goods* is well understood. Indeed, when discussing trade imbalances and production quotas and productivity, this is all that economic measuring apparatuses can see. There is no way for these categories, developed to measure first- and second-wave industrial output, to measure the value of third-wave information-age output. Or at least, the language used to measure these economic elements has not yet been naturalized. The new trends of globalization have moved more quickly than the representations of the phenomena have arrived: Indeed, that is what makes it a new trend and why it is a valuable project for technical rhetoricians to articulate the new trends. Postindustrial capitalism simply does not know how to examine itself: Indeed, there is no way for capitalism to critique capitalism from the inside. Rather, the capitalist enterprise can be seen as though it is unfamiliar or alien, a process called *defamiliarization*.

Defamiliarization was originally used in Russian formalist criticism. It puts distance between the critic and the cultural object being viewed, a way to make the familiar strange. The ability to make the familiar strange recontextualizes mundane ideas. Recontextualization can result in new insights, in innovative ways of seeing and, indeed, of invention. So, here I offer my strange analysis of capitalism.

It seems counterintuitive to see Marxism as a source of innovation for capitalism. However, postmodern thinkers, particularly Lyotard, observe that the revolutionary potential of either Marxism or capitalism is diminished. Indeed, there is little space for belief in any ideology. For Lyotard, the "grand narratives" of salvation, whether through capitalist eschatology or Marxist utopia, do not sway the postmodern mind. Therefore, postmodern rhetoricians engaged in the work of technical communication should know better than to seek professional fulfillment in political economy or ideology, through capitalist or Marxist ideals or other essentializing battlegrounds where platonic truth fights for the heart and mind.

The often cited, always renewing "crises" of the humanities fail to capture the American public's attention precisely because humanists have insisted on their disdain for utility, for art's ability to stand apart from (most often seen as metaphorically "above") the market, the agora. However, rhetoric embraces utility. Indeed, Plato so often has his character Socrates disdain rhetoric precisely because of its utility and its subsequent abandonment of eternal truths like beauty, ancient echoes of rhetoric/literature, high art/low art, pragmatism/Truth squabbles. Unfortunately, this is the battleground many academics find the most appealing—irresistible, in fact. And so there are many chapters in this book that argue for a capitalist rhetoric or a Marxist rhetoric or a critical rhetoric that will bring salvation, truth, and quiet eternal arguments over value, worth, and even beauty. What is beautiful? What is true? Very little about political rhetoric is beautiful, but there is much utility. Very little about rhetorical persuasion is based in truth, but there is much pragmatic power in a strong argument made well, delivered to a particular audience. And there is much power in shaping information.

In the quote that opens this chapter, Burke asserts that scholars and students of communication should not forget the powerful insight Marxist criticism offers in understanding capitalism. It is particularly important for students of technical communication to recognize the role rhetoric plays in restructuring economic communication and the ways in which communication defines relationships between people and their time, their technology, and their culture. Indeed, to recognize the constructed nature of the market system, and to see the assertion of capitalism as "natural" as a rhetorical assertion. As an economic system, capitalism influences the patterns of valuation and influences people's notions of what is and is not possible, as well as their sense of what is and is not desirable. And so, following Burke, it is important to recognize ways in which a self-conscious application of Marxist concepts can open capitalist rhetoric to scrutiny. Because capitalism and the free-market system, wedded to representative democracy, have become the preeminent economic-political system, it is all the more important to retain the intellectual and cultural distancing, the defamiliarization, that is provided by Marxist criticism as a critical tool for examining and reforming capitalism. The fall of the Soviet Union and subsequent end of its peculiar mix of authoritarianism and Marxist economic and political thought did bring an end to the Cold War era, the end of which some capitalists welcomed with an odd sense of economic salvation.

Salvation is a peculiar word to include in a title on rhetoric in an age of information. Since the Victorians considered the import of fossil evidence and the possibility that Darwin had discovered something in evolution, through (repeated) American reinvigoration of fundamentalist Christianity (see Bloom's *The American Religion* for more on this), and the postmodern questioning of science, there exists an interest in finding something *certain* to cling to. We want to know the *Truth*, eternally and forever, to know what is right and good and beautiful. This desire strives for a sense of knowing, once and for all, *something*, anything, that can be depended on and trusted to bring assurance. It is this that I call *salvation* in the title, a sense of certitude and of knowing that one is right and that doubts are just that, doubts and uncertainty in the face of assured knowledge.

Such assurance in knowledge would justify establishing a beginning of a new time and calling an end to an old time. The new time would be represented as an age of understanding and enlightenment while the old a darkened world of misapprehension and mistaken interpretation. The moment of salvation is a moment of revolution in which the old way comes to an end and a new era dawns in its place. It is a moment recognized as different, a pause in the flow of one era and the emergence of another. Indeed, the definition of history itself may change. It may appear that the substance of history has shifted, and shifted so dramatically, that language is insufficient to the job of describing the change. An historical development so important as to bring an end (or at least a pause) to history itself, requires some form of commemoration.

For the Jewish calendar, time started with the Genesis, and indeed is supposed to be a counting of days from the very beginning of time itself. The "common era" begins with the birth of Jesus Christ. The French Republican Calendar begins in 1789 with the fall of the Bastille. Each moment of labeling the year simultaneously reasserts the naturalness of the current regime, whether referring to the year as 3 or 1792, or 5552, context defines the values associated with each act of labeling. I wonder if a new calendar will be proposed for the information age, perhaps based on Moore's law, which states that processing power doubles every 18 months, with new 18-month-long years each named for Intel chips. January, February, and March might be renamed 286, 386, and 486, which would be followed by the renamed months of Pentium, Pentium II, and Pentium III, with perhaps an interruption by Athalon and Duron, followed by the next wave of processors. In any case, the beginning of this new calendar would need to be established: is it with the release of Intel's 4004 in 1971 (*CE*), or in a different ideological vein, the 1984 (*CE*) launch of the Macintosh, or perhaps 1980 of the common era will become year 1 of the Microsoft era to commemorate the copyright protection of DOS and the establishment of software as a saleable commodity. Microsoft's innovation in protecting the *intellectual* property of computer software rather than the *physical* property of computer hardware represents a shift from atoms to digits (see Negroponte) and illustrates a key innovation in the shift from an industrial to an information economy, representing the invention of whole new sectors of economic production. I return to the creation of new markets later on.

However one justifies the new timeline, the commemoration of a new historical epoch seems part of Western cultural identification. We want to know what year it is, and in doing so create the need to have the year's establishment justified. Toward the end of the Cold War, when it became clear that the Soviet Union was disintegrating both economically and politically, Francis Fukuyama asked if a new epoch was emerging, asking if the end of the cold war was indeed "The End of History?" *(The National Interest)*. Fukuyama was taken to mean that, with the fall of Russian communism and the disintegration of the USSR, democratic capitalism had triumphed and that official historical narratives would no longer concentrate on the struggle between competing political/economic systems.

History would change in a new era and would no longer be recognizable as history to those who had lived through the previous era. In the essay "The End of History?" Fukuyama writes:

> What we are witnessing is not just the end of the Cold War, or a passing of a particular period of postwar history, but the end of history as such: that is, the end point of mankind's ideological evolution and the universalization of Western liberal democracy as the final form of human government. (cited in Kimball)

The end of the Cold War means the end of all history. Western liberal democracy has vanquished Communism, and henceforth political institutions will be largely similar and take roughly the same form: that of the "winners" of the Cold War, of Western liberal democracies led by the United States. Roger Kimball's assessment of Fukuyama's essay appears in *The New Criterion* in 1992, and it is from Kimball's essay that I take this reference to Fukuyama.

Kimball's essay in *The New Criterion* develops its critique by tracing Fukuyama's adherence to Hegel, concluding that "the Hegelian system possesses tremendous *aesthetic* appeal." However, Kimball concludes "The inconvenient question is only whether the story it tells is true." Clearly, Kimball believes Fukuyama has offered a rich and compelling *tale* but does not do justice to history or to the history of ideas. The narrative of human events will continue, and ultimately the end of the battle between Russian Communism and American capitalism and democracy simply means the end of the narrative of these two 20th-century powers in this particular form. Indeed, as we begin the 21st century, we are still unsure what the new epoch will look like. An accident off the coast of China brought down a Chinese fighter and an American spy plane leading to speculation that China will be constructed as the new Communist foe of American economy hegemony. Perhaps we are witnessing the creation of the new era.

Fukuyama's analysis and declaration of the "end" of history contains a kernel of truth common to millenialist projections: History will never take *this* particular form again, and so now this unique set of identities and social relations have come to an end. Important to this chapter is the way in which Fukuyama's millenialist prediction of the end of history can be linked to the very Marxism Fukuyama has just buried. Kimball links Fukuyama's ideas to Hegel, imploring his readers to recall the link between Marx and Hegel: "And anyone familiar with the interstices of nineteenth-century German philosophy will remember that the end of History also figures prominently in the philosophies of G. W. F. Hegel and his disgruntled follower Karl Marx"(Kimball).

In burying Communism, Fukuyama has apparently reinscribed the relevance of Marxist inquiry. By reminding readers of the role of millenialism in Marx, Kimball teases out an interesting and valuable thread in the evaluation of millenialism itself. In so doing, he questions the belief that one's own age is in any substantive way different from the rest of history. The contemporary era only differs from the past in its particulars, and not in substantive ways that would indicate that different rules apply in one historical epoch that do not apply in current time. In his way, Fukuyama was proclaiming the salvation of the 20th century through the vanquishing of communism. Defeating the Soviet bloc somehow results in the establishment of the eternal rule of capitalism: thereby establishing an economic heaven, at least *haven*, on earth.

The urge to separate one's own era from others is not unusual, particularly when one sees one's own era as impure, or incomplete, or corrupt and seeks to attain a pure and renewed future. Indeed, the realization of a revolutionary moment often inspires the establishment of a new era.

The language of salvation is present in both Fukuyama's representation of global free markets as the end of history as well as Frederic Jameson's naming of the postmodern era as the "late age of capitalism." For the faithful free marketer, unfettered global trade will bring a golden age of "frictionless" capitalism in which economic agents compete bloodlessly for endless wealth in a never-ending upward spiral of prosperity. For the faithless Marxist critic, global trade spells the end of resistance, agency, intellectual depth, and cultural value. Yet these are two faces of the same coin: Both extremist views that see the *system* of economic accountability as central to the production or loss of wealth, and this "monetary psychosis" is what unites the two systems.

Jameson and Fukiyama are both older representations of the divide between resistant postmodern critique and the capitalist embrace of globalization. Both represent extremes of thinking, acting as straw arguments that are easily (from my authorial perspective) deconstructed. Although it is fairly easy to construct these two authors as two sides in debate, I use them here only as examples of the extremes of positions on economic globalization. Both attracted numerous responses of both praise and critique and are readily recognizable by populations of economists and humanists (Fukiyama and Jameson, respectively) as interesting and important position statements. Similarly, Giddens' "third way" charts a course between two extremes, neither of which is now tenable, if either ever were meant as a foundation for further inquiry.

Ironically, Fukiyama's strand of faith erases the human agency that is supposed to be one of market capitalism's highest values, abandoning initiative to trust in mystified "market forces." However, history as we know it will not end in either a golden age of unfettered global trade or in a proletarian revolution. Indeed, capitalism and market economics have been far more flexible than Fukiyama forecast as recently as 1989, changing the relationship between labor and capital far beyond what Marx ever could have foreseen. Indeed, innovation in technological and cultural formation is a variable that has brought down many persuasive forecasts on both the radical left and the right. The pace of invention outstrips the ability of the field of economics to forecast the future, maintaining the real risk in the system.

Jameson's "late age of capitalism" similarly shows the flaws in Marxism, although it does not therefore follow that Marx's own writings are irrelevant. On the contrary, understanding Marx in light of market innovations such as globalized capitalism and worker profit-sharing reveals valuable insight into how, where and why maintenance and engagement with markets is not only necessary but desireable.

Although individuals trading in the marketplace have agency and a certain amount of freedom to exercise their will, this constrained marketplace is regulated and governed by clear rules and expectation. Rather than a radically "free" market, economic freedom is constrained within agreed-on boundaries.

Central to Aune's critique of the free market is the equation of *free* with *no responsibilities*. For Aune, as for Gidden's third way, rights are tied to responsibilities. Indeed, something so complex as a global financial market or as simple as a Saturday morning neighborhood farmer's produce market is only as stable as its rules. Agreement about these rules, and the consequences of transgressing them, are precisely what makes trade possible: a rhetorically based technology of exchange. How one makes money, how one records whether one is ahead or behind, how groups and individuals compete, these are all rule-based and are rhetorically constructed. The sulfur dioxide and carbon dioxide markets are interesting to me as a rhetorician precisely because we are watching its construction—its rhetorical construction, before our eyes.

Ownership of private property theoretically allows owners could do whatever they wish with their property. However, community standards and zoning laws have restricted such freedoms. Sulfur dioxide and carbon dioxide markets have highlighted the distinction between market theory and market reality: Theoretically, companies should be allowed to use their resources to their advantage and bring products to market regardless of their environmental consequences. When air and water resources seemed inexhaustible and infinitely renewable, they were omitted from economic calculations. But now many are convinced that air and water systems have finite carrying capacity: air and water have been redefined as commodities, and as distasteful as that thought is for environmentally concerned citizens, it nevertheless stands as a victory for environmentalism. Sulfur and carbon dioxide markets create limits and restrict a company's ability to produce waste products and therefore restrict the use of private property.

Although the carbon dioxide emissions market is not yet enacted, the proposal seeks to balance the needs of the players in the market as it seeks to define terms and create boundaries as well as the actual definition of commodity (how much carbon dioxide constitutes a unit, how much carbon dioxide one should be "limited" to, etc). In this way, markets are revealed to be the constructed collaborative cooperative rhetorical social constructs they are—and must be defined as such. Any market that can be asserted as "free" and in which "free" means "unrestrained," has simply become a naturalized. Rules for stock and bond trading are naturalized, but they are rule-governed. Traders lose their freedom to engage in the market for breaking market rules, and indeed can go to jail (hence losing personal freedom) when they transgress rules of law by breaking the rules of the market. Yes, free marketeers want to eliminate rules but that is not (as Federal Reserve changes in interest rates demonstrate) to accept that rules are not important. Indeed, seen rhetorically, socially constructed rules are the raison d'être of markets. Without understandable, accessible, enforceable rules, the marketplace cannot exist. A marketplace is a nexus of agreements.

And this is why Giddens' *Third Way* thinking is so important. At this postmodern moment of cultural renewal, there is an opportunity to, as the sulfur and carbon dioxide markets demonstrate, incorporate some nontraditional rules into marketplaces, new late or otherwise capitalistic. Giddens' *Third Way* is important to the next section of this chapter. To this point, the argument of this chapter has been an exercise in defamiliarization: of making the familiar strange. In representing capitalism as an economic ideology with similarities and parallels to its primary 20th-century rival, Communism, it becomes possible to see capitalism as a symbol system. Its symbols are naturalized, internalized, so thoroughly accepted that they become confused with reality and with nature itself. Yet in recognizing the constructed nature of political economy, whatever its definition, its power is not reduced at all. Instead, we see it as (in Burke's terms) a screen or a frame that, like a lens, colors all we see through it. Living in a late age of capitalism, struggling to define and understand postindustrial society, and working with these structures as naturalized mundane conditions make them quite invisible to us as constructs, as systems of symbols and normalized relations.

INVENTING MARKETS:
NEW LANGUAGE, NEW VALUES

Opening new markets is an important development in postindustrial capitalism. Indeed, the defining company of second-wave industrialism, Ford, created the market for automobiles as it developed production methods. It enabled workers to purchase the very cars they were building by paying good wages. Critics of "Fordism," including Faigley in *Fragments of Rationality*, are quick to point to the social problems of mass production. But critics seldom discuss the innovation Ford represented at the time, enabling the consumer market by paying good wages and inventing worker profit sharing. This system continues when economic times are good, allowing Ford workers to share in economic profits as a January 2000 chapter in the *St. Louis Post-Dispatch* describes: "Record auto sales in 1999 not only mean record profits for the automakers but some hefty checks for the men and women who build the vehicles." Innovation has sustained capitalism. Profit sharing with workers distributes wealth through culture, redefining capital. Rather than seeing the ways in which this redefinition of relations changes Marx's critique, or seeing opportunities for cultural and political intervention, contemporary Marxists continue to wait for the end of capitalism after this "late" age of globalized capitalism. Like Christians waiting for the return of Christ, the wait for proletariat salvation may take longer than they had anticipated. However, as Anthony Giddens argues, there is opportunity for innovative redefinition of the market itself, of its core values such as individualism, agency, and risk. And there are opportunities to establish new environmental and cultural costs, commodities, as well as markets. Finding long-term sustainability will, perhaps, sustain market capitalism a bit longer than left critics would like. However, sustaining ecologically responsible markets that more effectively and more justly redistribute wealth seems an honorable goal when compared to the unrealistic alternatives of griping while waiting for utopia.

Third-wave capitalism relies on the creation of new markets for sustainability. For instance, the cable television industry developed in the late 20th century in competition with broadcast television. Free broadcast television, with its complex economic support model of industrial sponsorship, was itself a second-generation economic innovation. As mentioned earlier, Microsoft invented the software market by applying intellectual property concepts to computers. Intellectual property developed with commercial publishing to protect artistic production early in the first wave of industrialization. Extending intellectual property was an innovation of the information age that created new markets, defining a need in the marketplace for potential products. Law, industry, and technology come together to reveal a rhetorical role in economic innovation.

Two recent developments in environmental policy and protection illustrate the important role rhetoric has to play in capitalist culture in the information age. Burke's study of the "monetary psychosis" in capitalist culture opens a rhetorical possibility for manipulating the symbols of monetary value. Rhetoric's place in economic valuation, the argumentative dimension of economic worth, and reveals the necessary place of economic theory in a postmodern rhetor's education. Throughout the 1990s and into this new century, environmentalists and eco-friendly politicians have invented markets in the postindustrial economy for the measurement and control of industrial pollution.

It is important to remember here that the postindustrial economy does not mean that no manufacturing takes place. Indeed, as worldwide industrial production increases, the postindustrial economy refers to the information-based management of production, often in factories far from the consumption of the goods being produced. Dependent on competent communication over physical and cultural barriers, technical and business communicators are important to postmodern production in order to realize the savings and efficiencies promised. Postmodern capitalism relies on the technical communicator's ability to locate and describe challenges facing the production of goods and services, their delivery to the marketplace, and their reception by consumers.

In the 1990s, two new markets were invented through collaboration of politicians, environmental lobbyists, and the capitalist system of valuation. The first was created to limit the amount of sulfur dioxide released into the air, and has been regarded as the first successful pollution market. Sulfur dioxide is accepted as the main cause of acid rain, an environmental cause that energized involvement throughout the 1980s and into the 1990s. It made possible a re-examination of the economic and political understanding of industrial pollution in the United States and, indeed, throughout the world. Numerous references in environmental discourse would support this argument, but see especially Andrew Steer's 1996 report on the International Money Fund's recognition of the potential positive economic impact of environmental responsibility. Steer describes the emerging model of environmental reform:

> The new environmentalism—characterized by greater rigor in factoring environmental costs and benefits into policymaking—puts local people at the center of environmental strategies, diagnoses and addresses behavioral causes of environmental damage, and recognizes the political dimensions of environmental reform. (7)

Steer traces the collaboration between government and activists, and how this group convinced industry of the value of putting an economic value on pollution. The metaphor of the value of the environment becomes literalized when industry competes for the right to pollute, and pays for the right to pollute. Although these days the social value of broadcasting is questioned, there is an historical precedent in the sale of broadcast rights to radio and television companies—communication companies—interested in using public space (the air) to transmit media signals. Before the FCC proposal, itself the result of another collaboration between government, citizens and industry, there was no market for broadcast rights. The market for broadcast rights, and its multibillion dollar valuation, is the product of imaginative manipulation of the popular comprehension of an asset. In the case of sulfur dioxide, the ability to produce a measured amount of pollution becomes, similarly, an asset for which companies are willing to pay significant amounts of real money.

The creation of markets is, even to economists, difficult to explain. It remains an elusive process that depends on public engagement and government intervention both to gauge citizen interest and create effective regulation. Recognition that air and water are not free (or at least are not infinitely renewable) lies at the heart of the attempt to build pollution markets, yet "there is no theoretical construct in economics to establish markets" (Sandor, pp. 221-36). In his article "Toward an International CO2 entitlement Spot and Futures Market," Richard Sandor offers a strategy for creating a market for buying and selling the right to pollute even though there is very little precedent in economic theory for establishing new markets. Despite this gap in the literature of economics, Sandor relies on historical precedents to demonstrate that markets did indeed emerge and had profound cultural in addition to the intended economic results. Citing the creation of the Dutch East India Company in the 17th century through to the trading of futures in commodities in 19th-century Chicago, Sandor cites cultural examples of the need for new markets. He cites successful examples of market creation, and in particular mentions those markets that resulted in global shifts in economic power. Left unsaid in this essay, the implication is that successful realization of spot and futures markets for pollution will result in similar global shifts of power.

Sandor's paper is dedicated to defining terms for trading pollution rights in a new market, insisting that standardization and regularization of the terms and conditions of the market (the basic *rules* of the market) constitutes the primary roadblock to establishing a viable market. He locates nine elements necessary for any new market to be successful:

1. Establishment of a unit of trade (how much sulfur or carbon dioxide constitutes a unit, in this case, in tons).
2. Setting of standards for emission rates to determine how much pollution is currently being created.

3. Setting time measurement standards to establish the beginning and end of the month for measuring emissions.
4. Establishing price standards to determine the market to be traded in U.S. dollars.
5. Establishment of trading hours: the hours and days on which commodities can be traded legally.
6. Establishment of trading limits: limits on the number of units one entity can trade at any one time.
7. Establishment of a last trade day: no trading for the next month for the last three business days before the new month, e.g., May 2002 futures cannot be traded after April 26, 2002).
8. Establishment of record delivery: record keeping and measurement of actual pollution emitted (company's books are submitted to regulatory agency).
9. Establishment of position limits, which limit the number of contracts that can exist.

This list brings together the requirements for the sulfur and carbon dioxide markets as described in Sandor. Although this economic language of regulation establishes the units and groundrules of the market, it neither addresses the social exigency for—the need for—this market, nor does it describe the international discussion necessary to bring the market into being. Both these issues are discussed in the culturally informed, rhetorically based study of technology that characterizes technical communication. Most noticeably, Sandor's text elides the problem of difference between sulfur and carbon dioxide trading. It is a scientific problem, in that sulfur dioxide only exists as an industrial pollutant, whereas carbon dioxide is a byproduct of life. Human beings and other animals, most significantly livestock (also a source of methane, another pollutant), produce carbon dioxide as a byproduct of respiration. Whereas sulfur dioxide can be measured as a byproduct of industrial activity, it is unclear how (or even *if*) the carbon dioxide market will distinguish between industrial carbon dioxide production and respiratory production. More important than the scientific explanation (which is not a difficult matter) is the representational problem. What rhetoric exists to convince corporate, governmental, and regulatory organizations that a fair and stable definition of carbon dioxide emissions exist so that rights to industrial production of the gas can be bought and sold? This challenge of representation is a rhetorical limit on economic innovation, a challenge best met by experts in technical rhetoric.

Texts that address the role of technical communicators in environmental reform include Coppola and Karis' new collection *Technical Communication, Deliberative Rhetoric, and Environmental Discourse* and Herndl and Brown's *Green Culture*. And a new book by Bregman focuses on the *Environmental Impact Statement* as a rhetorical text. The environment and rhetoric meet at the creation of the environmental impact statement, and so technical communicators, often asked to contribute to these reports, have become increasingly interested and concerned with the representation of the environment in industry-sponsored and government-sponsored studies. Indeed, Heather Sehmel's dissertation explores the rhetorical dimensions of environmental impact statements. Technical communication's interest is already focused on the environment, and the creation of pollution markets represent the construction of economic value, together representing the inventive rhetorical solutions technical communicators will be asked to invent as the information age matures.

Pollution markets are an outcome of this complex network of transnational production and marketing arising from analysis of the ecological demands of consumer society. Technical communicators, as postmodern rhetoricians, make possible the market for both carbon and sulfur dioxide. Only by understanding postmodern capitalism and the way in which it assigns value to symbols, that is, how ideas become considered "real" in capitalist culture, can one begin to accommodate other ways of knowing in a system steeped in Burke's "monetary psychosis." By creating an information assessment that illustrates that citizens are willing to pay an economic price for a clean environment, technical communicators have the power to influence both the development of new markets within capitalist culture, but also to contribute to the ecological cause. I have shied away from addressing whether such innovations in market economics are good or bad, should be celebrated or resisted, precisely because it is beyond the scope of this chapter.

Ecology is just one example of ways in which rhetors are responsible for understanding and manipulating capitalist culture. Johndan Johnson-Eilola's often cited essay, "Relocating the Value of Work," builds on Reich's conception of the symbolic–analytic work that will be well-rewarded in the information age. For Johnson-Eilola's analysis, symbolic analytic work indicates one future for technical communication: one of building solutions to difficult problems. In this essay's analysis, such an ability to build solutions depends on the rhetor's ability to comprehend the challenge at hand and to envision solutions that open new possibilities, new markets, in the capitalist system. It will be increasingly important for postmodern rhetors to envision counterintutitive solutions, solutions that rely on understanding (in Heilbronner's words) what capitalism is, in an against-the-grain, counterintuitive mode that can reconcile seeming opposites such as environmentalism and market economics.

Only by knowing capitalism can we come to recognize rhetorical opportunities such as the creation of new markets, even pollution markets. In order to be understood by politicians and economics, rhetoric had to envision new ways of representing the environment. After many years of holding to the ineffable value of nature, environmentalists began to consider: What is the cost of a salt marsh? What would it cost to replace all the fish, the cost of cleaning sewage pumped into it, the cost of the lost recreational space, the cost of the stink. And what is this cost compared to the potential value of the condominiums or other development proposed? Perhaps we need to offer alternative modes of income, other opportunities for economic advancement—not because it is "right" but because of the implications of the "monetary psychosis."

CONCLUSION

Perhaps, then, Marxist Communism and free-market capitalism should not be seen as opposites any longer, but as the extremes along a continuum. Indeed, individuals offer innovation to the culture and, in trying to meet their needs in local situations, invent solutions that may have global application. Yet some needs cannot be met in purely market terms. In arguing for a "third way," Anthony Giddens argues that "Markets do not create or sustain ethical values, which have to be legitimized through democratic dialogue and sustained through public action." Indeed, in Giddens' third way, government and nongovernmental social agencies play an important role in sustaining civil society, and together act to establish and enforce the rules under which the market is both legitimated and run. The rules, built on rhetorical exchange, sustain the market. Giddens continues:

> A market economy can only function effectively within a framework of social institutions and if grounded in a developed civil society—a proposition that holds on a global level as well as more locally, the good society is one that strikes a balance between government, markets and the civil order. (164-5)

Giddens' third way opens opportunities for technical communicators in two ways. First, his reliance on "democratic dialogue" opens space for rhetorical action. As literate technical agents, rhetoricians can play numerous roles such as technological and cultural critic, in addition to the accustomed roles played by technical communicator. Professional technical rhetoricians can engage technologies in the public sphere, participating in ecological, technological, and cultural dialogue. Indeed, as technological experts, technical communicators have an ethical responsibility to the societies of which they are part. They must inform citizens of potential ecological and environmental dangers as well as threats to models of sustainability.

These rhetoricians can also play a part in economic innovation, both by constructing effective arguments for communicating worthwhile ideas and by calling attention to dangerous ideas cloaked in effective rhetoric. The problem remains defining *worthwhile* and *dangerous*; the perilous act of defining the *good* in a foundationless postmodern world. Giddens has called attention to efforts to redefine sustainability in ecological terms as well as widening democratic practice through dialogue.

The main objection I anticipate regarding this argument is the role I have assigned to Marxism. I can already hear critics questioning whether it is Marxism that contributes insight or the sheer power and wonder of capitalism itself that opens the possibilities for innovation. First, I assert that capitalism is an incredibly powerful, infinitely valuable, and insufficiently investigated context for communication. This volume tries to address the gap in scholarship for understanding rhetoric and communication in the context of market theory. Capitalism and the market theories supporting it, however, should be understood from as many perspectives and through as many frames as possible. Twenty-first-century market theory has a history, and in particular a history of conflict, with Soviet Communism throughout the 20th century. Capitalism's contact with socialist and Communist economies, and the influence they have exerted on each other, are issues that need to be continually investigated and discussed if only to defamiliarize, to denaturalize, capitalism to the students who study it as they live in its influence.

The postindustrial age is a postmodern age. It is an age of impurity, where answers are constructed with the cast-offs and remains of modernist projects of enlightenment. It is an age of bricolage, of taking bits and pieces of other ideas and cobbling together potential answers that work in context. This hybridity defines the distinction between the modern and the postmodern, not the end of history per se but the end of seeing the current era as anything but an extension of a long history of imperfect human cultures who themselves constructed the best answers they could in their contexts given the materials available to them. Digital technology and globalization mark the current era as unique, but these elements are added onto an already existing complex construction of contradictory discourses and contexts. Innovation, and the inspiration for invention, needs to come from wherever possible, and in the ongoing crisis of the current moment, Marxism cannot be cast off no matter who "won" the Cold War. By defamiliarizing our own market context to ourselves, we begin to see potentials for innovation and invention that are only possible in the impure, hybridized postmodern global economy.

Studying scientific development in the Soviet Union, Loren Graham offers a new way of understanding Marx in a market economy: "Perhaps now that Marxism has receded as a political threat, we shall be able to make this transition in understanding its sometimes contradictory effects" (102). I share Graham's hope that we can overcome intellectual McCarthyism and understand Marxism's capacity to reveal hidden, or forgotten, potentials and problems in capitalism while avoiding the trap Burke warns us about. Burke warns us to avoid the "negative accomplishment" of resisting Marxism out of misplaced patriotism, an idea much more relevant during McCarthyism perhaps, but no less intellectually valid in this post-soviet era of the globalization of capitalism. On some issues Burke is dated and so I refer to a contemporary investigation: Andrew Feenberg's *Transforming Technology* proposes alternative structure for technological and cultural innovation which are hybrids of capitalist market innovation and social democratic scrutiny. Many of these hybrids reflect Giddens' interest in developing a *Third Way*, moving beyond simple left/right political thinking. Market theory has much to teach the communication disciplines, but not at the cost of losing the critique of market capitalism that humanism has developed and continues to associate with Marx.

Technical communicators must retain their critical rhetorical training in order to articulate opportunities for markets and to explore the limits of the market. As rhetoricians, technical communicators play a limited role in the daily activities of the markets themselves, but have a distinctive ability to analyze ways in which culture both represents and relies on market forces for solutions to technological and social problems. Some market solutions will, indeed, be effective and will welcome the input of technical rhetoricians with an understanding of economic theories, practices and issues in order to have them operate effectively. Other market-based solutions will fail for a variety of reasons, and analyzing these failures requires clarity in economic rhetoric to articulate the limits of market solutions for social and other problems. The danger is in supposing economics has no relevance to technical communication or to training the next generation of practitioners.

REFERENCES

Aune, James Arndt. *Selling the Free Market.* Guilford Press, 2000.

Baudrilliard, Jean. *Simulacra and Simulation.* U Michigan P, 1995.

Bloom, Harold. *The American Religion.* Simon and Schuster, 1992.

Bregman, Jacob I. *Environmental Impact Statements.* 2nd ed. Boca Raton, FL: CRC Press, 1999.

Brown, John Seeley and Duguid, Paul. *The Social Life of Information.* Cambridge, MA: Harvard Business School Press, 2000. Available online [http://www.firstmonday.dk/issues/issue5_4/brown_contents.html]

Burke, Kenneth. *A Grammar of Motives.* U of California P, 1969.

CFTC Website. Commodity Futures Trading Commission. [http:// www.cftc.gov/ cftc/cftchome.htm] [quote from http:// www.cftc.gov/cftc/cft-cabout.htm]

Coppola, Nancy W. and Bill Karis, eds. *Technical Communication, Deliberative Rhetoric, and Environmental Discourse: Connections and Directions.* Norwood, NJ: Ablex, 2000.

EPA. "Greenhouse Gas Emissions Trading: A Company and Country-Eye View." http://www.epa.gov/globalwarming/publications/actions/cop6/emissions_trading.pdf

Faigley, L. *Fragments of Rationality: Postmodernity and the Subject of Composition.* U of Pittsburgh, 1992.

Feenberg, Andrew. *Transforming Technology: A Critical Theory Revisited.* Oxford UP, 2002.

Fukuyama, Francis. "The End of History?" *The National Interest* 16 (Summer 1989): 3.

———. *The End of History and the Last Man.* New York: Avon Books, 1991.

Giddens, Anthony. *The Third Way: The Renewal of Social Democracy.* Cambridge: Polity Press, 1999.

———. *The Third Way and Its Critics.* Cambridge: Polity Press, 1999.

Graham, Loren R. *What Have We Learned About Science and Technology from the Russian Experience?* Stanford UP, 1998.

Heilbronner, Robert L. *Marxism: For and Against.* Norton, 1980.

Herndl, Carl and Stuart C. Brown. *Green Culture: Environmental Rhetoric in Contemporary America.* Madison U of Wisconsin P, 1996.

Herrington, Tyanna K. *Controlling Voices: Intellectual Property, Humanistic Studies, and the Internet.* Carbondale: Southern Illinois UP, 2001.

Jameson, Fredric. *Postmodernism, or, The Cultural Logic of Late Capitalism.* Durham: Duke UP, 1991.

Johnson-Eilola, Johndan. "Relocating the Value of Work: Technical Communication in a Post-Industrial Age." *Technical Communication Quarterly* 5 (1996): 245-70 alt cit http://tempest.english.purdue.edu /tc.symbol/tc.symbol.start.html.

Kimball, Roger. "Francis Fukuyama & the End of History." *The New Criterion.* 10.6 (1992). http://www.newcriterion.com/archive/ feb92/fukuyama.htm

LaClau, Ernesto and Chantelle Mouffe. *Hegemony and Socialist Strategy.* 2nd ed. Verso, 2001.

Lyotard, Jean François. *The Postmodern Condition: A Report on Knowledge.* Trans. Geoff Bennington and Brian Massumi. Minneapolis: U of Minnesota P, 1994.

Negroponte, Nicholas. *Being Digital.* Knopf, 1995.

Reich, Robert. *The Work of Nations: Preparing Ourselves for 21st Century Capitalism.* New York: Alfred A. Knopf. 1991.

Rifkin, Jeremy. *The End of Work.* Los Angeles: J P Tarcher Press, 1996.

Sandor, Richard L. "Toward an International CO2 Entitlement Spot and Futures Market." In *Market-Based Approaches To Environmental Policy: Regulatory Innovations to the Fore.* Eds. R. F. Kosobud and J. M. Zimmerman. New York: Van Nostrand Reinhold, 1997, 221-36.

Sehmel, Heather Anne. *Websites and Advocacy Campaigns: Decision-Making, Implementation, and Audience in an Environmental Advocacy Group's Use of Websites as Part of its Communication Campaigns.* Dissertation completed 2002, UMI # AAT 3056111.

Selzer, Jack. *Kenneth Burke in Greenwich Village: Conversing with the Moderns, 1915–1931.* Madison: U of Wisconsin P, 1996.

Steer, Andrew. "Ten Principles of the New Environmentalism." *Finance and Development,* 22:4 (December 1996): 7.

Toffler, Alvin. *The Third Wave* (Reissue). New York: Bantam, 1991.

"Typhoid Mary" Online and in Your Town

University of Phoenix as a Burkean Scapegoat in Academe

H. Brooke Hessler
Oklahoma City University

> It is as if someone decided to accumulate the nightmares of every academic in America, stir them into one institution, and pronounce the result a university.
>
> *Professor Alan Wolfe, Boston University,*
> *regarding the University of Phoenix*

The University of Phoenix (UOP) is unapologetically focused on the bottom line; its students are customers; its faculty are primarily adjuncts using standardized syllabi tied directly to quantifiable assessment tools within a curriculum that privileges application over theory, vocationalism over liberal learning. Furthermore, at a time when most of academe is buttressing itself against economic pressures to do much more with less, Phoenix is turning a profit. No wonder it has become the university that academics love to hate.[1] The criticism surrounding this institution is often sardonic, composed with a passion and flair that makes reading it a guilty pleasure of mine. Cary Nelson casts Phoenix as the infamous icon of commodified

---

[1]One paradox of composing this chapter is that I must refer to academe as an entity distinctive from UOP while demonstrating that a merger has already occurred between the two. For the purpose of tracing the scapegoat phenomenon, I distinguish between the dominant academic culture of liberal education (referenced as more-traditional institutions, academe, academics, and nonprofits) and the culture of corporatization in education (referenced as proprietary institutions and for-profits).

education (4); credentialing board member Milton R. Blood coined the term *McEducation* to describe Phoenix's strategy of delivering mass-produced content at multiple locations with the efficiency of a hamburger franchise (Strosnider); James Traub, in the *New Yorker,* echoes the fast-food analogy, calling Phoenix "Drive Thru U," the leading purveyor of cheaply produced courses with limited critical substance (114). Such aspersion is nothing new to the institution's founder, John Sperling, who claims, "There are all sorts of forces that would like to see us destroyed"—including "the whole education industry" (Strosnider). In Burkean terms, Phoenix has become a scapegoat figure in academe.

Kenneth Burke describes scapegoating as a process or "mechanism" by which an individual or community transforms its social identity by projecting its faults onto an excluded other (*Grammar of Motives* 406). The process includes the following phases:

> (1) an original state of merger, in that the iniquities are shared by both the iniquitous and their chosen vessel; (2) a principle of division, in that the elements shared in common are being ritualistically alienated; (3) a new principle of merger, this time in the unification of those whose purified identity is defined in dialectical opposition to the sacrificial offering. (406)

In the case of Phoenix, the "iniquity" is corporatization: the adoption of businesslike priorities and behaviors by an academic institution. Signs of this corporate influence include the growth of vocational and pre-professional curricula, an increasing emphasis on efficiency (in all endeavors, ranging from budgeting to staffing to pedagogical assessment), and the development of entrepreneurial partnerships between academic and nonacademic organizations. By definition and by reputation, Phoenix is the ultimate corporate university. But its more significant role in academe may be that of scapegoat. As Alan Wolfe observes, "Academics who worry about the overly practical concerns of their students, threats to tenure, or the ramifications of institutions' increasing reliance on adjuncts now have a face to put on their fears."

For years, Phoenix has been the exemplar for those examining the pitfalls and possible benefits of a market-oriented education. During the plenary exchange on "Balancing Private Gain and Public Good" at the 2001 National Conference of the American Association for Higher Education (AAHE), the reputation and operation of Phoenix were the recurrent objects of discussion even though the speaker responsible for offering the for-profit perspective, Don Norman, was an executive of Cardean University (part of UNext.com), *not* University of Phoenix (Goldstein, Cantor, Norman). Plenary moderator Michael Goldstein dubbed Phoenix, "the Typhoid Mary of for-profit higher education," implying that its rapid replication of storefront campuses and online degree programs has triggered the proliferation of similar enterprises. This metaphor also suggests that Phoenix is a source of contamination—and a fatal one at that. Many fear that Phoenix's expansion will bring about the demise of some ailing institutions.

But it is inaccurate to view Phoenix as the initiator of proprietary behavior in academe, just as it is inaccurate to claim that for-profit educators are to blame for the vocational turn in higher education. Professional development has always been a service (if not the business) of the university. The majority of American institutions regularly exhibit a quasi-reluctant pragmatism that is in many respects indistinguishable from the marketing and management practices of industry. In the 25 years since the UOP charter, the nonprofit academic community has demonstrated just as much entrepreneurship as Phoenix, only with less economic success and with far more internal wrangling over the right and true nature of its work (see Table 6.1).

Like most of my colleagues in rhetoric, composition, and technical and professional communication, I am trained as a humanist scholar–teacher in a field that is regularly viewed as a site of "practical" knowledge within a liberal arts curriculum. Like those rhetoricians, I seek to illuminate the humanistic contributions of our work to audiences—public and academic—who have not been trained to recognize and interpret them. So I approach the rhetoric surrounding Phoenix as an opportunity to obtain further insight into a bifurcated discourse that is generating misunderstanding within public and academic audiences.

This chapter is not a defense of the University of Phoenix, but rather an attempt to reframe its role in the broader arena of institutional change. When examined in terms of Burke's scapegoat process, academe's reaction to Phoenix reveals that the for-profit/nonprofit dichotomy is primarily a matter of values rather than behavior. That is, although both kinds of institution are mindful of the marketplace and both enact a form of public service, educators within nonprofits tend to retain a pious identification with the liberal arts tradition that perceives vocationalism as a kind of blasphemy. Meanwhile, many outside academe remain unaware (or unconvinced) of the social benefits of liberal learning. Criticizing educational quality at for-profit institutions enables traditional educators to voice concerns about the academic capitalism within their own institutions. If brought full circle, the process of scapegoating Phoenix can help liberal arts educators articulate a clearer social purpose for their work. Observing the scapegoating process enables us to achieve two goals: to more clearly understand the marketlike behaviors that seem most threatening to academe's liberal learning ideals, and to identify opportunities for fields of writing to bridge the gap between academic and public expectations for higher education by creating and disseminating knowledge of value to communities in and beyond the academy.

TABLE 6.1. Evolution of a Nemesis: The Rise of the University of Phoenix During a Period of Academic Change

University of Phoenix	Period	American Higher Education
	1970 – 1979	
1971 – John Sperling and Jorge Klor de Alva begin working together at San Jose State University, developing a humanities program for under-prepared students (Sperling *Rebel with a Cause*, 64).		**1970** – Slightly more than 6% of all first-time freshmen are older than 21 (Levine and Nidiffer).
1974 – Sperling founds the ICRD to help traditional colleges and universities establish and teach programs for working adults. ICRD launches a program at the University of San Francisco. ICRD is converted into the for-profit company, IPD (Sperling *Rebel with a Cause*, 70-75).		**1973** – K. Patricia Cross and James Hitchcock publish articles in *Change* magazine alerting the academic community to the "new clientele" for higher education: adults, part-timers, ethnic minorities, and lower academic achievers, most of whom are seeking vocational advancement.
1976 – Sperling draws up the charter for UOP (Traub, 114). The university receives accreditation from the NCA (Fischetti et al., 48).		**1976** – The Carnegie Council on Policy Studies in Higher Education reports a growing trend of specialization in undergraduate coursework: students are concentrating on courses in their major field of study with a reduction in general education and breadth electives (Rudolph).
1977 – First classes are held at the Phoenix Campus in Arizona.		
	1980 – 1989	
1980 – First interstate expansion: the Northern California Campus in San Jose.		**1983** – The National Commission on Excellence in Education publishes *A Nation at Risk*, which accuses American higher education of failing to produce a well-prepared workforce.
1989 – UOP establishes its Online Campus for distance learning.		**1987** – Allan Bloom publishes *The Closing of the American Mind: How Higher Education Has Failed Democracy and Impoverished the Souls of Today's Students*.

138

1990 – 1994

1991 – Klor de Alva joins the board of the Apollo Group, Inc. (parent company of UOP).[a]

1993 – Enrollments reach 25,000 (Fischetti et al., 48).

1994 – Apollo Group first offers shares on NASDAQ, opening at $2 per share (Traub).

1990 – Approximately 47% of undergraduates are adults between 22 and 64 (Levine and Nidiffer). Ernest Boyer publishes *Scholarship Reconsidered: The Priorities of the Professoriate.*

1994 – Bennington College President Elizabeth Coleman downsizes the college and abolishes tenure (part of an emergency plan to stabilize the college in the face of shrinking enrollments and a $1 million deficit.) (Levine and Nidiffer). Oklahoma City Community College initiates a 24-hour class schedule (Levine and Nidiffer).

1995 – 1999

1997 – Apollo stock reaches $40 per share. Sperling reportedly jests, "Wall Street is our endowment" (Fischetti et al. 49).

1998 – Enrollments reach 42,000[a] Klor de Alva is appointed president of UOP, resigning his post as an endowed professor of anthropology at University of California at Berkeley[a]

1999 – Pennsylvania permits UOP to open campuses in the state, despite local institution complaints that the area is already saturated with schools (Selingo).

1996 – Bill Readings' *The University in Ruins* is published and soon becomes one of the decade's most influential polemics on the corporatization of liberal learning.

1997 – American Association of University Professors subcommittee publishes its report on distance learning, which cites Traub's *New Yorker* article on UOP to illustrate its concerns that distance education fosters a convenience-oriented, consumer-driven relationship with higher education.

1999 – Joseph D. Duffey, former president of American University and former chancellor of the University of Massachusetts at Amherst, becomes the head of an international for-profit university venture with Sylvan Learning Systems (Lively and Blumenstyk).

TABLE 6.1. Evolution of a Nemesis: The Rise of the University of Phoenix During a Period of Academic Change
(Continued)

University of Phoenix	Period	American Higher Education
	2000 – 2004	
2000 – Klor de Alva is appointed president and CEO of Apollo International to oversee the company's expansion into Europe, Latin America, and Asia (Wilson). The Online Campus graduates its first class.[b]		**2000** – Cornell University incorporates eCornell, and Columbia University launches Fathom—both are for-profit, online learning companies (Carr and Kiernan; Carlson, "Web Company Founded"). The American Association for Higher Education reports that 662 for-profit institutions are awarding degrees and 971 institutions are offering virtual courses (reported as a sidebar in Newman, 18).[c]
2001 – Klor de Alva joins the Board of Directors of the American Association of Higher Education. UOP begins marketing its courses through America Online. Approximately 50,000 students are enrolled in the online program alone. Television news program *60 Minutes* features a largely favorable segment on web-based education with UOP as the model (Stahl).[c]		
2002 – Enrollments are now estimated at 133,000, including the Online Campus and more than 100 locations in the United States, Canada, and the Netherlands. Fiscal year-end revenues increase 30% to $1 billion (Farrell).		**2003** – Columbia University's Fathom.com closes. Commenting on the failure, *The Chronicle of Higher Education* says Fathom's course offerings were "not career-oriented enough" (Carlson, "After Losing Millions", Carnevale and Olsen). A massive spike in tuition costs is reported as both public and private institutions respond to decreases in educational funding and increases in accredited competition (Rooney).

UOP, University of Phoenix; ICRD, Institute for Community Research and Development; IPDK, Institute for Professional Development; NCA, North Central Association of Colleges and Schools; CEO, chief executive officer.
[a] UOP press release, February 27, 1998.
[b] UOP, 2000 Fact Book, 14. <http://www.phoenix.edu/factbook>.
[c] The segment is so favorable that UOP now features the segment in streaming video on its Online Campus Web site: <http://online.uophx.edu>.

140

MERGER:
SHARING THE INIQUITY OF CORPORATIZATION

Burke claims that communities perpetually cycle through conditions of order, guilt, victimization, and redemption—this is his Iron Law of History (*Rhetoric of Religion* 4-5), and the scapegoat is its medium. As the terminology implies, Burke views this process as morally inflected. A community's values define proper action; members of that community invariably fail to live up to those standards; they sin; they feel guilty for their sins; they search for a way to purge their guilt; they select a scapegoat, an entity that appears to be the instigator or epicenter of their own iniquities; they cooperate with fellow sinners to rid their community of the scapegoat, thereby purifying themselves and restoring order.[2] Although academe includes a diverse range of perspectives on the nature and purposes of higher education, the ideals of liberal learning as a means of "liberat[ing] the mind from the bondage of habit and custom, producing people who can function with sensitivity and alertness as citizens of the whole world" (Nussbaum 8) remain the guiding principles of this community. Corporatization is a devil term because it summarizes the iniquities that undermine the liberal learning tradition: actions that reinforce the conventional power structures of an industrialized society, training students narrowly for work in that economy rather than preparing them for a broader understanding and engagement of humanity. Academic critics and commentators frequently adopt the language of virtue and vice to explain the phenomenon. For example, Frank Newman equates protecting the humanistic aim of liberal learning with "saving higher education's soul"; Alan Wolfe accuses nonprofit institutions of making "a pact with the devil" in order to secure increased enrollments. Such rhetoric frames corporatization as a disruption of academic culture, the initial phase of this community's scapegoat process.

The mission of cultivating humanity through a liberal arts curriculum that prepares students to be versatile, productive, and responsible citizens is a sacred trust within the liberal learning tradition. Yet throughout history educators have incorporated other objectives into their work, especially that of training students for specialized professions despite their institu-

---

[2]Several variations on this theme are presented throughout Burke's corpus, including the previously cited verse on the Iron Law of History (*Rhetoric of Religion* 4-5) and his treatment of Original Sin and Redemption in *Permanence and Change* (283-86). Burkean scholars offering summaries and critiques of the process include Rueckert on Dramatism (128-62); Foss, Foss, and Trapp on The Rhetoric of Rebirth (194-97), and C. Allen Carter on The Rod, The Ladder, and the Skull (3-27).

tional commitment to a broader sort of preparation. A 1937 study by the American Association of University Professors concluded:

> the character of educational institutions has changed in the past thirty years. Business, professional, and vocational interests have assumed a more important place. An aura of practicality hangs over the campus. The educational institution is more of the world than ever before. . . . As all the data thus far have shown, the ups and downs of the world of business have their counterpart in academic matters. Men are hired or dropped, salaries are raised or cut, and tenure is more or less secure as general economic conditions fluctuate between prosperity and depression . . . (Finkin 22)

We remain enshrouded by practicality. Unable or unwilling to persuade the public that academe should transcend—not serve—the marketplace, colleges and universities continue to accommodate the expectations of those who ultimately pay their bills.

Academic capitalism has evolved from this relationship, for many non-profit institutions (and their faculties) not only court certification-seeking consumers, they aggressively pursue external funding for proprietary research projects (Slaughter and Leslie). Compelled to negotiate within the realms of humanism and capitalism, many educators are attempting to strike a self-preserving compromise that makes it difficult at times to differentiate between the pious adherents to nonprofit, liberal learning and those bold sinners, the profit-seeking academic entrepreneurs. The incorporation of Ivy League enterprises such as eCornell and Fathom.com suggests that, in the words of Michael Goldstein, "We can't dichotomize for-profit and nonprofit anymore. We are they; they are us." In short, such institutions have reached the Burkean condition of *merger* in our community consciousness.

The embodiment of this merger is Jorge Klor de Alva, who resigned an endowed faculty position at the University of California at Berkeley to take the helm of UOP—an event that warranted a cover story in the *Chronicle of Higher Education* (Shea). In a cautious profile titled "Visionary or Operator?" Christopher Shea observes that "[t]he questions people have about Phoenix's new president are not unlike the ones that are posed about the university itself: Is Phoenix—is Mr. de Alva—driven by a desire to educate or to be enriched? Can the goals coexist?" Now serving as chief executive officer of Apollo International (another division of Phoenix's parent company) and as a board member of the American Association for Higher Education, Klor de Alva remains an academic insider with footing in both camps. His notoriety mirrors his institution's increasing influence—and its infamy. Shea reflects, "It's hard to judge how much the Jorge-bashing says about the man as opposed to the institution he now represents. There's something peculiar about the attacks. Many of the people now undermining him, after all, treated him like a star just a few years ago." In moving from a prestigious academic post to a comparatively suspicious one, Klor de Alva defied convention as thoroughly as Phoenix did when it began selling shares of stock in its university.

From a Burkean perspective, it is appropriate and perhaps inevitable that Klor de Alva emerges as an academic antihero, a champion of UOP, just as Phoenix itself has become the representative of academic corporatization. Such roles are charged with celebrity or infamy, as is befitting a scapegoat, for as Burke says, "the scapegoat is 'charismatic', a vicar. As such it is profoundly consubstantial with those who, looking on it as a chosen vessel, would ritualistically cleanse themselves by loading the burden of their own iniquities on it" (*Grammar of Motives* 406). Every litany detailing the transgressions of Phoenix becomes an inventory of like behavior by nonprofit institutions. Wolfe admonishes,

> Go back and look at the list of "sacred cows" for which Phoenix is said to have so little respect, and you will discover how few of them turn out to be sacred after all. Night classes, trimesters and summer terms, distance learning, commuting students, extension campuses, reliance on adjuncts, substitutes for tenure, contracting for profit, and emphasis on practical courses—all were pioneered by the most-prestigious, and expensive, universities in America. (B4)

Denouncing Phoenix is, in this regard, an articulation of guilt—a rhetorical byproduct that may help more traditional institutions to isolate, define, and concretely address their own unacceptable practices.

DIVISION:
ALIENATING THE PURVEYORS OF PRACTICAL EDUCATION

Academe's rhetorical dissociation from for-profit behavior leads it into the *division* phase of the scapegoat process, where the characteristics of corporatization are "ritualistically alienated" through public discourse condemning Phoenix as the nemesis of liberal education. In recent years, academics seeking to mobilize support have begun to rely on Phoenix as a recognizable foe, an immediate and symbolic threat to their values and institutions. In his critique of the corporatization of faculty employment, Stephen Watt warns that the erosion of faculty autonomy and working conditions will make the academic experience "nothing like Cardinal Newman's idea of a university, or nothing like that education for which families and students borrow money to attain, but more like the ideas that led to the University of Phoenix's credentialing mill" (152). In a convocation address, President Jane Jervis of Evergreen State College describes the intensified demands on liberal arts colleges to "prove that our product is worth the price" in comparison to new academic competitors such as proprietary and online institutions. She calls Phoenix "a formidable challenge to traditional institutions, and even to non-traditional ones like Evergreen."[3] In a 2001 faculty colloquium presentation at Northeastern Illinois University, Timothy Scherman cautions his colleagues, "If we don't want the State to foist on us the same poverty-stricken, dehumanized University of Phoenix definition of our students as consumers and clients . . . we will have to define what we mean to give our students beyond 'work' skills . . ." (8). A few months later, plenary moderator Michael Goldstein summarizes the mood of his AAHE audience with the quip, "All those here who see University of Phoenix as a threat to your way of life and civilization as we know it raise your hands." The resolute hands and nervous laughter filling the ballroom that day affirm the power of Phoenix to unite even those educators who disagree on virtually everything else.

As academics rhetorically distance themselves from Phoenix-style values, two themes are especially prominent: consumerism and vocationalism. Among nonprofits and for-profits exhibiting consumerism and vocationalism, the key difference is not so much behavior but attitude: When nonprofits appeal to students as consumers they fear they are compromising their true calling; when for-profits do so they fulfill their true calling. Hence, as Phoenix executive Craig Swenson observes, the terms *customers* and *markets* have become "the cusswords of academe," connoting pandering and profit-seeking in the name of education (34). Such blasphemy depends on the perspective of the educator. Whereas Phoenix's opponents view consumeristic terms as indicators of dehumanization and exploitation (e.g., Scherman; Nelson and Watt), Swenson maintains that acknowledging the economics of the relationship gives students the respect they deserve.

---

[3] Jervis' reference to Phoenix is noteworthy because the institutions are, in fundamental ways, operating in such very different realms: Evergreen is a public, residential liberal arts college in Olympia, Washington, an area that is still outside the expansion radar of Phoenix, an institution that specializes in adult commuter students pursuing professional certification. Phoenix's most likely threat relates to its role in the evolving culture of accountability: Whereas Evergreen's notoriety involves interdisciplinary learning paths and the use of unconventional qualitative and reflective assessment methods, Phoenix is winning public and legislative support for demonstrating academic quality through standardized curricula and mostly quantitative performance measures.

That division of opinion is likely to remain, for the foreseeable future, a litmus test for distinguishing "us" from "them." Klor de Alva claims that the for-profit model is more responsive to student priorities and potentially more responsible to society's needs because it offers people the lifelong learning they require for professional and economic advancement. In contrast, Scherman argues that institutions like Phoenix prepare students for their next jobs but for little else. Citing a recent article by the Phoenix president, Scherman responds, "I'd like to think that when we say our students are 'life-long learners' that we mean more than Klor de Alva does—that out of sheer necessity in a fastpaced economy that threatens to leave them behind, they are forced to stop to retool themselves every two years or so just to stay employed—and that we'll take advantage of that need with a sort of planned educational obsolescence, supplying them with just enough to get by for a couple of years" (7). In sum, although for-profits claim to give students the education they want; nonprofits claim to give students the education they need.

Or, from the perspective of the intellectual community, nonprofit, liberal learning institutions give students the education they *should* want even though they may not be sufficiently educated to realize it. With this assertion, I state explicitly what many critics of for-profit education indicate implicitly. Calling into question the sophistication and judgment of the typical Phoenix student, these writers wryly assess both the institution and its alumni as they differentiate *true* education from mere training. James Traub's *New Yorker* article, "Drive-Thru U: Higher Education for People Who Mean Business," is among the most quoted examples. Traub calls Phoenix, among other things, a "para-university" because it "has the operational core of higher education—students, teachers, classrooms, exams, degree-granting programs—without a campus life, or even an intellectual life" (114).

The sardonic tone of the Traub article (refer to Fig. 6.1, its associated cartoon) is a familiar feature of Phoenix-wary commentaries, as is its characterization of Phoenix's founder as a rough-and-tumble entrepreneur with an irreverent attitude toward academe's ennobling "life of the mind."[4] Regarding his early decision to accommodate student preferences for practitioner–instructors, Sperling explains, "You were going to have to draw your faculty from the world they were familiar with—the world of work. If you had a Ph.D. that didn't mean shit" (Traub 118). If the doctoral diploma is an unnecessary distinction for Phoenix faculty, so too is the scholar's

---

[4]The Phoenix mythology is further enriched by the fact that both Sperling and Klor de Alva began their academic careers as working class kids who acquired prestigious credentials (Cambridge and University of California, Berkeley) and were tenured at more traditional institutions before defecting to the realm of proprietary education.

library. To emphasize the contrast between the traditional professor and Sperling's practitioners, Traub describes his library-perusal during a Phoenix interview:

> When [the instructor] walked out of his office for a minute, I glanced at the three books he had on his shelf. Their titles were "Training and Performance," "The Miracle of Personal Leadership," and "Team and Organizational Development." (118)

Traub's observation reinforces the stereotype of intellectual life at Phoenix: Its faculty neither produce nor treasure weighty scholarly volumes, and their pedagogy is "roboticized" by strict adherence to a common syllabus that encourages them to enliven their lessons with professional anecdotes while remaining anchored to the easily accessible texts selected by Phoenix headquarters (Leatherman; Farrell).

The replacement of intellectualism with vocationalism is a recurrent charge against the Phoenix model. Traub describes the students' "lack of intellectual, as opposed to professional, curiosity" with an almost audible sigh (121). The plainspoken Phoenix president, William Gibbs[5] reinforces Traub's impression,

> The people who are our students don't really want the education. They want what the education provides for them—better jobs, moving up in their career, the ability to speak up in meetings, that kind of stuff. They want it to *do* something for them. (114)

In a similar vein, *Chronicle* reporter Kim Strosnider quotes a recent Phoenix graduate (a police lieutenant who was also the commencement speaker) praising his alma mater and criticizing the comparatively impractical approach of conventional institutions: "In a regular four-year college, you deal with a lot of theory," he concludes (A32). That Phoenix students have little regard for theories and theoreticians is presented as symptomatic of an institution that grants academic credit for practical experience while teaching almost exclusively practical courses.

The paradox of vocationalism is that many representatives of nonprofit, liberal learning institutions are both morally opposed to overtly practical

---

[5]Gibbs, whose pre-Apollo career was in industry rather than academe, was Klor de Alva's predecessor as president of UOP. In July 2000, Klor de Alva took the post of chief executive officer and president of Apollo International; Laura Palmer Noone was appointed president of UOP.

"The people who are our students don't really want the education," the president of the U. of P. says.

Figure 6.1. Dissociating intellectualism from capitalism: Phoenix dis-
places liberal education. A cartoon from the frequently
quoted New Yorker article critiquing the for-profit institution's anti-intellectualism (Thompson; Traub).

courses and highly protective of those in their own catalogs. After all, the
terms *practical* and *profitable* are now used interchangeably in the academic
policy literature to indicate staple courses with high enrollments (see, e.g.,
Immerwahr; Goldstein, et al.). According to a recent study of publicly
funded universities, one of the chief fears of administrators and faculty is
that Phoenix and others will "cherry-pick" practical programs—offering
them more cheaply and/or more conveniently to career-oriented students
(Immerwahr; Schmidt). In short, the principal threat of for-profit competition is that liberal learning institutions may be forced to survive on their
liberal arts curricula.

PURIFIED IDENTITY:
CLARIFYING THE ROLES OF NONPROFIT, LIBERAL EDUCATION

Of course, it is highly unlikely that any institution—even the most elite liberal arts college—would completely rid itself of practical and pre-professional studies, if absent from credit-bearing courses then such preparation will be available from a career services office, campus computer lab, or faculty mentor. Most colleges claim their graduates will be polished and equipped to enter or continue their chosen career. So the question is not—nor has it ever been—whether such experiences belong on a traditional campus but how those experiences can be meaningfully integrated into a rigorous academic foundation. This is where the third phase of the scapegoat process can help us make a more sensitive assessment of the Phoenix threat. Burke says that a *purified identity* is formed when our community defines itself in "dialectical opposition" to the scapegoat (*Grammar of Motives* 406, *Philosophy of Literary Form* 27). In other words, in considering the scapegoat, we are not viewing the static portrait of a monster, but rather the realtime image of a repulsive community offspring who will continue to grow and change in response to the world we share. This image of the scapegoat is most valuable as we become attentive to the salient similarities and differences between us. To whatever degree they disagree with for-profit education, observing Phoenix's approach gives nonprofits an opportunity to clarify their social purpose and redefine their roles and relationships.

Although each university and college has its own unique character, some fundamental commitments distinguish most nonprofit, liberal learning institutions from their for-profit competitors:

- maintaining resources and artifacts of public interest;
- advancing and refining knowledge in all fields of study, and sharing that knowledge with the public;
- preparing students for opportunities and responsibilities beyond the workplace;
- serving as community stewards;
- making some (or all) kinds of academic study more accessible to under-served populations.

How each institution interprets and fulfills these commitments will vary widely and may even appear to overlap a bit with the stated missions of some for-profits. As an example, Sperling claims that Phoenix's core value is to make higher education available to those not served by the nonprofits (see, e.g., Sperling; Sperling and Tucker).

Faculty and administrators of public institutions recently reported that they feel pressured to "emulate the for-profits, and shed much of their public mission" in order to compete for student enrollments in the higher revenue programs (Schmidt; Immerwahr). But halting all market-driven behavior is an unlikely solution to this problem because one academic's vocational subject is another academic's liberal art. For instance, Wolfe argues, "[only] when colleges and universities voluntarily relinquish to places like the University of Phoenix those subjects and approaches that they never should have adopted in the first place will American higher education once again resemble the institutions whose ideals attracted most academics to their calling" (B4). His conclusion becomes more complicated when we review Wolfe's list of less desirable subjects and approaches: in addition to pre-professional courses such as hotel management are academic service courses such as "survey research for political scientists" and "expository writing for departments of English." The belief that a purified liberal arts institution could dispense with composition courses is maintained by for-profits and nonprofits alike. At the AAHE plenary discussed earlier, Cardean University executive Don Norman used the composition course to illustrate the value of proprietary instruction. He began by asking the rhetorical question, "Who likes to teach introductory writing?" He then proceeded to explain that institutions such as his specialize in offering high-quality, high-volume introductory courses developed by people who actually enjoy teaching them, presumably in contrast to those relegated to teach first-year composition in conventional institutions (Goldstein et al.). This shared assumption equates writing courses with practical instruction at a time when practicality is being used to designate whether a subject is a form of education or training and, by the same token, whether that subject falls within the preferred territory of nonprofit or for-profit institutions.

At issue is whether courses associated with writing, applied research, and professional culture can be retained within the "redeemed" structure of a liberal learning institution when such subjects appear to fall so neatly into the buckets of practicality and vocationalism. Within this context, one of the most imperiled subjects would be technical and professional communication. Interestingly, this predicament illustrates Peter Drucker's claim that the key dichotomy of values and aesthetic perceptions in postcapitalist society is between intellectuals ("those concerned with words and ideas") and managers ("[those concerned] with people and work") (9). Operating between industry and the academy, capitalism and humanism, scholars of workplace writing are doing work that is "too theoretical" for most for-profit curricula, and "too practical" for the liberal arts. Although, as Locke Carter claims in his introduction to this volume, it is clearly important to demonstrate the value of writing studies for the knowledge work done beyond campus, so long as this field operates within liberal learning institutions it must also demonstrate value to traditional humanistic inquiry—not just philosophical consistency, but recognizable scholarly interconnectivity. Demonstrating, for example, how autoethnographic research on narrative in the workplace may contribute to theory-building in other subfields of narrative studies may help reformers integrate a more diverse range of textual studies into the revisioned liberal arts.

CONCLUSION: INCREASING THE VISIBILITY OF LIBERAL EDUCATION

For-profit schools have competed with nonprofit schools in America since the Colonial era. Writing in 1900, educational historian Edmund James concludes that for-profit education "embodies all the defects and the excellencies of the American character" (Ruch 107). Exploitation and entrepreneurship, vocationalism and idealism—all the characteristics perceived by the historian are now evident in both for-profit and nonprofit institutions, as perhaps they were all along. If today's competitive crisis is remarkable, it may be because technology has given us more venues for expressing our collective anxiety and more options for defending or extending our turf. It is unsurprising that many nonprofits are resorting to extensive media campaigns to market their institutions, taking their cue from the UOP to establish a consistent "brand identity" that is attractive to prospective students (see, e.g., Kotler; Ruch 151-2). Although academics may find these campaigns superficial and distasteful, the core strategy of differentiation is one worth noting. Phoenix is highly successful at attracting working adults because it persuasively presents its distinctive advantages for those students. Liberal learning universities and colleges could do more to persuasively present their distinctive advantages to students and to the public.

One way to begin is by increasing the visibility of academic projects and programs that are both widely relevant and institutionally distinctive. The following are a few of the more interesting trends—all of which are familiar territory for rhetoric, composition, and technical communication:

- Specialized Web sites tied to an institution's geography, curriculum, or culture. A well-known example is "The Valley of the Shadow: Two Communities in the American Civil War," a visually compelling repository of letters, public documents, and other artifacts from the politically divided communities of Augusta County, Virginia and Franklin County, Pennsylvania. The site is used by researchers of all ages, worldwide, to examine the context and consequences war, and is maintained by the University of Virginia's Center for Digital History (Ayers).

- Electronic portfolios for outcomes assessment. Scholars of rhetoric, composition, and technical communication have been particularly instrumental in refining and promoting the portfolio genre for demonstrating learning outcomes to students, teachers, and stakeholders. Electronic portfolios are especially helpful for communicating "non-quantifiable" outcomes to a public accustomed to numbers-driven reports. These portfolios are used to illustrate the goals and accomplishments of institutions as well as students (Cambridge et al.), and may be enriching the way informational portfolios are designed outside academe.

- Increased marketing of staple programs. To counter the "cherry-picking" phenomenon discussed earlier, programs that manage high-enrollment courses such as introductory composition, technical communication, and pre-professional requirements are using campus websites, promotional videos, and other means to attract and retain students and to forge partnerships with other programs (see, e.g., Howard).

- More extensive alliances with local corporations and service organizations. Whether for internships, service-learning, or participatory action research, institutions are deepening local relationships to offer their students experiences that are unique to the communities near campus. Here, too, is an opportunity to reinforce the unique identity of an institution through its association with a well-known industry, social project, or landmark. The most sophisticated models incorporate the knowledge and expertise of multiple disciplines.

Ideally, this local emphasis will lead to alliances with underserved populations who can contribute important perspectives on the relative value of academic work for the communities near campus. These students are overlooked as institutions scramble to recruit well-prepared and well-heeled prospects.

If liberal learning institutions intend to operate in fulfillment of their social responsibilities, with or without the threat of competition or reduced enrollments, then each must clarify its relationship with the underprivileged and less educated students who tend to lie outside the radar of most nonprofits, as well as with the working professionals who lie squarely within it. Additionally, these institutions must attend to the real and perceived relevance of their programs. Increasing the visibility of interesting and important work is an important step in that direction. The next step is to redesign programs to channel broad disciplinary knowledge into the complex problems encountered in our communities.

Refining the scope of liberal education will likely involve an altogether different understanding of "private gain" and "public good" as academics observe that competition for students and resources is arising within as well as outside their campus community and adopting increasingly unusual forms. Whereas Phoenix's current model has become a familiar opponent, its next incarnation may be an "educational shopping mall" or media conglomerate (Scherman). Considering Burke's scapegoat mechanism within the framework of academic corporatization helps us appreciate the importance of viewing the process as recursive rather than linear, for as institutions pause or conclude their comparisons to Phoenix alternative competitors arrive. In his article on the rise of the professional guild as a source of training and credentialing, Clifford Adelman claims, "In our frenetic fascination with the likes of the University of Phoenix and virtual degree delivery, we have been looking for challenges in the wrong direction" (23). A new scapegoat may be on the horizon.

REFERENCES

Adelman, Clifford. "A Parallel Universe, Explained: Certification in the Information Technology Guild." *Change* 32.3 (May/June 2000): 20-9.

American Association of University Professors, Committee R on Government Relations. Report. "Distance Learning." *Academe* 84.3 (May–Jun. 1998): 30-8.

Ayers, Edward L. "The Valley of the Shadow: Two Communities in the American Civil War." Digital Archive Online. 2001. <http://www.iath.virginia.edu/vshadow2/>.

Bloom, Allan. *The Closing of the American Mind.* New York: Simon and Schuster, 1987.

Boyer, Ernest L. *Scholarship Reconsidered: Priorities of the Professoriate.* San Francisco: Jossey-Bass, 1990.

Burke, Kenneth. *A Grammar of Motives.* Berkeley: U of California P, 1969.

———. *The Rhetoric of Religion: Studies in Logology.* Berkeley: U of California P, 1970.

———. *The Philosophy of Literary Form: Studies in Symbolic Action.* 3rd ed. Berkeley: U of California P, 1973.

———. *Permanence and Change: An Anatomy of Purpose.* 3rd ed. Berkeley: U of California P, 1984.

Cambridge, Barbara, Susan Kahn, Daniel P. Tompkins, Kathleen Blake Yancey, eds. *Electronic Portfolios: Emerging Practices in Student, Faculty, and Institutional Learning.* Washington, DC: American Association for Higher Education, 2001.

Carlson, Scott. "After Losing Millions, Columbia U. Will Close Online-Learning Venture." *Chronicle of Higher Education.* 17 Jan. 2003, A30.

———. "Web Company Founded by Columbia U. Opens a Beta Version of Its Site." *Chronicle of Higher Education.* 1 Dec. 2000, A42.

Carnevale, Dan and Florence Olsen. "How to Succeed in Distance Education." *Chronicle of Higher Education.* 13 June 2003, A31.

Carr, Sarah and Vincent Kiernan. "For-Profit Web Venture Seeks to Replicate the University Experience Online." *Chronicle of Higher Education.* 14 April 2000, A59.

Carter, C. Allen. *Kenneth Burke and the Scapegoat Process.* Norman: U of Oklahoma P, 1996.

Cross, K. Patricia. "The New Learners: Changing Perspectives on Quality Education." *Change* (Feb 1973). In *Learning from Change: Landmarks in Teaching and Learning in Higher Education from* Change *Magazine, 1969-1999.* Ed., Deborah DeZure. Sterling, VA: Stylus, 2000, 58-61.

Farrell, Elizabeth F. "U. of Phoenix Sees Surge in Revenues and Enrollments." *Chronicle of Higher Education.* 25 Oct. 2002, A31.

Finkin, Matthew W. "Tenure and the Entrepreneurial Academy: A Reply." *Academe* (Jan. – Feb. 1998): 14-22.

Fischetti, Mark, John Anderson, Malena Watrous, Jason Tanz, and Peter Gwynne. "Gas, Food, Lodging . . . Education?" *University Business.* 1.1 (March/April 1998): 44-51.

Foss, Sonja K., Karen A. Foss, and Robert Trapp, eds. "Kenneth Burke." *Contemporary Perspectives on Rhetoric.* 2nd ed. Prospect Heights, IL: Waveland P, 1991, 169-207.

Goldstein, Michael, Nancy Cantor, Don Norman. "Balancing Private Gain and Public Good: Perspectives From Across the Table." Plenary panel. American Association for Higher Education National Conference. Marriott Wardman Park Hotel, Washington, DC. 25 Mar. 2001. Compact disks HE01-PS1. Conference Media, 2001.

Hitchcock, James. "The New Vocationalism." *Change* (Apr. 1973). In *Learning from Change: Landmarks in Teaching and Learning in Higher Education from* Change *Magazine, 1969-1999.* Ed., Deborah DeZure. Sterling, VA: Stylus, 2000. 62-4.

Howard, Rebecca Moore. "Selling the Writing Program." Plenary address. Council of Writing Program Administrators Conference. Park City, UT. 11 July 2002.

Immerwahr, John. "Meeting the Competition: College and University Presidents, Faculty, and Legislators View the New Competitive Academic Arena." Providence, RI: Public Agenda and The Futures Project, 2002.

Jervis, Jane. "Opening Address." Evergreen State College. 16 Sept. 1998.

Klor de Alva, Jorge. "Remaking the Academy in the Age of Information." *Issues in Science and Technology Online* 16.2 (Winter 1999). 10 Jun. 2003. <http://www.nap.edu/issues/16.2/klor_de_alva.htm>.

Kotler, Philip and Karen Fox. *Strategic Marketing for Education Institutions.* Englewood Cliffs, NJ: Prentice-Hall, 1995.

Leatherman, Courtney. "U. of Phoenix's Faculty Members Insist They Offer High-Quality Education." *Chronicle of Higher Education.* 16 October 1998, A14.

Levine, Arthur and Jana Nidiffer. "Key Turning Points in the Evolving Curriculum." *Handbook of the Undergraduate Curriculum.* Eds., Jerry G. Gaff, James L. Ratcliff, and Assoc. San Francisco: Jossey-Bass, 1997, 53-85.

Lively, Kit and Goldie Blumenstyk. "Sylvan Learning Systems to Start a Network of For-Profit Universities Overseas." *Chronicle of Higher Education.* 29 Jan. 1999, A43.

National Commission on Excellence in Education. *A Nation at Risk: The Imperative for Educational* Reform. Washington, DC: US Government Printing Office, 1983.

Nelson, Cary. "Between Meltdown and Community: Crisis and Opportunity in Higher Education." *Academic Keywords: A Devil's Dictionary for Higher Education.* Cary Nelson and Stephen Watt. New York: Routledge, 1999, 1-14.

Nelson, Cary and Stephen Watt. *Academic Keywords: A Devil's Dictionary for Higher Education.* New York: Routledge, 1999.

Newman, Frank. "Saving Higher Education's Soul." *Change* 33.5 (Sept./Oct. 2000): 16-23.

Nussbaum, Martha C. *Cultivating Humanity: A Classical Defense of Reform in Liberal Education.* Cambridge: Harvard UP, 1997.

Readings, Bill. *The University in Ruins.* Cambridge: Harvard UP, 1996.

Rooney, Megan. "Higher and Higher." *Chronicle of Higher Education.* 9 May 2003, A35.

Ruch, Richard S. *Higher Ed, Inc: The Rise of the For-Profit University.* Baltimore, MD: Johns Hopkins UP, 2001.

Rudolph, Frederick. *Curriculum: A History of the American Undergraduate Course of Study Since 1636.* 1977. San Francisco: Jossey-Bass, 1993.

Rueckert, William H. *Kenneth Burke and the Drama of Human Relations.* 2nd ed. Berkeley: U of California P, 1982.

Scherman, Timothy. "What Do You Mean Our Students Aren't Customers?" Northeastern Illinois University. University Day. Faculty Colloquium. 2001.

Schmidt, Peter. "Study Notes Tensions Facing Public Colleges." *Chronicle of Higher Education.* 18 Oct. 2002, A28.

Selingo, Jeffrey. "Pennsylvania Surprises Colleges by Letting U. of Phoenix Open Campuses in State." *Chronicle of Higher Education.* 26 Mar. 1999, A43.

Shea, Christopher. "Visionary or Operator? Jorge Klor de Alva and His Unusual Intellectual Journey." *Chronicle of Higher Education.* 3 July 1998, A8.

Slaughter, Sheila and Larry L. Leslie. *Academic Capitalism: Politics, Policies, and the Entrepreneurial University.* Baltimore: Johns Hopkins UP, 1995.

Sperling, John. *Rebel with a Cause.* New York: John Wiley, 2000.

Sperling, John and Robert W. Tucker. *For-Profit Higher Education: Developing a World-Class Workforce.* New Brunswick, NJ: Transaction P, 1997.

Stahl, Leslie. "Online U." *60 Minutes.* 18 Feb. 2001.

Strosnider, Kim. "For-Profit University Challenges Traditional Colleges." *Chronicle of Higher Education.* 6 June 1997, A32.

Swenson, Craig. "Customers and Markets: The Cuss Words of Academe." *Change* (September/October 1998): 34-9.

Thompson, Richard. Cartoon. "Practical Experience is Power." *New Yorker.* 20 Oct. 1997, 114.

Traub, James. "Drive-Thru U." *New Yorker.* 20 Oct. 1997, 114-23.

Watt, Stephen. "Faculty." *Academic Keywords: A Devil's Dictionary for Higher Education.* Cary Nelson and Stephen Watt. New York: Routledge, 1999, 132-52.

Wilson, Robin. "U. of Phoenix Chief Takes a New Post in the Company." *Chronicle of Higher Education.* 31 July 2000. Today's News Online. <http://chronicle.com/daily/2000/07/2000073102n.htm>.

Wolfe, Alan. "How a For-Profit University Can Be Invaluable to the Traditional Liberal Arts." *Chronicle of Higher Education.* 4 December 1998, B4.

7 Meeting a Demand

Technical Communicators' Invitation to Discourse

Donna Spehar
Texas Tech University

Traditionally, colleges and universities stand apart from the world of commerce. Their mission and goals for graduate programs include factors that go beyond teaching specific disciplinary content, to include a wide range of social and personal experiences that are designed to produce what society and industry perceives as a well-educated and responsible citizen. Although responsive to the demands of government and the business sector, these accredited institutions maintain their independent status in order to foster critical analysis of public and private methods and practices as well as provide course content. However, advances in technology over the last decade make it possible for the academic content of entire accredited degree programs to be delivered to the convenience of students' homes. Such convenience, on the other hand, raises the question of devaluing some of the less tangible elements of a traditionally delivered education, such as knowledge management, networking, collaborative techniques, social skills, and emphasis on civic responsibility.

Recent changes in governmental policies recognize the value of graduate degrees awarded solely on coursework completed in distance programs by relaxing the strict guidelines of federal student loan programs as well as reducing mandated contact hours between student and provider ("Ten"). In fact, the U.S. Department of Education's Technology Office policy statement encourages the formation of consortia of existing accredited colleges and universities under a for-profit information management provider as a means to standardize delivery and provide wider choices for students (e-Learning). In October 2001, HR 1992: The Internet Equity and Education Act, which passed with a bipartisan vote of 354–70, modified the Federal Aid packages to bypass the 50% rule. This existing rule required that more than half of coursework in a degree or certificate providing program be presented in traditional face-to-face classrooms for the student to qualify for federally assisted student loan programs. Relaxing the strict loan guidelines makes distance learners a more attractive potential customer for emerging for-profit based course delivery consortia and challenges traditional providers to attract students by emphasizing the benefits of a university education over the expedience of nontraditional Internet-based programs. Furthermore, the changes also raise the question of how such a partnership structure between nontraditional course providers and for-profit management companies can be seen as a threat to valued university goals because their curriculum concentrates on genre training and software use, often bypassing the elements that involve human judgment that Aristotle called *phronesis.*

Still, it is these less tangible skills that differentiate the expert from the practitioner in the field of technical communication. They are not *techne,* which is the art of producing something, or the *praxis,* the production itself, but the underlying knowledge and beliefs that the individual communicator brings to each task. In the fourth chapter of Nicomachean Ethics, Aristotle describes this *phronesis,* or prudence, as an underlying principle to both by first pointing out that it cannot be either a science or an art because "the sphere of action is variable and not an art, because all art is productive and action is generally different from production" (1140a). He ties the idea to human good, which is the essence of valued-added elements in technical communication—good for the society, producer, and user:

> It remains therefore that prudence should be a true rational and practical state of mind in the field of human good and evil; for while the end of production is different from the production itself, it is not so with action, as the right action is itself an end. It is in this view that we consider Pericles and people like him to be prudent as having the capacity of observing what is good for themselves and for mankind; and this is our conception of such persons as are successful in administering a household or a State. (1140b)

Can a graduate education that does not explore these intangible elements produce the kind of expertise that is competitive in the workplace? Or, perhaps are these kinds of elements not considered a part of the technical communicators' valued skills by the workplace? To explore these ideas we turn to research and contemporary workplace literature that define the ideas of knowledge creation and expertise.

Popular management books, such as Jim Collins' *Good to Great* and Etienne Wenger, Richard McDermott, and William Snyder's *Cultivating Communities of Practice*, emphasize the idea that rhetorically based management skills and knowledge creation techniques make the difference between success and failure in competitive markets. Why, then, cannot the same valued-added perception be transferred to the process and documentation development within companies? Dreyfus and Dreyfus, in *Mind over Machine*, define five levels of performance that a learner progresses through while learning new tasks:

1. Novice learners take appropriate actions by following the rules they have been presented regardless of the context in which they must be applied.
2. Advanced beginners have some experience and question rules based on context, i.e., look for guidance beyond the rules.
3. Competent performers rely on their experiences and knowledge to apply the rules within given contexts and look for guidance only when there is a wide departure from set procedures.
4. Proficient performers identify problems within the context that they are asked to apply the rules and suggest solutions or changes.
5. Experts behave intuitively changing rules to fit the context often without requesting analytical evaluations from outside sources.

These levels of expertise conform loosely to the guidelines described by Collins in his discussion of "a genius with a thousand helpers." In this model of practice if, or when, the genius moves on to a new job or company, the enterprise he or she leaves behind fails because the helpers are all operating at the advanced beginner stage. On the other hand, if the company has made employment decisions based on level of expertise, then losses of central players can be overcome rapidly (63). Wenger et al. take a more explicit approach by exploring a knowledge-pool structure for developing an effective workforce and for recognizing the dynamic nature of knowledge and building tools to foster distributed cognition (132). A graduate education, from a traditional provider, should build the skills of a proficient performer: one who recognizes the context of a situation and has the skills to build strengths in co-workers while still developing his or her own. This is a strength that could, and should, be emphasized to the current and future employers of these students.

EXPLORING THE DICHOTOMY

As an academic technical communicator, I see a philosophical split between traditional university distance-based graduate program providers and nontraditional university providers that parallels the split in our own profession between teaching productive tools and value-added skills. In "Conversations with Technical Writing Teachers," Bonita Selting explores the relationship of teaching software tools courses, or teaching technology as part of a rhetorically based course, in an "age of technological determinism." Hers is not a theoretical article, but one based on "teacher lore" that "steps under the layers of theory on how to teach technology in the technical writing classroom to add some voices to the conversation about how much technology we should teach at all" (253). Based on a survey of 64 practicing teachers in the field, her results indicate that there is not one answer to this question, but that the respondents generally reject the idea of being teachers of technology even though it was the consensus that students need to use technology.

Working technical communicators often value the technology over the value-added elements of the profession: the opposite to Selting's survey results. One example can be observed in the popular technical writer's listserv, TECHWR-L. Johnson-Eilola and Selber recognize how this group of practicing technical writers rejects discussions about ethical issues and civic commitment. They demonstrate that members of this group express impatience with issues that do not directly relate to *praxis*- and *techne*-based discussions and react to the introduction of topics that explore ethical or civic duty issues by either withdrawing from the list or refusing to discuss topics of a social consequence. In fact, owners of the listserv exercise their right to manage topics of conversation by closing issues that cause heated ethical or political discussion. It seems that members of this list do not recognize these kinds of issues as central to the professional persona, the *phronesis*, of the members. This dichotomy between what the university values and the workplace evokes consideration of "Foucault's assertion that discourses write authors, not vice versa" (289), and raises the question of whether or not, denied legitimacy by peers, professional expectations in these nontangible areas are devalued. From this viewpoint, the nontraditional skills-based education would seem adequate for entry into the profession. However, it raises the question of whether or not the students would enter the workplace with those skills that would allow them to become proficient performers.

By opening a dialogue between traditional academic and workplace stakeholders about the challenges to traditional goals that are lacking in nontraditional distance-based graduate education providers, the academic world can accomplish at least two important goals:

1. Demonstrate the practical value of *phronesis* in potential employers.
2. Develop understanding of particular strengths that the workplace values.

Open discourse is one method by which technical communicators can develop and maintain a professional persona that is valued by both academia and the workplace. However, this task is not as simple as inviting the stakeholders to a roundtable discussion and providing a few seed questions to stimulate discussion because each has different goals and venues of communication. The goal of traditional educators in technical communicators is long term, striving to prepare students to enter the workplace with both the technical skills required to accomplish a task and the nontangible skills to do so in a productive and ethical manner (Flyvbjerg 58). As communicators, the educators generally hold their professional conversations in public forums, such as publications, conference presentations, online discussion lists, and workshops.

The goal of employers, when hiring technical communicators, is to find proficient performers and experts to develop information that explains their products or concepts to potential users. Immediate workplace concerns are short term: profit, production, and perhaps quality in the form of end-user satisfaction. The long-term goal of fostering expertise in their employees is less evident. Effective documentation is important to them, but not crucial in the sense that they see it as paramount to accomplishing their ultimate goal of producing a competitive product (Schriver 78). At management levels, conversations are centered on product development and sales, rather than documentation, and often occur at private discussions and meetings rather than public forums. Of course, much of what they discuss is about specific product development, and it would be counterproductive to share the information with the competition in public forums. Discussion between these two central stakeholders, then, begins from opposite places and is disseminated in different ways. The workplace wants to discuss visible end-products and is proprietary about their research, whereas technical communication educators want to discuss methods and approaches for the effective communication of information and share their research. Just as the workplace probably does not read the discipline's growing body of professional technical communication literature with any regularity, educators in the field are seldom invited to intracorporate strategy meetings. So, employers must be provided with evidence and reasons to reinforce their subjective perception of return on their invested time and money in terms that they value, just as the university needs to maintain those unique features that allow its students to develop *phronesis*.

Examining traditional programs reveals a concentration on skills that should reflect their long-term goals. Students progressing through both traditional and distance university-based graduate programs in technical communication are exposed to the following:

- Production software: word processors, presentation tools, on- and off-line publishing tools, and programming languages.
- Genre training: design, formatting, and editing of common workplace documents.
- Process analysis and testing: techniques such as contextual inquiry, participatory design, and analytical interviewing techniques.
- Workplace practices: ethical and legal problematizing about issues that affect both individual and employer responsibilities.
- Communication techniques: exploration of rhetorical issues based in classical sources that have evolved into current management theory including such practices as information management and knowledge enabling.

In contrast, techwriter-certification.com, a for-profit educational consortium that contracts with accredited institutions, offers an Internet-based master's specialist certificate that is "is ideally suited for those employed in the technical writing industry who seek or are at the management level" (techwriter). Completion of this certificate requires coursework in basic writing and editing skills, graphic manipulation (CorelDraw and Snagit), Robohelp, usability, management of multilingual documentation, and XML. Other popular providers, such as JER Group, Inc. and Online-Learning.com, have course offerings that are similar. Clearly, students from the university-based programs emerge with backgrounds that go far beyond the issues that are addressed in these programs, which concentrate on *praxis* and *techne*.

The content of these online courses reflects the workplace need to have employees trained in information design and production. To further ensure success, employers hire people they feel are well qualified and invest in further training to meet specific needs and compensate or train them based on profit- and need-based decisions. For example, Saba Corporation provides technical infrastructure to corporations that want to establish in-house training courses for employees. In the fiscal year ending May 2001, their revenues rose to $53.1 million, an increase of 195% over the previous year (Wilson). The service package offered at a small firm like Saba is not unique. SmartForce, a rapidly growing international corporation that partners with software developers, provides individualized in-house training programs that they call "Learning Solutions" (Smartforce). In fact, a simple search of the Internet reveals dozens of companies, large and small, prepared to help employers provide tools training for their employees. In essence, this intracorporate emphasis on *praxis* and *techne* (i.e., genre and tools) issues demonstrated by the workplace's willingness to invest money in training, defines the limited perception of a technical communicator's more intrinsic skills by emphasizing short-term goals. As participants in the conversation, employers can provide educators with insights into real workplace needs while benefiting from looking at the long-term profitability of employing people with strong rhetorical and communication skills, which traditional educators value and emphasize.

This dichotomy creates an exigency because the answer must come from a variety of sources: academia, working professionals, and management. It is here that professionals in the field, such as members of professional organizations and discussion groups, might become a bridge to open a conversation that strengthens perceptions of real needs for all stakeholders. Identifying a "starting place," however, is not easy. As technical communication professionals, the differences between university training and "professional" training raise many questions. Two central issues, however, are compelling because they are dependent on viewpoint. The first is practical and employer-based. What value does the workplace give intangible skills such as those mentioned earlier: knowledge management, networking, collaborative techniques, social skills, and emphasis on civic responsibility? The second is philosophical and addresses the professional persona of technical communicators. Is the future of graduate technical communication education merely to provide competent workers, or is it to maintain the philosophy that its role is to assist in building responsible and responsive members of society?

OPENING A DIALOGUE

To answer the first question, one must look to the workplace and hiring practices. The workplace's willingness to invest in training programs like those provided by Saba and Smartforce, demonstrates that basic writing skills and competence with production software are critical for technical communicators. However, if a practitioner's skills do not go beyond these two areas of competence is he or she truly a technical communicator, or instead a well-trained technical writer? In December 2002, a small informal survey of technical communication jobs advertised in several online sources revealed a concentration of production-type qualifications and requirements, but very little emphasis on less tangible communication skills (Table 7.1). Of the employers mentioned in this table, only two refer to "strong communication" skills, and then in only a passive manner, such as "Will work with software and test engineers to gather information and present it clearly and effectively to a target audience." The jobs represented in Table 7.1, using compensation as an indicator, represent a wide range of responsibility and experience levels; yet, each also seems to undervalue the intangi-

TABLE 7.1. Employer Expectations for Technical Communicators

JOB TITLE	EDUCATION	EXPERIENCE	TOOLS	STATE	SALARY
Technical Writer (ASIC)	n/a	5 yrs	AA, AI, FM, V, MSP, MSO	NH	$60 hr contract
Technical Writer – Manufacturing	BS	3 yrs	MSO	NY	nego.
Sr. Information Processing Analyst	Certificate or Experience	2 yrs	MSO, D, CD	NJ	$80,000
Technical Writer	BA/BS and Experience	3 yrs	MSO, PS, RH, DW, HTML	CA	$70,000
HTML/XML Technical Writer		4 yrs	MSO, V, HTML, XML	IL	
Technical Writer		3 yrs	MSO, FM	TX	
Technical Writer			MSO, PM	CA	$40,000 contract
Technical Writer		3 yrs	MSO, FM	TX	
Technical Writer	BS/BA		MSO, RH, VS	FL	
Technical Writer		5 yrs	MSO	IN	$39 hr
Jr. Tech Writer	BS/BA and Experience	2 yrs	MSO	MN	temp
Technical Writer	BA or AA with Exp.	2yrs	MS0, MSP, V	IL	$30 hr

AA, Adobe Acrobat, AI, Adobe Illustrator, AP, Adobe Photoshop, D, Documentum, DW, Dreamweaver, CD, Core Dossier, FM, Framemaker, V, Visio, MSP, MS Project, MSO, MS Office Suite, PM, Page Maker, RH, Robohelp, VS, Visual SourceSafe.

ble attributes acquired through traditional university graduate training. Note also that although the terms technical communicator were used to search online job offerings, in all but one instance the title "Technical Writer" appears to be the professional title of employers' choice.

Professional technical communication associations, such as the Society for Technical Communicators (STC), no longer use the term *technical writer* as a designator for their profession, preferring instead *technical communicator*. Yet, the workplace does not seem to have accepted this terminology.

In fact, conflicts in terminology can easily lead to misunderstandings about competencies and skills. From the broad label *technical communication* to the simple term design, professionals in the field of providing usable data and clear information to readers disagree about the meaning of common terms. In *Dynamics of Document Design*, Karen Schriver points out that, in all forms of written technical communication, the design is often something applied to an existing body of compiled information. This observation underscores the classical Aristotelian viewpoint that proof (i.e., data and information) exists outside the field of rhetoric. Yet, in the historical sense, other classic rhetoricians and the Sophists quickly disagreed with this view and included gathering data and compiling information as part of the initial stage of the rhetorical paradigm, *inventio*. We, of the postmodern world, employ the Greek term for invention, *heuresis*, in ways that mean a set of actions designed to pass knowledge effectively. Thus, through the very words we use, we indicate that the heart of our profession goes far beyond taking an existing set of words and shaping it into some format that is pleasing to the eye and soothing to the mind.

Such disagreements about basic terminology haunt the emerging field of *technical communication* by blurring the lines between what practitioners can do, based on academic training, and what employers expect them to do, based on perceived workplace need. A strong argument can be made for technical communicators actively redefining themselves by emphasizing their competencies rather than by the products that they can produce or the electronic tools that they can manipulate (Wick). What must be considered, however, is that the business world will only participate in a conversation if they perceive the outcome will be to their benefit. Therefore, it is incumbent on professionals in the field of *technical communication* to find ways to emphasize the value of their training and demonstrate how such a redefinition of the field adds value to the employer's goals as well as the employees' personal satisfaction. This active sharing of information should encourage employers to open their minds to the unique strengths that university-educated technical communicators can bring to their enterprises, and recognition that these skills go beyond applying structure to information gathered and sorted by others.

Changing the perceived image cannot occur if the university and university trained professionals merely talk about what competencies they can bring to the workplace in academic terms. To begin a dialogue between the stakeholders, here, some common grounds of communication must be established. In *Dialogue and the Art of Thinking Together*, William Isaacs states: "It is a contradiction in terms to use a top down, control oriented approach to try to manufacture learning and empowerment instead of creating conditions there they naturally emerge" (338). In other words, professionals cannot dictate the terms of the discussion. Instead, they must demonstrate that their intangible competencies add value to the overall endeavors of their employers. Furthermore, they must become listeners to discover the terms that the business world uses to express the intangible skills of technical communicators and incorporate those terms into their own vocabularies in an effort to become information, as well as document, managers. Then, they must share the language of the workplace with the academic world through discussions, publications, and presentations. In the workplace, technical communicators often sit outside special interest groups or departments as the documentation expert and necessarily provide guidance in maintaining established goals and keeping conversations focused on producing collective information. To accomplish these productive conversational skills, Von Krogh, Ichijo, and Nonaka believe that more emphasis must be placed on them by management training and business focused education programs (127). Furthermore, technical communicators need to provide a method of communication designed to foster knowledge creation because such knowledge-management theories can only be applied when all the stakeholders are using common terminology.

Just as professionals in the field must find ways to demonstrate the value of their rhetorical and communication skills in ways that the workplace will understand and value, academia must find ways to open the dialectic door by observing and asking what employers demand as core educational competencies, *praxis* and *techne*, and emphasize the strengths in critical thinking and rhetorical courses, *phronesis*, brings to these skill-based concepts. North and Worth call these *domains of knowledge* and *skills that transfer*:

> Domains of knowledge involve sets of facts and concepts, along with an understanding of how to perform actions within a domain. Skills that transfer extend across general domains of work activities, such as project planning. Of the two, skills that transfer are far more important because domains of knowledge change rapidly, especially in the areas of technology and media. (144)

Yet, it is the domain of knowledge that receives emphasis in programs provided by employers and nontraditional providers. If technical communicators are going to take an active professional role in the workplace, skills that transfer provided at the university are invaluable because they form foundational abilities: to reason, to think creatively, to make decisions, to solve problems, to take individual responsibility, to self-manage, to act ethically, to work in a social environment (146). This does not mean that domains of knowledge are devalued. Certainly, a strong balance of the two are one thing that defines the expert over the practitioner, but as Bereiter and Scardamalia point out, the set of expert competencies are most emphasized in the academic setting. Their research, based on the working behaviors of a group of engineers, demonstrates that expert learners carry on a program of progressive learning. Inconsistencies between existing beliefs and new knowledge are not resolved by problem-solving changes to existing structures, but by efforts to construct new knowledge structures that can deal with newly recognized complexities (181). Graduate students, here, are a valuable conversational conduit between the workplace and academia. Not only do they bring their newly acquired skills and ideas to the workplace, they also bring the ideas of the workplace to their educational activities. Ultimately, new knowledge structures reinforce the long-term goals of all stakeholders.

Although nontraditional education providers appear to concentrate on domains of knowledge rather than skills that transfer, they are successfully communicating with the workplace. In fact, because as profit-based enterprises and part of the business sector, they have already started a conversation with technical communicator employers, and those conversations shape the expectations for all technical communication professionals. They do not need to make extra efforts to meet evolving needs because their own needs change along the same lines as employers. Working professionals, too, are joining the conversation. Eric Ray, in the January 2002 TECHWR-L online newsletter, proposes ways for people to become technical writers outside of the traditional university path. He emphasizes outside reading that concentrates on *praxis* and *techne*, such as software experience and hardware knowledge. More importantly, for the purposes discussed here, he defines what he, as an academic and practicing professional, sees that employers are looking for when they hire new employees and offers the following advice:

> [Y]ou can think of your learning task as building a mental framework (or schema) into which everything else must fit. Exactly what your schema will work like or look like is an open question—it depends completely on your prior knowledge and what you learn over the years—but you'll know you're getting there when you start seeing the interconnections among technologies rather than the individual (and individually confusing) bits and pieces.

Without specifically identifying it, or perhaps not recognizing it, Ray's framework concept describes the proficient practitioner from Dreyfus and Dreyfus that leads to the expert skills that Bereiter and Scardamalia emphasize. Although traditional education does not replace experience, it does foster ease in building the kind of schema that this author describes.

If academia stands outside this exchange, it risks the redefinition of qualities that go beyond *praxis* and *techne* as experience based attributes. Furthermore, it defaults in its role of providing independent critical analysis of corporate practices and policies. It is incumbent, then, for traditional university distance providers to explore newly emerging programs with an eye toward overall goals and particular curriculum that will help them stay abreast with the corporate expectation, and at the same time find ways to enhance the corporate value for the critical thinking and rhetorical foci that academia provides. Furthermore, they must compete for recognition by corporate entities, just as they do for competent students, by looking for ways that they can form complementary relationships that emphasize the unique strengths of the academy and fill the dynamic needs of the workplace.

DEFINING A SPACE

The potential affiliation between those seeking post-baccalaureate training and the university is particularly important for people who work in the field of technical communication. Having achieved a position in the field, these professionals must continue their education in order to maintain or develop the skills needed in the workplace. Employers often contract with other corporate providers for workshops or computer based training designed to meet this need. Nontraditional providers, such as techwriter.com also compete in this marketplace. In other words, the university provider is only one choice available to students, and often academic technical communication programs are not locally available, so the need for distance-based coursework is a critical alternative. Without distance-based postgraduate programs, the choice for students is limited to the kinds of continuing education that will facilitate practical goals of the employer rather than the professional development of the employee.

Distance-based university courses, which can be more costly and time-consuming, allow students the opportunity to develop the skills that they need in the workplace as well as work toward a personally enhancing degree. Furthermore, these courses expand their *phronesis* by helping them recognize that their strengths go beyond genre and tools issues. It is this added value, and the prestige that accompanies it, that makes the university choice more attractive to students. The cost, however, can be daunting and so potentially commercial providers maintain the edge over the university as long as employers place equal value on the two types of providers. For instance, most individual university graduate distance courses cost more than $500, and a total of at least 12 courses plus exit examinations of some kind are required. The entire certification program provided by techwriters.com, mentioned earlier, can be purchased for less than $1,000.

Time, also, is a factor for those seeking to continue their education while maintaining their professional activities. University distance programs cannot be completed quickly because, following the traditional schedule, a limited number of courses are offered each semester. Commercial providers enjoy more latitude in shortening courses or allowing students to work at their own pace to complete individual classes or certifications because the content of their course offerings is product-based and can be focused on particular workplace needs. Because traditional programs are subject to graduate school, government, and accreditation guidelines, they are less flexible. In fact, building skills that are variable by situation, *phronesis*, requires more time and effort than working through application tutorials because generally there is no product-based "right" answer. As a profession, technical writers should seek ways to emphasize the enhanced attributes provided by university-based continuing education courses are more valuable in order to attract students to programs. To do this successfully, we must find ways to demonstrate to the business world that such attributes enhance the overall contributions of technical communicators to their endeavors.

EXPLORING DISTANCE PROGRAMS FROM TRADITIONAL PROVIDERS

To attract quality students, universities have always competed against one another by developing unique programs and emphasizing how their traditions can enhance attendees' lives and reputations. To maintain these time-honored goals of higher education, university providers of technical communication programs recognize the need to compete with private providers in the distance-learning arena, and are approaching the task by researching effective means of delivery. Thus, many have adopted a wait-and-see attitude about distance delivery methods and approach changes with caution while the research continues. Although this is a foundational factor, there is another important influence on the apparent slow pace of distance program development.

The academy, like industry, suffers from a lack of qualified instructors to develop and deliver programs that meet the growing student demand in the field of technical communication. A rigorous commitment to quality in university-based master's degree programs may be one reason that only five degree-granting programs are currently offered to distance students: Mercer University, New Jersey Institute of Technology, Rensselaer Polytechnic University, Texas Tech University, and Utah State University. The reputation and rigor of a university-based graduate degree in technical communication should provide students a professional persona in that peers, as well as employers, perceive as a valuable asset. Maintaining the rigor and content of campus-based university programs within distance education venue is one way to encourage this perception.

Although these programs are unique, each emphasizes the values of competence, professionalism, and personal responsibility. A close examination of these program goals and mission statements, posted at the university Web sites, reveals a rubric for defining overall values and expectations associated with earning a university graduate degree in technical communication. This rubric will be applied in the following section of this analysis to the newly emerging for-profit or nontraditional distance-only degree providers with an eye toward analyzing how corporate industry values phronesis as part of a technical communicators skill set. Common features of traditional university-based programs are as follows:[1]

- Provide educational opportunities for people in the workplace with multidisciplinary backgrounds.
- Deliver course materials to classes through both synchronous discussion and asynchronous methods.
- Present instruction about current electronic technologies.
- Emphasize analysis, theory, and ethics as integral parts of an overall education.
- Parallel onsite programs in content and expectation.
- Prepare students for leadership roles.

Each program sets admission standards that require acceptance by the onsite graduate school that include having earned a bachelor's degree and demonstrated ability for success in graduate work based on a writing sample and some form of standard placement testing: GRE, HCI, GMAT.

---

[1]For goals and missions statements of these four university-based graduate-level distance programs see:
- Mercer University Distance Education Home Page. http://www.mercer.edu/mstco/Philosophy/phil3.htm
- Rensselaer Polytechnic University. http://www.rsvp.rpi.edu/academics/degrees/mstechcomm.shtml
- Texas Tech University http://www.english.ttu.edu/tc/
- Utah State http://english.usu.edu/dept/instruction/programs/grad/#Technical Writing.

Completion of these programs requires from 30 to 36 hours of credit (based on the kinds of exit activities students must complete) that are divided between practical (design and tools courses) and theoretical (foundational, rhetorical, ethical). One university, Mercer, requires work experience in the field.

The resulting rubric has four areas of emphasis for acceptance to a program and completion of a degree that mirror the abilities that are outlined by North and Worth:

1. Preparedness—demonstration that the entrant can meet the expectations of graduate level coursework and research requirements.
2. Ability—students are expected to demonstrate the ability to express ideas and apply knowledge in both conversational and formal writing situations.
3. Mastery—students are expected to learn genres and tools that enhance their ability to perform in the workplace.
4. Tradition—students develop relationships with other students and onsite faculty members while completing course work that reflects the value of personal and civic responsibility.

This resulting rubric reflects the ideas of E.M. Noam, who proposes that "technology cannot facilitate effective teaching and learning, but that the cornerstones of good teaching must always involve 'mentoring, internalization, identification, role modeling, guidance socialization, interaction, and group activity'" (cited in Mehlenbacher et al. 168). In this statement, Noam points the way for Ronald Phipps and Jamie Merisotis, researchers for the Institute for Higher Learning Policy, who conclude their "What's the Difference?" report with the idea that technology cannot replace the human factor in education (38). These researchers reject the idea that distance-based education can recreate the traditional classroom experience because of the reduced interaction between participants. Even though this study was produced in 2000, it fails to recognize interactive Internet capabilities that allow for synchronous classroom participation, such as Net Meeting, Yahoo Classrooms, and educational MOO spaces. Furthermore, the goals of university-based providers refute the idea that distance format courses provide solitary learning experiences, and the interactive structures that these programs rely on provide the cornerstones that Noam emphasizes.

Driscoll and Reid also reinforce Noam by providing a definition for an interactive web based program that they label "Web/Virtual Synchronous" that is the *phronesis*-centered model for existing university graduate programs:

These programs bring the instructor and students together online at the
same time of day or night to participate in live discussions, debates,
brainstorming, role playing, software demonstrations, and panel discussions. A variety of synchronous tools such as Internet relay chat
(IRC), application sharing, whiteboards, and audio conferencing and
video conferencing on the Web are used to engage learners. (76)

Furthermore, such programs bring students together using these same
assignment schedule and tools to work and study for common coursework.
Thus, this extended sense of community fosters the development of social
interaction, networking opportunities, and ethical practices that are seldom
achieved without interaction on multiple levels.

EXPLORING DISTANCE PROGRAMS
FROM NONTRADITIONAL PROVIDERS

In a way, the resistance to traditional programs is understandable because
of the nature of the corporate structure. Mary Kwak points out that corporate information officers are often unsuccessful until they learn to adapt
their behaviors to the intangibles of a company culture (2). Kwak's observations provide reasons why de-emphasizing skills and behaviors that are
not tools or genre-focused occurs. Because technical communication is an
emerging profession, it is most easily defined in terms of the end product.
Her contention allows us to ask whether, as professional technical communicators, we are allowing our culture (i.e., our public persona) to be
restricted by a tangible end product rather than demand that intangible
skills, such as application of ethical and rhetorical principles, become part
of the professional expectation.

The plethora of new distance-learning providers on the Internet can be
easily revealed by a simple search of the using key terms such as technical
writer, communicator, distance learning, and university consortium. For
my purposes, I explore the goal and mission statements of two large consortiums of existing programs, Western Governors University (WGU) and
eArmyU (eAU), to find differences and similarities with traditional uni-
versity-distance programs. Consortiums are a new structure for distance
delivery developed by corporate sector management companies that contract with existing colleges and universities to provide developed distance
degree programs. Like existing traditional providers, they struggle to find
course providers and faculty mentors for their technical communication
programs. I chose these two consortiums because both have the following
characteristics:[2]

- Enroll student populations from across state boundaries.
- Are successfully negotiating the accreditation process and are able to offer Associate, Bachelor's, Master's, and Doctoral Degrees.
- Have a strong tie to government agencies.
- Do not develop any independent course offerings.
- Are administered by for-profit information management corporations.

This consortium structure is not organizationally unique. At least 13 similar consortia appeal to smaller populations (Consortia). Gary Berg, of Chapman University, describes these information management systems as large brokerages for technologically delivered coursework (4). However, it is unique that they appear to de-emphasize the relationships that would reinforce the tangible and intangible elements of a graduate education that are demonstrated by the emphasis rubric of goals and expectations that emerged from evaluation traditionally based distance degree programs: preparedness, ability, mastery, and tradition. Exploring ways that these non-traditional providers approach the university-based goals reveals that they center their program development on *praxis*, *techne*, and expedience.

Traditional Provider Emphasis 1

- Preparedness: Demonstration that the entering student has ability in the field and can meet the expectations of graduate-level research requirements.

Both WGU and eAU emphasize credit toward degree completion for life experience. Although eAU ties this credit closely to military experience, training, and standardized assessment, WGU is more eclectic. In fact, it appears to create its own standards:

> The benefit of this competency-based system is that it makes it possible for you—if you are already knowledgeable about a particular subject— to make progress toward completing a WGU degree even if you lack college experience. WGU recognizes that you may have gained skills and knowledge on the job, through years of life experience, or by tak-

---

[2]For goals and mission statements of the consortium providers see:
- eArmyU http://www.pwcglobal.com/servlet/printFormat?url=http://ww w.pwcglobal.com/extweb/industry.nsf/docid/71022C160747CC1D85256A 370052CBC1
- Western Governors' University http://www.wgu.edu/wgu/about/vision_ history.html

ing a course on a particular subject. This competency-based system does not use credits in awarding degrees. Instead, students demonstrate their knowledge or skills through assessments. For that reason, you will not be able to transfer credits to WGU—at least not in the usual sense. Rather, you may earn a WGU degree or certificate by demonstrating—through WGU assessments—what you learned while you were earning those credits at another institution. ("Understanding")

This statement raises critical questions about the value of traditional university training. Can competency in be measured in areas that do not rely on skills and genres? It would seem that intangible elements, such as community responsibility and ethical behaviors, would be very difficult to measure. However, traditionally these elements are reflected in a potential employee's resume, job history, and letters of recommendation from employers, instructors, and colleagues.

Furthermore, the idea of credited courses is challenged by the WGU policy of not accepting credit from other colleges and universities, and instead establishing their own guidelines for competencies in all areas. This policy statement also raises the question of who the consortium chooses to set the standards and create the competency assessments. This practice concerns Gary Berg who sees it as an administrative nightmare (5). Technical communication professionals need to consider whether or not such standardization fosters analytical and creative thought processes. Graduate degrees are often looked on more favorably if they are earned at an institution other than the one where a student earned a bachelor's degree. The reasoning behind this preference is that the student has taken advantage of the opportunity to expand his or her viewpoint by exploring the ideas of more than one university's department emphasis or strength. By not valuing this idea of expanded viewpoint, WGU seems to be stating that there is only one right answer—the one that their provider values and defines. Finally, the WGU Web site expresses a clear warning that other institutions may not accept the "assessment-based" work completed with this consortium ("Transfer"). This disclaimer is a further indication that the focus of the program is not necessarily to strengthen or enhance the profession of technical communicator, which would benefit all, but to merely provide some kind of entry level key for helping the individual student find a job.

Traditional Provider Emphasis 2

- Ability: Students are expected to demonstrate the ability to express ideas and apply knowledge in both conversational and formal writing situations.

There seems to be no clear statement about these qualities in either WGU's or eAU's public web presentations. In June 2001, The eAU program offered a master's degree program in technical communication. It has since disappeared because they are still looking for a provider willing to meet the requirements of their contract with the U.S. Army. The army requires that soldiers be able to access the core of course information on a flexible 24-hour basis, which eliminates any kind of scheduled class meetings. At the same time, PricewaterhouseCoopers (i.e., eAU) is dependent on the course provider's accreditation to affirm degrees earned through the program, so they must avoid .com providers with less than stellar credentials. Here, it seems, our professional standards are upheld not by the consortium provider, but by the expectations and traditions of college and university providers.

WGU's technical communication program is also on hold because of a lack of providers. Their reasoning, however, does not seem to be based on philosophical issues. They offer coursework in technical writing at the graduate level but do not have a fully developed degree program. In Spring 2002, one course was offered: Professional Writing and Applied Research. The provider for this class is the U.S. Sports Academy, and the platform is audiotape, telephone conferencing, e-mail, and the postal service ("Professional"). Thus, it barely qualifies as a web-based course, but it does meet the criteria of expressing ideas and applying knowledge in both conversational and formal writing situations because an extended research paper is the product centered goal of the course. What is lacking here is any collaboration with peers or contact with the professional community beyond communication between the student and the teacher of record.

The lack of technical communication distance graduate coursework from these large for-profit consortiums could represent a future danger. Both eAU's inability to find a provider willing to compromise its standards, and WGU's single course offering bring up the question of quality. As for-profit distance providers become more prevalent, is it possible that small accredited colleges and universities will develop less than adequate programs to meet the demand? In other words, if the for-profit distance education providers become the standard for graduate education in the field of technical communication, will the existing standards set by university programs become compromised? All universities struggle with funding for their onsite as well as their distance programs. Therefore, the profitability, rather than particular expertise in the field, of becoming a provider for a consortium could become a factor in curriculum development.

Traditional Provider Emphasis 3

- Mastery: Students are expected to learn genres and tools that enhance their ability to perform in the workplace.

Both consortiums considered here place heavy emphasis on workplace skills. Because they do not currently provide technical communication programs, particulars are impossible to explore. However, the purpose of this analysis is to consider whether or not there is more to the discipline than workplace skills, and there is no indication in the goals or mission statements that such an emphasis would exist.

In fact, WGU's Web site index page presents the following testimonial from Novell Industries vice president of education, Debbie Maucieri:

> There is a recognized 'War for Talent' in the IT industry today. It requires all companies, including Novell, to focus on attracting and retaining highly skilled and talented individuals. Continuous learning and the ability to upgrade and enhance skills 'real time' is a critical issue to employee retention. Novell has joined forces with Western Governors University to provide a real-time continuous learning platform for our employees. Together we will offer Novell employees the ability to learn anytime, anywhere. That is the mission of WGU, to provide a blended learning experience that is skill/proficiency based, and Novell's employees love the experience. ("Western")

The heavy emphasis on skill and proficiency from a large employer of technical communicators speaks for itself. Here again, the question is raised about valuing *praxis* over *techne* in the workplace. WGC's prominent placement of this testimonial underscores the idea that technical communicators need to consider how their intangible skills are valued in the workplace.

At eArmyU, the goal is to have a well-trained and effective military force, and the long term benefits to the individual students are not clearly emphasized. Because they have not yet found a provider for the technical communication program willing to operate within the constraints of their scheduling, there is no graduate program in place at this time. However, because *praxis* is the focus of this emphasis, it is reasonable to assume that any technical communication program developed would satisfy this emphasis.

Traditional Provider Emphasis 4

- Tradition: Students develop relationships with other students and onsite faculty members while completing course work that reflects the value of personal and civic responsibility.

As discussed, WGU places huge emphasis on the needs of the individual and the rejection of traditional university requirements. As a consortium, they administer and provide support services. They do not develop courses themselves, but partner with existing universities and corporations:

> WGU gives its affiliate education providers a world-wide stage for their distance-delivered .courses. We also support those courses with our unparalleled Online Bookstore, Central Library and student support services [working with] institutions such as Washington State University, Northern Arizona University, and ActiveEducation. ("About")

Therefore, the structure of individual courses is dependent on choices made by the provider. In fact, the rhetorical emphasis on provider is clear in this statement about organization. At a time when the U.S. Department of Education calls for learner-centered distance programs by making grants available for institutions developing programs and low interest rate loans for students (e-Learning), WGU aims its persuasive message to providers and represents student services as supportive of course design rather than students' needs.

PricewaterhouseCoopers (PwC), who designed and administers eArmyU, is built on a different structure, discussed earlier, because of contractual agreements with the Army that require 24-hour access. To support their students, PwC provides mentors, who are educators in the field, for each enrollee, but not the designers of the course:

> What makes eArmyU.com unique is its ability to bring together programs from 20 universities across the country into one seamless integrated learning experience for the student. Never before has such robust functionality been combined with a full suite of student services in one cohesive environment. Ultimately, the portal provides an experience that will encourage students to enroll efficiently, to learn effectively, and to work successfully toward their degree. ("eArmyU")

In practice, the mentor functions as a tutor and advisor, managing the student's entire academic career. Thus, personal contact does allow the student to form some personal relationship with the provider, but not with other students. David Norton, in "How Changes in Discursive Patterns Affect the Value of Technical Communication in Cross-functional Team Settings," proposes that work teams produce "goods, services, or bodies of knowledge that are 'more valuable' than those that could be produced if they worked alone" (77). From this viewpoint, distance education providers, such as the eAU consortium that allow students to always work alone, could actually perform students a disservice by underpreparing them for actual workplace situations.

EMERGENT EMPHASIS

Accreditation is an emphasis that was not raised when developing the rubric from traditional university providers because they fall under the umbrella of established university graduate schools. For consortiums, however, it is a pressing problem. WGU and eAU approach this requirement in different ways. PwC relies on the accreditation of the university, which provides the courses to extend accreditation. They can do this because they use a traditional crediting system and conventional criteria for admittance in to the programs. On the other hand, WGU has a unique system of crediting life, work, and academic experiences. In November 2000, WGU was granted Candidate for Accreditation status by The Interregional Accrediting Committee (IRAC) ("Accreditation"). Their online literature states that "Candidate for Accreditation status is critical for a degree-granting University in that its students [become] eligible for tuition reimbursement from corporations, the military, and government entities" ("Accreditation"). On June 6, 2001, WGU celebrated accreditation by the Distance Education and Training Council (DETC). An examination of the list of schools that the DETC extends accreditation to reveals that the majority of their members are high schools and religiously based institutions. On February 25, 2003, WGU announced that it had been granted accreditation from IRAC at the associate, baccalaureate, and master's degree levels, a rigorous process that WGU had pursued for five years. Accreditation raises many questions that are beyond the scope of this paper, but when considering the balance of *praxis* and *techne*, lack of accreditation may tip the scale toward an emphasis on the latter.

CONTINUING THE DIALOGUE

Throughout this analysis, the questions about balancing *praxis* and *techne* are raised as a legitimate discourse issues for technical communicators to address with stakeholders in the profession. Because the issues affect several groups, each with its own needs and goals, it can be defined as a public sphere. In *Vernacular Voices*, Gerald Hauser defines public sphere in a way that such eclectic stakeholder groups are included:

> A public sphere may be defined as a discursive space in which individuals and groups associate to discuss matters of mutual interest and, where possible, to reach a common judgment about them. It is the locus of emergence for rhetorically salient meanings. (61)

It seems clear that issues about the breadth and depth of a curriculum in an emerging professional field, such as technical communication, need to be resolved through just such public discourse. Recognizing the need for discourse, however, is only the first step.

Jeffrey Grabill's article, "Shaping Local HIV/AIDS Serves Policy through Activist Research: The Problem of Client Involvement," addresses the next step, which is bringing members of the sphere to the discussion table. He looks at a reluctant, disinterested, and underprepared community that is encouraged to participate in forming public policy. Perhaps the same set of threatening characteristics are confounding issues for corporate employers and successful technical communicators who have come to this profession through the workplace rather than through formal technical communication training. An integral part of the conversation should address the idea that the public and private sector businesses do not understand the issue. Currently, many successful technical communicators may feel ill-prepared to address educational issues beyond production tools because they came to their positions without formal university training. Technical communication, after all, is an emergent field that grew along with the development of electronic communication. One indicator that this may be true is that there seems to be little scholarship in professional journals, such as *Technical Communication* and *IEEE Transactions on Professional Communication* that discusses corporate expectations for university-prepared employees. This lack is not an indicator that the issue is of no interest, but that traditional providers are not perceived as part of the solution. Grabill believes that no "rhetorically salient meanings" can emerge unless representative members of all facets of a public sphere contribute to the conversation (34). Is it possible that employers do not see the questions raised by academia to be an issue? If so, then concerted effort to become participants in the conversation must be initiated from academia through professional organizations such as the STC as well as with individual corporate employers.

To begin this conversation, traditional providers must bring ideas to the table that complement and interest the corporate world beyond what is currently provided. Following the guidelines Brandenburger and Nalebuff set for co-opetition, university programs must look for symbiotic, or complementary, relationships that can strengthen what they have to offer employers as well as graduate students. Efforts must go beyond merely standardizing language and terminology, by looking at the purposes behind the communication focus. Dicks recognizes that there is an entirely different focus to the language set between the two discourse communities. The business and industry language set stresses speed and efficiency reflecting the business world's desire to get a job done quickly and confounds academia's slow moving decision structures that are based on committee deci-

sions and long-term budgeting (Table 7.2). Neither of these approaches are
going to change, but it is the value added elements of a traditional education that will allow developing professionals to recognize the difference and
optimize the approaches of both.

Corporate providers are not going to fade into the woodwork because
traditional providers enter the conversation, so academia must learn to
emphasize their existing strengths by capitalizing on intrinsic elements, as
well. Already, companies, such as SmartForce, provide specific content,
administrative services, and infrastructure for corporations that are tailored
to content and goals of employee training programs (Wilson), so merely
providing flexible curriculum will not suffice. For a distance-learning
provider, symbiotic relationships will be harder to define because they are
not based on the traditional recruiting tools of local civic and social attributes (see Brandenburger and Nalebuff 27), but instead on uniqueness, reputation, information dissemination practices, and cost.

In *Competetive Strategies*, Michael Porter points out that one generic
strategy for success is to emphasize the unique qualities of a product (37).
Existing graduate distance-learning programs provide this in their dedica-
tion to synchronous learning practices. North and Worth's study of
employers expectations for entry level skills from 1993 to 1998 reveals that
although the demand for technological skills remains steady and high, the
demand for interpersonal and critical thinking skills has steadily risen
(149). One possible symbiotic element, then, is to demonstrate that continued traditional education can strengthen this important personal asset by
capitalizing on providing personal access to relevant scholars who may not
be willing to partner with nontraditional providers. Of course, these
courses would be more difficult to orchestrate and expensive to develop,

TABLE 7.2.   **Business and Academia Discourse Differences**

BUSINESS AND INDUSTRY	ACADEMIA
Active	Passive
Concrete	Abstract
Inductive	Deductive
Instrumental	Rhetorical
Product, Result	Process
Presentational	Reflective
Direct	Indirect

Source: Dicks, R. Stanley. "Cultural Impediments to Understanding: Are
They Surmountable?" *Reshaping Technical Communication*. Barbara Mirel
and Rachel Spilka, Eds. Mahwah: Erlbaum (2002): 16.

but the result in terms of skills that transfer is dramatic. For instance, in one *Ethics in Technical Communication* course offered in the Texas Tech program and taught by Dr. Sam Dragga, the course was assigned Dombrowski's text, *Ethics in Technical Communication.* When the class met in a synchronous MOO session to discuss the text, Dombrowski joined them as a participant in the 2-hour discussion. This added value was possible because of the professional relationships between Dragga and Dombrowski and is an example of academia building on its strengths to add value to its students' experience. It would be possible, in survey courses that explore two or three theories on *praxis* or *techne* issues, to develop this kind of discussion with existing scholars, complete with synchronous discussion, so as to offer the kind of focus that fosters the skills associated with *phronesis*. Such courses might be more useful to an entry-level manager than a focused asynchronous course or short workshop based on only one currently popular method. By strengthening and expanding traditional structures to include individual student access to experts in emerging topics in the field of technical communication, an existing strength can be made into an enticing element for support while fostering those long-term skills that transfer.

A second symbiotic element might be to develop a strong tie with technology researchers and providers in order to monitor innovation. Barbara Mirel of Lucent Technologies points out that there is a "widespread impression that most academics are at least three years behind the times in regard to effects of tools and technology on information development" (cited in Spilka 207). Private corporations have long partnered with academia for research in the sciences. Perhaps, as Spilka suggests, it is time for technical communication programs to form a partnership with technology developers by contracting to assist in the areas of development and testing (217). If, indeed, the overall perception of academic training in *praxis* is weak, it might be that the issues of *techne* are moot. Therefore, it is incumbent to join in the conversation of what corporate employers expect entry level employees to bring to the workplace in order to form any kind of relationship at all. In *Active-Practice: Creating Productive Tension Between Academia and Industry*, Bernhardt complicates Spilka's proposal by pointing out that the purpose of research in academia and in the workplace conflict, forming yet one more dichotomy. Academia trades in research. Its purpose is to share knowledge developed through research. Business, on the other hand, survives by keeping their research to themselves, which limit "how specific external reporting may be [causing] industry [to take] many issues off the table for discussion" (85). Research is not an issue with for-profit providers, so this becomes a complicating issue when academia attempts to develop joint research projects. These conflicts make it difficult to design projects that will meet the needs of all stakeholders. One area of cooperative research that academia can enter is user testing. Whereas the workplace concentrates on results, academia concentrates on methodology, compromising the needs of neither. With clear guidelines, then, the needs of all can be met.

Certainly, these are not the only issues that need to be explored; they are merely examples of ways to establish a stronger position in the growing marketplace. One appeals to students, with their long-term needs, and the other appeals to the workplace with their more immediate needs.

CONCLUSIONS

In "Resistance to Change: a New View of an Old Problem," Peter De Jager proposes that "Two corporate cultures resist merging into a single cohesive whole. Some people would rather continue to struggle with old, outdated tools than adopt some new technology, even if they know it would make life easier" (24). I wonder if this is not true of the relationship between corporate employers and distance-based technical communication academic programs, also. The exigency that De Jager's observation points out can certainly compel us to open the door and engage in a conversation about perceptions and expectations. However, there is a danger accepting new methods and technologies, also. Jimmie Killingsworth cautions us to be wary of extrapolations and predictions based on past performances, because they are often too narrowly focused (166). By looking for new relationships that strengthen overall programs, traditional-based distance providers widen rather than restrict their viewpoints while opening themselves to meet the needs of the marketplace more completely.

This examination merely invites a longer conversation about distance-based graduate technical communication programs. The philosophical focus and practice of distance education providers are particularly relevant to the field of technical communication because of the nature of working with rapidly evolving technology. Post-baccalaureate continuing education for professionals is essential, and distance learning programs offer a convenient platform to satisfy this need. Yet, for those just entering the field, some of the more traditional elements of education, such as foundational rhetoric and ethics, seem essential. In order to strengthen the perception that technical communicators are more than document producers, conversations between traditional course providers and potential employers must take place. Thus balancing the focus of the profession between the strength of well developed *techne* and *praxis*, and the value-added skills that transfer, *phronesis*, providing that "capacity [for] observing what is good for themselves and for mankind " (Aristotle 1140b).

REFERENCES

Aristotle. *Nicomacean Ethics*. Trans. J. E. C. Welldon. Amherst: Prometheus Books, 1987.

Bereiter, Carl and Marlene Scardamalia. *Surpassing Ourselves: An Inquiry into the Nature and Implications of Expertise*. Chicago: Open Court, 1993.

Bernhardt, Stephen. "Active Practice: Creating Productive Tension Between Academia and Industry." In *Reshaping Technical Communication*. Eds. Barbara Mirel and Rachel Spilka. Mahwah, NJ: Erlbaum 2002, 81–90.

Berg, Gary A. "Public Policy and Distance Learning in Higher Education: California State and Western Governors Association Initiatives." *Education Policy Analysis Archives* 6.11 (June 1998) http://olam.ed.asu.edu/epaa/v6n11.html (June 2001).

Brandenburger, Adam M. and Barry J. Nalebuff. *Co-opetition*. New York: Currency, 1996.

Collins, Jim. *Good to Great: Why Some Companies Make the Leap and Others Don't*. New York: HarperBusiness, 2001.

Consortia. (2001) http://dir.yahoo.com/Education/Distance_Learning/Colleges _and_Universities/Consortia (August 2001).

De Jager, Peter. "Resistance to Change: A New View of an Old Problem." *The Futurist* 35.3 (May/June 2001): 24–7.

Dicks, R. Stanley. "Cultural Impediments to Understanding: Are They Surmountable?" In *Reshaping Technical Communication*. Eds. Barbara Mirel and Rachel Spilka. Mahwah, NJ: Erlbaum 2002, 13–26.

Dreyfus, Hubert and Stuart Dreyfus. *Mind over Machine: The Power of Human Intuition and Expertise in the Era of the Computer*. New York: The Free Press, 1988.

Driscoll, Margaret and John E. Reid, Jr. "Web-Based Training: An Overview of Training Tools for the Technical Writing Industry." *Technical Communication Quarterly* 8.1 (Winter 1999): 73–86.

Flyvbjerg, Bent. *Making Social Science Matter*. Cambridge: Cambridge UP, 2001.

Grabill, Jeffery. "Shaping Local HIV/AIDS Serves Policy through Activist Research: The Problem of Client Involvement." *Technical Communication Quarterly* 9.1 (Spring 2000): 20–50. http://www.attw.org/TCQarticles/9.1/9-1Grabill.pdf

Hauser, Gerald A. *Vernacular Voices*. Columbia: University of South Carolina Press, 1999.

Isaacs, William. *Dialogue and the Art of Thinking Together*. New York: Currency, 1999.

Johnson-Eilola, Johndan, and Stuart A. Selber. "Policing Ourselves: Defining the Boundaries of Appropriate Discussion in Online Forums." *Computers and Composition* 13 (1996): 269–91.

Killingsworth, M. Jimmie. "Technical Communication in the 21st Century: Where Are We Going?" *Technical Communication Quarterly* 8.2 (Spring 1999): 165–74.

Kwak, Mary. "Technical Skills, People Skills: It's Not Either/Or." *Sloan Management Review* 42.3 (Spring 2001): 16.

Mercer University Distance Education Home Page. http://www.mercer.edu/mstco/
    Philosophy/phil3.htm (September 2001).
Mehlenbacher, Brad, Carolyn R. Miller, David Covington, and Jamie S. Larsen.
    "Active and Interactive Learning Online: A Comparison of Web-Based and
    Conventional Writing Classes." *IEEE Transactions on Professional
    Communications* 43.2 (June 2000): 166–81.
North, Alexa Bryans and William E. Worth. "Trends in Entry-Level Technology,
    Interpersonal, and Basic Communication Job Skills, 1992–1998." *Journal of
    Technical Writing and Communication* 30.2 (2000): 143–54.
Norton, David. "How Changes in Discursive Patterns Affect the Value of
    Technical Communication in Cross-functional Team Settings." *IEEE
    Transactions on Professional Communication* (February/March 2000): 77–89.
Phipps, Ronald, and Jamie Merisotis. "What's the Difference? A Review of
    Contemporary Research on the Effectiveness of Distance Learning in Higher
    Education." *Institute for Higher Learning Policy* (1999).
Porter, Michael E. *Competitive Strategy.* New York: Free Press, 1998.
PricewaterhouseCoopers. "Army University Access Online Participating Colleges
    and Universities." (2001) http://www.pwcglobal.com/servlet/printFormat?url
    =http://www.pwcglobal.com/extweb/industry.nsf/docid/C10F63333415E1998
    5256A370069825E. (July 2001)
Ray, Eric J. "Becoming a Techie Writer." (2002) http://www.raycomm.com/tech-
    whirl/becomingatechie.htm. (January 2002).
Rensselaer Polytechnic University. http://www.rsvp.rpi.edu/academics/degrees/
    mstechcomm.shtml (July 2001).
Schriver, Karen A. *Dynamics in Document Design: Creating Text for Readers.* New
    York: Wiley, 1996.
Selting, Bonita. "Conversations with Technical Writing Teachers: Defining a
    Problem." *Technical Communication Quarterly* 11: 3 (Summer 2002): 251–56.
"SmartForce: Learning Solutions for the Human Enterprise." (2002)
    http://www.smartforce.com/corp/marketing/ (July 2002).
Spilka, Rachel. "The Issue of Quality in Professional Decomentation: How Can
    Academia Make a Difference?" *Technical Communication Quarterly* 9.2 (Spring
    2000): 207–20.
tech-writer certification.com http://www.techwriter-certification.com/courses.htm
Texas Tech University. Technical Communications Master of Arts Program.
    http://www.english.ttu.edu/tc/ (November 2001).
US Department of Education. "Ten New Distance Ed Projects Expand Higher Ed
    Access." (6/25/01) http://www.ed.gov/PressReseases/06-2001/06252001.html.
    (07/14/01).
US Department of Education Office of Educational Technologies. "e-Learning:
    Putting a World-Class Education at the Fingertips of All Children–A National
    Education Policy." (January 2001) http://www.ed.gov/Technology/elearning
    /index.html. (May 2001).
Utah State Technical Writing Graduate Program Purpose and Goal Statement. (July
    1999) http://english.usu.edu/dept/instruction/programs/grad/#Technical
    Writing. (July 2001).

Von Krogh, Georg, Kazuo Ichijo and Ikujiro Nonaka. *Enabling Knowledge Creation*. Oxford: Oxford UP, 2000.

Wenger, Etienne, Richard McDermott, and William M. Snyder. *Cultivating Communities of Practice*. Boston: Harvard Business School Press, 2002.

Western Governors University. "Accrediting." http://www.wgu.edu/wgu/academics/accreditation.html (August 2001).

———. "About WGU." http://www.wgu.edu/wgu/about/index.html (August 2001).

———. "Professional Writing & Applied Research." http://www.wgu.edu/wgu/smartcatalog/class_description.asp?classkey=13791&pipe=&AAP=&aapenroll=&10106=&sitecode106=&backurl (August 2001).

———. "Understanding Competencies." http://www.wgu.edu/wgu/academics/understanding.html (July 2001).

———. "Transferring Credit." http://www.wgu.edu/wgu/union/transfer.html (August 2001).

Wick, Corey. "Knowledge Management and Leadership Opportunities for Technical Communicators." *Technical Communication* 47.4 (2000): 515–29.

Wilson, Lizette. "E-Learning Firms Put Heads Together." *San Francisco Business Times*. (09/24/01) http://sanfrancisco.bcentral.com/sanfrancisco/stories/2001/09/24/sotry6.html (October 2001).

New Process, New Product

Redistributing Labor in a First-Year Writing Program

Susan Lang
Texas Tech University

Do writing programs have irreconcilable labor issues? One might think so, given that the vast majority of instructors at mid to large size universities have limited, if any, teaching experience, and an equally limited desire to teach writing as they work toward degrees in other areas such as literature and creative writing. Add to this mix a very small administrative structure (sometimes as little as one faculty member working with one part-time secretary) and it seems only fitting to label such a situation as unworkable. Instruction in such programs becomes fragmented despite the best efforts of program administrators to ensure a comparable and quality experience for students because regardless of experience level, classroom instructors expect to exercise a significant deal of sovereignty over their various sections.

As Fred Kemp writes elsewhere in this volume, English departments have historically resisted any attempt to think systemically. Although courses within the department are bound together, however loosely, as components of a major or minor program of study, the conduct of individual sections is left largely to those faculty members who teach them. Perhaps a few faculty members might assemble to discuss a particular course, but rarely do such gatherings move beyond a local level. It is an unstated rule that faculty, especially once they are granted tenure, are the captains of their own courses.

Examining the larger consequences of such a structure on departments at large is beyond the scope of this chapter. My purpose here is first to consider how inadequate and, indeed, ill-suited, such ideas are when applied to the first-year writing programs that are usually housed within English departments. Then, I describe the initial planning and implementation for a bold initiative undertaken by the Texas Tech University (TTU) First-Year Writing Program that is designed to deal with many of the problems faced by writing programs largely taught by graduate instructors and adjuncts. This initiative, currently in the second phase of preliminary testing, seeks to maximize both the human and technological resources of the Writing Program and to break away from the constraints that are imposed by the cohort teaching model. This initiative presents a dramatic shift in terms of writing instruction by accomplishing the following:

- Testing pedagogical assumptions, particularly in regard to the cohort teaching structure, regarding the teaching of writing.
- Offering program instructors a more systematic way of gaining professional teaching skills.
- Providing program administrators more effective means for ensuring the current and future success of composition students and instructors.
- Making available a comparable student experience in and between the two first-year writing courses, ENGL 1301 and ENGL 1302.

PROGRAMMATIC BACKGROUND

As with most first-year writing programs, the TTU writing program operates under a cohort teaching structure, with each instructor responsible for all of the duties (classroom contact hours and preparation, grading and evaluation of all student work, office hours, etc.) connected to one or more sections of either 1301 or 1302. Sections contain a maximum of 25 students; most Graduate Part-Time Instructors (GPTIs) are assigned either one or two sections, with contract lecturers staffing up to 5 sections per semester. Enrollment levels average 2,000 to 2,700 students each semester. In Spring 2001, the program had 18 sections of 1301 and 92 sections of 1302. In Fall 2001, 80 sections of 1301 and 36 sections of 1302 were offered. Nearly all of these sections are taught by GPTIs who spend an average of 2 years teaching composition before moving on to teach other courses. Because GPTIs also teach technical communication and literature in the department, the annual turnover of instructors in the first-year composition program averages between 25% and 30%.

Since the late 1980s, TTU composition program faculty, led by Fred Kemp, have been exploring ways to effectively use computers in writing pedagogy. For much of the 1980s, the common conclusion of writing instructors and many program administrators was that one key to the integration of computers into writing courses was for these courses to take place in a computer classroom. However, as the 1990s dawned, it became clear that especially in large writing programs, many institutions had reached a computer classroom "ceiling"; that is, programs with many sections of writing courses and numbers of students reaching into the thousands realized that they needed more computer classrooms than it was possible to build or to convert from existing physical facilities in order to accommodate all sections of their courses. This simple fact made it clear that if students were to be offered a comparable experience in all sections of writing classes, a new paradigm for teaching writing with technology would need to be developed, one that combined the innovative use of technology with a pedagogy capable of being implemented both in and out of computer classrooms.

Since Spring 1998, the Texas Tech Online/Print Integrated Curriculum (TOPIC), a web-based application for managing and interacting with course material and student writing developed by Fred Kemp, has been used by an increasing number of instructors and students in Writing Program courses. Initially, TOPIC was conceived as a cross-platform utility for exchange of documents among students and instructors. Since 1999, both instructional and course management functions of the application have been added and upgraded. Most recently, the writing program has expanded TOPIC functions to include more programmatic management tools.

In terms of implementation, prior to Fall 2000, the use of TOPIC by first-year writing instructors was optional, although encouraged. As more administrative functions were added, such as attendance records and full, flexible grading capabilities, TOPIC was more frequently referenced by program administrators in resolving student complaints and grade disputes and was found to be an effective way of doing so without the need to call in the individual student and instructor, along with gradebooks, student work, and other documents. Consequently, beginning in Fall 2000, instructors were required to keep attendance records and grade records on TOPIC, although they could choose whether or not to have students submit written work or to provide written feedback to student work on TOPIC. As more instructors and students used the TOPIC program, it became increasingly clear to program directors that discrepancies in pedagogy and student experience existed. Thus, in Fall 2001, the Writing Program mandated that all 1301 and 1302 instructors also have students submit drafts of major writing assignments on TOPIC; instructors were also required to place their written feedback to student writing on TOPIC.

This incrementally expanded use of TOPIC has helped make explicit several things that Writing Program Administrators (WPAs) assumed but could not verify. For example, although the Writing Program has the ability via TOPIC to provide instructors with a medium in which to read and respond to student documents, as well provide comprehensive syllabi that include instructional rationales and classroom activities for each class and assignment, it is still unable to assure quality and consistency in two areas—instructor response to student feedback and delivery of classroom content in face-to-face meetings. This quality and consistency is essential to both the first-year composition students and to the GPTIs who teach them. In reviewing instructor feedback to students and observing classroom instruction, it has become evident that despite these mechanisms, the level of instruction is not equal, and in some cases, not up to acceptable standards. Part of the problem is that GPTIs are not attending the university for the purposes of gaining experience in teaching writing. They are, first and foremost, students of literature, creative writing, rhetoric and composition, and technical communication and rhetoric; to that end, they (and who can blame them) privilege their academic studies above their teaching, especially if they are studying in areas other than rhetoric and composition. Additionally, until recently, it has been impossible or nearly so for WPAs to effectively intervene in problematic teaching practices in a proactive way; usually WPAs are restricted to reacting to a situation near to or at the conclusion of a semester. When this happens, GPTIs are unable to gain important experience in terms of teaching proactively so as to avoid problematic teaching practices. As a result, students' learning experience is diminished and the reputation of the First-Year Composition program becomes scarred.

Like many writing programs at large institutions, the TTU first-year writing program has ongoing responsibilities to its students and its student-instructors. For undergraduate students, the TTU program faces the ongoing problem of how to deliver a comparable experience so that a student in Section X has a similar experience to the student in Section Z. Using TOPIC, a common text, and syllabi are initial, significant steps; but as noted previously, important variants can occur in classroom delivery and in responding to student writing. For GPTIs, the program has the responsibility to provide professional development in the teaching of writing. Depending on the circumstances, GPTIs can be exempted from taking the department's pedagogical preparation course, ENGL 5360 (History and Theories of College Composition). Although not a desirable situation, it pales in comparison to the fact that students who have successfully completed ENGL 5360 are frequently unwilling or unable to teach the recommended curriculum. This means that some instructors enter the program and continue to teach according to the methods developed at other institutions, methods not necessarily condoned by the TTU writing program or in line with the aims of the 1301 and 1302 classes. From a programmatic perspective, this variety in instructional theories and/or content means that the comparable experience of the undergraduate students is compromised, and that WPAs are often asked to justify instructional methods or assignments that they have not sanctioned, or even been made aware of, in some cases.

Furthermore, under the cohort teaching structure, instructors are expected to spend 10 hours a week per section on teaching-related activities to fulfill the conditions of their appointment. As the Table 8.1 illustrates, these requirements are easily met and often exceeded, given that instructors

TABLE 8.1.   Breakdown of Instructor Time Under Existing Cohort System

Tasks	Time (weekly)	Number of times required during semester	Time for semester
Class-meetings	2.5 hrs	15 weeks	37.5 hrs
Grading • Preliminary Drafts	5 min/draft *25 drafts = 125 min or 2 hr 5 min	8 prelim drafts (1.1, 1.2, 2.1, 2.2, 3.1, 3.2, 4.1, 4.2)	16 hr 40 min
Grading • Critiques	5 min/critique *25 students = 125 minutes or 2 hr 5 min	13 – 16 critiques	27 hr 5 min- 33 hr 20 min
Grading • Final Drafts	20 min/draft *25 students = 500 min or 8 hr 20 min	4 final drafts	33 hr 20 min
Grading • Final Exam	20 min/exam *25students = 500 min or 8 hr 20 min	1 exam	8 hr 20 min
Subtotal for class meeting and grading			**129 hr 10 min**
Class Prep	90 min	16 weeks	24 hr
Meeting with students	12 min	15 weeks	3 hr
Mentoring by program administrators/professional development	30 min	Varies by individual choice	~4 hr
Subtotal for other activities			**31 hr**
Total time involved			**160 hr**

are responsible for preparing for and meeting with students as well as responding to student work. A typical breakdown of instructor efforts for a single section of a composition course and based on a current enrollment of 25 students appears in Table 8.1.

Several items in Table 8.1 deserve further scrutiny. First, we should note here that the class prep time assumes that classroom instructors are using syllabi, schedules, and assignments prepared and/or recommended by the WPAs. The prep time for those who choose to prepare their own syllabi may vary. Additionally, the figures presented in Table 8.1 show that instructor-contracted time is maxed out at an enrollment of 25 students. Any increase in enrollment under the current plan requires opening more sections of courses and hiring more personnel, or asking instructors to work unpaid overtime in order to meet the needs of their students. The only alternative for the instructors is to decrease the amount of assigned work to their students that requires instructor evaluation.

Not reflected in the table of instructor effort are the following additional problems that arise under the cohort system. First, forecasted increases in enrollment will require that more instructors be hired, either by increasing appointments of GPTIs or by hiring lecturers. Increasing graduate enrollment does not ensure the program of quality teachers, and it is difficult to find and hire qualified lecturers, given TTU's location several hours from major metropolitan areas. Additionally, the current cohort structure means that sections must be added or dropped on a last minute basis; finding qualified instructors at the last-minute often means asking for existing personnel to take on an overload, or else the program takes a chance by placing an untested instructor in the classroom. Furthermore, if a classroom instructor is unable to perform his or her duties and must be removed, an individual must step into this classroom and take on all duties, placing a burden on the now-overloaded instructor. Finally, in the interest of recruiting and retaining graduate students, the English Department is investigating the possibility of reducing teaching loads of master's apprentices and GPTIs from a 2/2 load to a 2/1 load. This change will require re-evaluating the way in which courses are delivered or it will mean that the program will need to rely on additional untenured lecturers. Finally, TTU is moving toward abolishing the CLEP test for first-year writing, thereby introducing up to 500 more students each year into 1301/1302 courses.

All of these elements clearly point to one fact—the cohort teaching system in first-year writing courses is quickly becoming outmoded in terms of what it can offer instructors and students. For instructors, especially those entering the writing classroom, and in some cases, the American Higher Educational System, for the first time, mastering the diverse skills needed in order to manage a classroom and respond to student work can seem an overwhelming task. Equally daunting are the time management problems that arise, problems that are usually "solved" by either (a) assigning fewer writing projects, or (b) defaulting to a "read-and-discuss" pedagogy in which the focus of the classroom activities and writing assignments turns away from writing itself to the content of whatever is read and discussed by the students and instructor. The primary advantages of this latter option are that it enables instructors to engage in a classroom structure with which they are familiar, and it allows instructors to more quickly evaluate student work because evaluation can become primarily content rather than rhetorically based. One frequent result, then, for the student in such classes is that the student leaves the course with either the sense that writing is still a matter of giving the instructor positions that he or she agrees with, or that writing is still a mysterious operation that is beyond the reach of all but a select few. Additionally, students find that in comparing notes on their classes, some students have a far different experience because they like (or dislike) their instructor's personality more or less than their peers, or because they have fewer or different assignments, or because their instructor assigns grades according to a different rubric. In short, any notion of objectivity that students see in other courses or departments seems lost in the writing course. Such consequences reduce the writing class to nothing more than a requirement that students fulfill, often with excellent grades, but learn very little about writing that they then transfer to other situations or courses.

THE INITIAL PROPOSED SOLUTION: PLANNING STAGES

The proposed solution seeks to address many of the issues, both pedagogical and administrative, that arise from the cohort teaching structure. It assumes that the central activities in a writing course involve classroom meetings and evaluation of student documents. It also tests the assumption of whether these activities need to be performed by the same individual. The essential, defining characteristic of this solution lies in the phrase *redistribution*, whether that redistribution be of teaching responsibilities, class meeting time, reading and responding to student documents, or class size. No longer will a single instructor be responsible for a discrete number of students as well as the entire set of duties and responsibilities surrounding that group of students. Instead, the various tasks and responsibilities will be distributed among the entire pool of ENGL 1301/1302 instructors, thereby providing a more efficient and effective means of instruction. Whereas other schools are in the process of outsourcing evaluation of writing, and thereby finding ways to move writing instruction out of the duties of full-time faculty and into the hands of lecturers, TTU's initiative redistributes the tasks among the same labor pool in order to take advantage of the talents of individuals in that pool. Such distribution will also enable the writing program to incrementally train new instructors; new hires will first work as Document Instructors and gain proficiency in reading and responding to student documents before being asked to assume responsibility as Classroom Instructors, who will work with up to 140 students. However, movement from Document to Classroom Instructor should not be interpreted as a one-way progression. Graduate instructors who have no desire to teach in the classroom (i.e., some students enrolled in the M.A. in Technical Communication (MATC), who will be returning to industry on completion of the degree) or who are at various points of dissertation research and writing may choose to remain in or return to Document Instructor positions.

In its most basic form then, the program contains the following features, each of which is discussed in more detail in the following pages:

- Students meet once each week with a Classroom Instructor, who engages students in classroom activities that directly support the students' work on each writing project.
- As students submit documents to TOPIC, the documents are loaded into a distribution mechanism that is then accessed by all Document Instructors, who read, respond, and evaluate each document. Although the Classroom Instructors also engage in grading, they do not, under this system, necessarily respond to the work of the students in their sections.
- The student documents and Document Instructors' feedback assists in the further structuring of classroom activities in subsequent weeks' meetings.

Initial assessment of benefits of the proposed solution include the following:

- Comparable experience for students
- Incremental professional development for GPTIs

  ◊ Incoming GPTIs trained first in responding to student writing
  ◊ These GPTIs will observe and receive training in classroom delivery before being given responsibility for even a single section

- Greater ability for administrators to deliver/be accountable for a program responsible to needs of all users

  ◊ Decreased reliance on lecturers/GPTIs who resist the recommended curriculum

- Fiscal benefits which can result in increased leverage for the First-Year Composition program

Initial assessment of liabilities of the proposed solution include the following:

- Losing the "personal touch" of FYC; however, although no one has proven that such an atmosphere either exists programwide or contributes to the improvement of student writing, it remains a powerful myth
- Need to justify new method of teacher training
- Perceived gap in what is being taught in classroom/what is being evaluated because evaluation comes from different individuals

  ◊ Such gaps already exist in cohort system, in which instructors and students often enter a tacit agreement that enables students to receive grades without mastering course content and meeting objectives that the teacher prefers not to teach or does not understand well enough to teach

CLASS SIZE AND CLASS MEETINGS

The first redistribution, then, involves class size and meeting time. Unlike in the cohort system, in which adding even a single student can add up to 4 hours additional grading time, adding students to the classroom under the proposed solution does not unduly increase the burden on the Classroom Instructor. Thus, under the proposed system, the class size for both ENGL 1301 and 1302 would increase from 25 to 35 students per section. This change alone will yield a significant decrease in the number of sections offered for the current enrollment of both ENGL 1301/1302. As Fig. 8.1 indicates, this change would mean that 28 sections of ENGL 1301 and 12 sections of ENGL 1302 would no longer be necessary.

The second change in terms of class redistribution is that students meet with a Classroom Instructor once a week for a period of 80 minutes. Thus, in addition to reducing the total number of sections offered for both ENGL 1301/1302, we are also reducing the number of meetings required

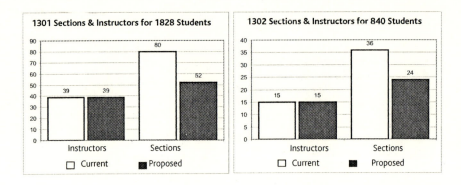

Figure 8.1. Enrollment figures for 1301/1302. (Enrollment figures for Fall 2001 are used as the basis for all calculations. Any minor discrepancies are due to rounding numbers.)

for each individual section. The end result is that fewer Classroom Instructors would be needed for face-to-face meetings with students. For example, if 13 of the 39 ENGL 1301 instructors became Classroom Instructors and each taught four sections of the course, all face-to-face meetings would be covered for the current enrollment. Thus, GPTIs working on a half-time appointment who are assigned to classroom instruction would devote approximately 5.5 hours per week to face-to-face meetings with students (80 minutes per meeting x 4) for the duration of the semester. The remainder of their time (14.5 hours) would be divided between classroom preparation (approximately 1 hour per week, given that Classroom Instructors would be working with the same course materials for each section as well as well-developed pre-existing syllabus) and grading/responding to student writing.

ASSESSMENT OF STUDENT WRITING

All personnel assigned to ENGL 1301/1302 will engage in the assessment of student writing, which will take place online. The amount of grading accomplished by each individual will vary according to his or her other assigned duties. Key to this solution is that the hours freed by reducing class meeting times can be reassigned to evaluation of student work; thus the program can provide all students with two evaluators for their documents. This development is discussed later in the chapter.

Those instructors not assigned to meet face to face with students would spend the majority of their time grading and responding to student writing. For example, ENGL 1301 students currently generate 29 separate documents during the course of a semester (8 preliminary drafts, 16 peer critiques, 4 final drafts, and 1 final exam). When multiplied by the number of students currently enrolled in ENGL 1301 (1,828), a total of 53,012 separate documents are generated each semester. A quick calculation reveals that using a pool of 26 instructor-responders, none of whom are in the classroom, would mean that each responds to approximately 2,038 documents.

Although this number may seem extreme, it should be noted that instructors who carry a half-time appointment (two sections of 25 students each, for a total of 50 students) must grade approximately 1,450 documents, plus meet face to face with students, prepare for class, and so on. A comparative breakdown of the time responsibilities of Cohort Teachers, Classroom and Document Instructors, along with systemwide hour comparisons is presented in Fig. 8.2.

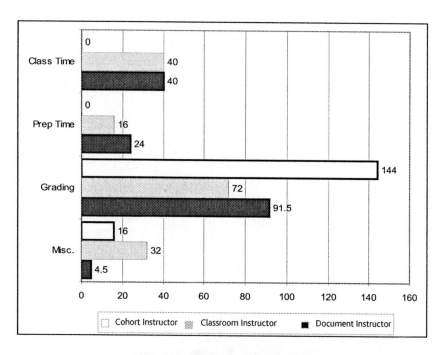

Figure 8.2. Hourly effort (semester) for GPTIs with one-quarter time appointments. (The category of "Misc." may involve such items as training, mentoring by program administrators, or office hours.)

SYSTEM COMPARISONS

The final section of this initial discussion provides a comparison of the contract hours involved in both the current and proposed system. Both assume a total of 18,560 contracted hours, which represents the number of appointments made to staff the 116 sections of the program in Fall 2001.

Figure 8.3 shows that under the proposed system, decreasing both the number of sections as well as the meeting time of each section allows classroom preparation time to decrease by nearly 90% under the proposed revision and class meeting time by 65%. These hours, which are now represented in the "Remaining Time" column, can be used in a number of ways—to decrease reliance on term lecturers or to reduce GPTI workloads, for example. However, simply reducing the workforce does not necessarily enable the Writing Program to increase the quality of instruction. Instead, the Writing Program chose to apply some of those hours to supplying all documents with a second evaluation by a document manager. Doing so

System Hour Comparison

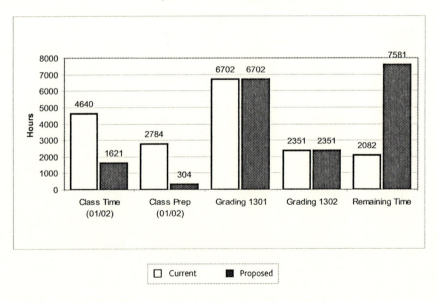

Figure 8.3.   System hour comparison.

would, in theory, bring a new level of objectivity to the evaluation of student writing as two individuals would, independently of each other, assess and assign a grade to a student document. It was planned, at this point, that the two grades would be averaged and the averaged grade given to the student.

However, at this point the question was raised as to whether or not adding an additional grader would deplete the hour surplus and thereby remove some of the potential fiscal benefits of the system. It was determined that the second grade would be added based on a holistic reading of the student document. The second reader would have access to the student document and to the comments made by the first reader, but would not have access to the grade itself. Thus, the second reader's task would be to scan the document and the comments and assign a grade, a task that should take no more than 5 minutes per document, given that most were 1,200 words or less. Based on the Fall 2001 enrollment, for the 1301 course, the second readings should take 1,341 hours, and the 1302 second readings should require 1,020 hours. This would still leave more than 5,000 surplus hours.

The planning then, would seem to indicate that the proposed solution was a feasible one; however, what would implementation, even on a small scale, look like? In the next section, I describe what became the first pilot study for the solution.

IMPLEMENTATION: THE FIRST PILOT STUDY

During the early days of the Fall 2001 semester, it became clear that one of the department's new GPTIs was unable to coordinate classroom activities or respond effectively to student writing. Preliminary discussions of the proposed solution had begun, and when it became clear that one of the program directors would need to intervene and take on a third 1301 class, hereafter referred to as "Section 19," the decision was made to try what was then termed "Group Grading." Three members of the composition faculty, along with two advanced doctoral students, agreed to respond to all Section 19 student drafts in order to test the feasibility of the Document Instructor role.

Primary concerns during this iteration of testing included the following:

- Ability of the Document Instructors to agree on the objectives of evaluation for each set of documents (first and second preliminary drafts, final drafts).
- Objectives set, the ability to construct grading criteria that would enable individuals to evaluate drafts in a consistent manner.

These concerns were resolved via a series of meetings between the five individuals involved. Lists of 5 to 15 criteria for each draft were developed and incorporated into the evaluation mechanism. To measure the evolution of consistency among the graders, two parameters were set; in grading preliminary drafts, the grades of the first two responders were averaged, unless the grades were more than five points (on a 1 – 100 scale) apart. Then the document was given to a third reader for evaluation. On final drafts, the grades with a spread of more than seven points were sent to a third reader for reconciliation. Out of the 197 documents evaluated, 29 (14.7%), required a third reading. Although these numbers were encouraging, they were the result of having five experienced readers, most of whom participated in the development of grading criteria, score, and comment on the drafts. A second pilot study that involved less experienced Document and Classroom Instructors as well as a larger number of students would provide key information concerning a number of factors, including the degree and scale of necessary training for all participants, communication between participants, and various human factors issues, as well as providing more statistical information regarding the efficiency of the redistribution of labor.

THE SECOND PILOT STUDY

The second study took place during the Spring 2002 semester and involved 3 Classroom Instructors, 6 Document Instructors, and approximately 160 students. Early discussions reinforced intrinsic difficulties of engineering a paradigm shift in the labor pool—the traditional and assumed authority of the cohort classroom instructor was impossible to maintain, and both Classroom and Document Instructors felt this stress of restructuring. Much of the work of the first few weeks was focused on improving communication between the participants in order to alleviate this tension. A few weeks into the semester, these pressures receded into the background; they did not disappear entirely, but certainly became less dominant and allowed more group members to focus on other issues of implementation.

Early statistics indicate an impressive level of efficiency that would be difficult to achieve in a cohort teaching situation. With approximately 1,150 documents graded, the percentage of third readings had actually dropped from 14.7% in the initial pilot study to 11%, a surprising number given the increased number of and decreased experience level of Document Instructors. Average turn-around time fluctuated between 3 and 6 days, comparable to the turnaround time in the most efficient of the cohort classes, and superior to the time in most classes. Also significant is that despite the tensions between Classroom and Document Instructors, only six documents (0.5%) had grades changed by the Classroom Instructors.

Perhaps one of the most significant findings thus far concerns the time and effort put forth by the participants in the project. Readers might recall that appointments are made with the assumption that instructors will put forth approximately 10 hours per week for each one-quarter-time appointment. When teaching under the cohort model, it is easy to work above or below that weekly level, depending on the number of students enrolled and the instructor's own work habits. In this new initiative, tracking time and effort has produced some promising results. Through the first 7 weeks of the semester, Classroom Instructors worked an average of 60% of their appointment time, whereas Document Instructors' efforts ranged from a low of 28% to a high of 48% of their appointment time, with an average effort of 37%. Given that five of the six Document Instructors had no teaching experience, and the other Document Instructor had never taught in this particular writing program, those figures are staggering.

And what of quality of the Document Managers' feedback? A key point of tension in this pilot study arose because Classroom Instructors were concerned about having to mediate the feedback of others, feedback that might not, in their eyes, measure up to what they themselves would write. And the comments of many of the Document Instructors, particularly at the outset, were typical of the comments written by new teachers—brief, general comments about the student's work with few specific suggestions for improving the student writing. What changed, however, was the fact that these neophyte Document Instructors had each of their comments read by at least three individuals—the student, the Classroom Instructor, and a program Assistant Director—and received immediate feedback on their comments if problems were detected. Thus, even in the earliest phases of the project, it became evident that problems with commentary, which often went undetected until too late to help the students, were intercepted and remediated to the advantage of both Document Instructor and composition student—this in itself is a key difference from those cohort classrooms where trouble went unnoticed until too late to help either instructor or student.

CONCLUSION

Clearly, this initiative will continue to yield provocative data and findings about the nature of writing program administration and writing pedagogy for some time to come. What is most critical to note at this juncture is that the project enables WPAs and participants to see for the first time how pedagogy and labor interact in the teaching of writing. Traditional considerations of labor in first-year writing programs have focused primarily on such issues as instructor autonomy and academic freedom at the expense of other, heretofore implied problem areas such as actual measures of efficiency and quality of instruction. Student evaluations and classroom observations have typically served as the benchmarks of measurement for all but the newest of instructors, who will have some discussions with WPA staff concerning syllabi, assignments, and grading practices; the problem remains that of these evaluation tools, only student evaluations are conducted with any systemic regularity. The core responsibilities of writing instructors, conducting class meetings and responding to student documents, are often largely undocumented over the course of an instructor's career.

The composition initiative at TTU provides, for the first time, a vastly more complete picture of the pedagogical and labor process. The initiative began as a result of local exigencies that were showing that the cohort model was becoming progressively less capable of delivering a comparable, quality experience to the first-year writing students (if, indeed, it ever has been capable of doing so), even when instructors were provided with detailed syllabi, assignments, and classroom activities. This situation is by no means localized to TTU; writing programs nationwide suffer the same erratic instruction and have had neither the time nor technology to institute a comprehensive study and evaluation of labor practices. Instead, programs operate on a model of good faith, where everyone—administrators, instructors, and students—is expected to "do the right (best) thing" and all will be well. Unfortunately, such is almost never the case—witness the calls over the last decade or so to eliminate first-year writing—not because students have no need of the course, but because it could not be effectively taught and administrated—until now.

Although beginning out of local need, the composition initiative quickly moved out of response mode and into a more proactive examination of the labor involved in writing program teaching and administration. In re-engineering the division of labor involved in the teaching of writing, WPAs have confirmed that in both classroom teaching and responding to student writing there exist inefficient use of human resources; many new instructors are not ready to deliver quality classroom instruction *and* respond effectively to student documents. Neither is easy, and when asked to do both, novice instructors generally do neither task well. Hours are wasted making comments that have little effect in modifying student writing behaviors and in developing lectures for the classroom, when such time could be more efficiently used in developing a single set of skills for responding to student writing over the course of one or two semesters *before* moving into the classroom to interact face to face with students. Although the original focus of the initiative was on instruction rather than labor issues, it has become clear to administrators that the project may achieve significant results in terms of making instructional labor practices more efficient. Decreasing the amount and magnitude of misdirected efforts on the part of composition instructors will have ramifications far beyond the writing program; observers external to the program will see a unit with fewer bottlenecks, miscommunications, and complaints from those who see instructors responding to needs other than those of the first-year writing student. The project also answers the questions of many who seek to understand and assess the work of writing programs; data capture enables all involved in the program to adjust and adapt in response to student needs—a far cry from the single teacher working alone in the classroom.

POSTSCRIPT

Since the initial manuscript was submitted, several important events regarding this new program have occurred. The first of these is that the program described in the chapter now has a name—Interactive Composition Online (ICON). The second event, or change, is that ICON has rapidly scaled up from the modest pilot projects to cover the entire first-year composition program at TTU. During Fall 2002, the first semester of implementation, 2,871 students, 35 Classroom Instructors, and 23 Document Instructors composed and responded to 100,319 drafts, peer critiques, and writing reviews. In Fall 2004, 2,664 students, 33 Classroom Instructors, and 46 Document Instructors participated in 83 sections of composition classes, generating 97,067 pieces of student writing. The third event came as Texas Tech's Extended Studies (ES) program adopted ICON. Instead of working as separate entities, ES students now participate with onsite students as all of them turn in their writing assignments via the ICON web interface and have it evaluated by the same instructors who teach in the onsite program. Turnaround times average 32 hours, 16 minutes for regular drafts and 2 hours, 30 minutes for ES drafts.

Although the ability of ICON to scale up has drawn attention to the program and impressed many in the Texas Tech community, one of the primary tasks of the ICON development team in the coming years will be to closely examine the quality of student writing and teacher instruction in the program. Thus far, anecdotal evidence suggests that despite initial misgivings from the students about the amount of writing required and the reliance on an online document submission and retrieval system, a significant number of them are finding the courses challenging, instructive, and beneficial. Furthermore, ICON has thus far enabled the program to sustain an intensive writing workload without asking teachers for an unreasonable amount of grading; thus, ICON does support much of the scholarship in composition studies, which suggests that the more students write, the more their writing improves.

Clearly, however, research into the delivery of any writing curriculum is bound to be questioned by those who want to ensure that the quality of student writing increases. To ensure the improvement of the quality of student writing, a more in-depth and longitudinal research will be required. Currently, the ICON development team is developing a research project that will track randomly selected students who have participated in ICON at some time during its first 4 years of implementation. Ideally, this project will allow the team to study students' progress throughout their stay at TTU. Students who participate will be asked to submit writing assignments from their sophomore-, junior-, and senior-level courses for assessment in order to examine how well the criteria-based curriculum appears to prepare them for other college-level writing. Another planned study will involve the relationship between instructor comments (which are currently evaluated independently of the student texts by members of the program staff) and any perceived changes in quality of student writing. These, as well as additional projects still in the planning stages, should provide valuable evidence concerning the impact of ICON on student writing.

Some projects already underway measure the impact of ICON on instructors. Dr. Kathleen Gillis is conducting research to gain a better understanding of how both experienced and inexperienced instructors respond to the use of ICON via dynamic change processes. Gillis' study will provide those interested in adopting ICON or its successors with valuable information about instructors' perceived concerns. Another ongoing initiative mentioned in the previous paragraph is the assessment of instructor comments independent of the drafts. Comments are evaluated according to a Likert scale, which will locate individual instructor strengths and weaknesses. Not only is this sort of research valuable for understanding how students learn to write, it also provides important information that can help writing program administrators develop more effective teacher training models.

In summary, a project born of necessity, like ICON, is often the easiest to market. That is, responding to well-defined needs makes it easier to develop programs, products, or processes whose potential is quickly recognized by clients (be they students, instructors, or retail shoppers). Although many may see such projects as high risk, the truth of the matter is that rapidly changing computer technology is strongly influencing our own expectations of education as well as those of our clients. Not surprisingly, then, writing program administrators must display a willingness to experiment with new methods of developing and delivering effective instruction.

Balancing Constituencies

Being Able to Act

Barry Maid

Marian Stone
Arizona State University East

Historically, academic programs have been designed entirely from a theoretical perspective driven by forces within academic disciplines. However, when given the opportunity to create a new Multimedia Writing and Technical Communication program at Arizona State University (ASU) East, we decided to base the curriculum not only on discipline-based theories but also on a variety of different market forces. Additionally, perhaps the best decision we made was to not create a program that, like most academic programs, was created and then became "set in concrete." On the contrary, we were committed to create a program that could quickly respond to new or changing needs. We were able to do so because we acknowledged that we, at all times, need to continuously be sensitive, not only to market needs, but to the constant shifting nature of our markets.

Although it is important for technical communication programs to be sensitive to the markets that affect them, we feel it is even more important to be able to respond quickly to market changes. We have also seen in the first 3 years of the program that faculty expertise must be used to make key decisions in how to respond or not respond. For example, like many technical communication programs, we have had students demand courses in specific software. Although the market is clearly there, our professional expertise tells us that we need to teach all kinds of web development skills in our courses. However, we do not need to offer a 3-hour course in Dreamweaver. On the other hand, when it became clear that our on-campus offerings were limiting to our students because of time and distance, we quickly jumped into the business of online classes.

When our program was initially conceived, and this is evident in the historical sections of this chapter, the U.S. economy—especially the technology sector—was booming. Now, there has been several years of economic downturn. We are also seeing a shifting in the needs of the markets that will likely hire our students. What seems to be serving us best is the attitude we developed, by necessity in our start-up phase, of being able to react quickly. Looking back, now 3 years past the program's initial approval, the fact that we were and continue to be willing to make quick changes, as allowed within ASU's rigid structure, has enabled us to establish ourselves and to show growth despite talk of economic gloom and doom.

In designing the Multimedia Writing and Technical Communication program we did not ignore the best minds in the discipline (that, itself, constitutes a certain kind of a market); however, we also chose to focus on who our students were likely to be, what their perceptions might be, as well as trying to respond to views held by already practicing professionals who might soon be hiring our graduates. We have also discovered that we need to understand the role that technical communication and business communication courses play in our relationships with our students and our colleagues at ASU.

Initially, the Multimedia Writing and Technical Communication program became thinkable because by stressing interdisciplinarity it showed it could exist by using many existing resources within ASU, by meeting the needs of a student population that seemed "lost" with regard to an academic major that would provide them with entry into a career, and, finally, by meeting the needs of local industry. In other words, the program was able to solve the needs of dissimilar and, at times, contradictory markets. In fact, we see being able to do so as being an important rhetorical act. We have shaped our new program with the intended purpose of delivering much needed skills to the multiple markets (audiences) of potential students and their future employers.

THE PROBLEM WITH WRITING

The act of writing (unless pages are being constantly generated by continuously updated databases) tends to fix things in time. Writing about a program whose hallmark seems to be emerging as "being able to react quickly to change" is, in many ways, an exercise in futility. We can write it, but then tomorrow it changes. We can report on the history and the present state, although that present state will likely change quickly. We already know that some of the assumptions that we believed and that appear in the historical information presented here have either changed or were wrong.

For example, initially large numbers of communication and journalism majors were seen as potential students. The reality of the situation is that most of those students are traditional college students. Traditional college students are less likely than returning students, or older community college students with workplace experience, to be interested in technical communication programs. Likewise, when looking at existing ASU populations, the decision to propose a bachelor's program first made sense. In reality, based on the emerging realization that there is a great interest in graduate education in technical communication in the metropolitan Phoenix area, we might have been wiser had we begun with a master's program. That was a case of looking at only one market instead of all of them. In the planning and initial stages of building the program, we were working on the assumption that many of our students would move into jobs with identifiable high-tech employers in the area. Established industry giants such as Motorola, Intel, and Honeywell seemed to be a good fit for our students. Additionally, new software companies seemed to be starting up every day in Scottsdale and Chandler. All that changed. Our students still see those corporations as well as Boeing and Lockheed Martin as potential employers. However, they are also beginning to look at writing for health-related industries — especially the emerging biodesign operations. Finally, the poor economy has prevented us from hiring the needed tenure track faculty. It has forced us to move into online classes faster than we might have liked. However, that movement has opened up other interesting possibilities in responding to the needs of the Valley of the Sun.

TWO HISTORIES: MARIAN STONE

Our program history, like our program, was based on an understanding of market forces. As early as 1993, I, then a technical communication faculty member in the Department of Manufacturing and Industrial Technology at ASU, joined 21 academic and industry members of the Society of Technical Communication's (STC) Professionalism Committee in conducting research on technical communication. The committee concluded that technical communication's body of knowledge was derived from various disciplines, including composition, reading, and rhetorical theory, graphic and instructional design, management theory, systems theory, and cognitive psychology (Skelton and Andersen). Based on this research, I recognized the demand for a broad and interdisciplinary program with faculty expertise in a number of key disciplines.

My idea was that it would be an effective use of resources to develop a program that would attract new students to the university, but not require new faculty hires. Also, because no technical communication program existed in Arizona, there would not be competition in the state. These seemed ideal management conditions to begin a program.

In 1997, during my year-long sabbatical in which I developed ASU's first online technical communication course, I read Karen Schriver's book, *Dynamics of Document Design*, and agreed with many of her findings. In that text, Schriver, an internationally recognized expert in document design, said that no program existed where faculty worked in their own department, developed an interdisciplinary curriculum, and had expertise in visual and verbal rhetoric. I now feel more confirmed for my idea for an interdisciplinary program, and believe even more strongly in it.

Returning from my sabbatical in 1998, I saw an opportunity for an innovative program in a new multidisciplinary college, East College, that was just forming. I approached the dean, David Schwalm, and asked him if he might accept me in East College to start building the program. Sensing that Schwalm had keen vision, flexibility, an understanding of the market-place, and an open-minded receptivity to new ideas and because he had a background in rhetoric and had formerly served as the Writing Program Administrator (WPA) on ASU's main campus, I felt confident he under-stood the issues and concerns in the field. Moreover, Schwalm was also the vice provost of ASU East's campus, so he had a global awareness of the administrative and political issues the program would confront on campus.

Working together, Schwalm and I were able to envision what would be needed to achieve the goal of building the applied, interdisciplinary pro-gram on ASU's newest campus. In some ways, it was an ideal situation since I was the first professor in East College and easily had direct contact with the dean. For months, we met and corresponded by e-mail and tele-phone. Although Schwalm was not entirely familiar with all the issues in the technical communication field, he had a national reputation in the rhetoric/composition community and I was able to provide him with the research he needed to better understand technical communication.

Then in 1998, while serving on the board of STC's Phoenix Chapter, I decided to invite Schriver to Phoenix to hold a workshop on designing for quality for the STC community. Because Schriver was going to be in Phoenix, I recommended to Schwalm that it seemed an ideal opportunity to use Schriver as consultant for the proposed program. Schriver thus became a key subject matter expert who provided important input in the early planning and conceptualization of the program.

Subsequently, we developed a Request for Planning Authorization and submitted it to the Arizona Board of Regents (ABOR) for approval. ABOR granted us the authorization to proceed with planning for the bach-elor of science in multimedia writing and technical communication. In our proposal, we explained that the program we designed would incorporate rhetoric, technical communication, graphics, cognitive psychology/human factors, and technology in order to graduate verbally and visually literate information designers/technical communicators who are able to embrace technology.

Initial Limited Market Thoughts

The proposal indicated that we anticipated the program to be attractive and high demand. We identified part of our initial market as being some of the 1,000+ majors in general communication and 1,300 majors in journalism and telecommunication that currently existed on ASU's Tempe campus. By attracting these students, we argued it would ease the enrollment pressure on the programs and directly serve students who were interested in technical communication. Although not specifically addressed in the original proposal, we also understood that the program was also a potential academic home for many of the overwhelming number of undecided majors at ASU as well as for the numerous students transferring from one of the many Maricopa Community Colleges (the second largest community college system in the nation). In fact, we are presently confident that students from the community colleges and returning students (students who may have started college years ago but never finished) represent a large part of our market. We also argued that ASU is in the heart of the "Silicon Desert," an area of the country with many high-tech and information industries. Therefore, we anticipated great interest in the program and a high placement rate for graduates. All of these factors helped to fashion the idea of a program that was brought together by pressures from a variety of markets.

Once approval to plan was in place, we at ASU East decided we needed to hire a senior faculty member to assume the leadership role in planning and developing the program, staffing, and building and maintaining connections with industry. In April 1999 I chaired the search committee to seek that senior hire.

On May 11, 1999, Schwalm, in his role as vice provost of Arizona East University and dean of East College, posted an ad for an associate/full professor in multimedia writing and technical communication on the WPA-L listserv. The ad was to appear in the May 21, 1999 edition of the *Chronicle of Higher Education*. Schwalm had been talking about the possibility of such a position in a new program for some time, probably trying to let senior faculty around the country think about what it would mean to move to a new campus being built up from an old air force base where they would have to start an entirely new program.

TWO HISTORIES:
BARRY MAID

I was one of the people who read the WPA-L post. I was then a professor of rhetoric and writing at the University of Arkansas at Little Rock (UALR) Reading the ad caused me to do some deep soul-searching. I realized I had a good job with good colleagues at UALR and was very comfortable—maybe a bit too comfortable. I talked with family. I also talked about the job with colleagues when I attended Computers and Writing in late May. Finally, I decided to apply for the job, wondering if it was possible that ASU would have someone in place by August 1999.

Except for a postcard acknowledging my application, I heard nothing from ASU East. Finally, at the end of the summer, I received a phone call from Marian Stone in her role as head of the search committee. She invited me to come to ASU East for an interview to be held on August 27, 1999. I happily accepted the invitation. Marian also told me that as part of the interview process they would like me to present a 20-minute multimedia presentation. I asked her how she was defining multimedia. Her response was that it was up to me. The realization of what it meant to build from the ground up began to sink in.

I put together a presentation I called, "Just Because You Can, Doesn't Mean You Should." I used "bells and whistles" to show that "bells and whistles" are not always the best choice. I created a Web site that used a javascript-enabled password protection script and then moved to a Flash movie. I demonstrated image editing, audio and video streaming, as well as the use of an educational MOO. It must have worked because ASU offered me the job starting in January 2000.

Still, the one thing that I carried with me from the interview was the knowledge that there was no technical communication program of any kind in the entire state of Arizona. I was accepting a job to build a new program in a market where no such program existed but the need for such a program seemed great. For me, the desert had suddenly turned very green.

I arrived at ASU East January 2, 2000. My first job was to create a curriculum that would be the heart of the Permission to Implement proposal that needed to be submitted to the ABOR in order for ASU East to be allowed to offer a degree in technical communication.

It may be the dream of all faculty members who wonder about an ideal curriculum to be put in a situation where they get to start from scratch. Yet, it is a position that is full of potential pitfalls. I had two distinct advantages in creating the curriculum at ASU East. First of all, I had an experienced, knowledgeable colleague, Marian Stone. Second, since in Fall 1998, ASU East had brought in a consultant, Karen Schriver, to give suggestions about the development of the program as well as the possible curriculum, I had a concrete starting point for curricular development. In fact, Schriver's report was one of the first things the East staff sent me once I had accepted the position. Along with that help, I had the charge of David Schwalm, in his role as Dean of East College, that I think not only of a BS degree but also of a Bachelor of Interdisciplinary Studies (BIS), Bachelor of Applied Science (BAS) as well as an undergraduate and a post-baccalaureate certificate. The task kept growing. David kept telling me to keep it "lean and mean," and to make sure it had ultimate flexibility. Those members of the WPA-L listserv who have read Schwalm's comments for years know that he is a very wise man.

A MULTIPRONGED ATTACK

The first real task we faced was to define the program. We accomplished that by writing what became known as "The Sentence." One sentence might not seem like much, but it was an important start. "The Sentence" read, "In the Multimedia Writing and Technical Communication program, students will learn how to produce, to design, and to manage information, using both traditional and developing technologies." "The Sentence" was harder to write than might be expected. It needed to fill a multitude of roles. It needed to define the program both within and outside the academy. Within the academy, we needed to explain ourselves to our colleagues in other disciplines (without stepping on anyone else's turf). We also had to tell the administration, who had supported us, that the administrative support was justified. Explaining ourselves to our external constituencies was, and remains, more difficult. Part of the reason for this is because there are multiple external groups with multiple needs. Additionally, although the Multimedia Writing and Technical Communication program is an applied program, it is still an academic program within an academic institution. The program's goals are, therefore, necessarily going to be somewhat different than those of industry. That does not mean that partnerships cannot or should not exist, but simply that, even at this most basic level, those partnerships must be thoughtfully conceived and carefully nurtured. It also means that although we wanted to be sensitive and responsive to market needs, we also did not want to compromise our own knowledge of what needs to be in an academically viable program. From the beginning, we wanted to be clear that we were creating an academic program with roots in rhetoric. We were not training students to only become experts in using the current versions of RoboHelp or Framemaker.

Initially, we identified our primary outside constituencies as our potential students—at that point, and even today, a loosely defined and rather amorphous group (they include the community colleges that produce many of their potential students in this group). Originally, we expected our relationships with the Maricopa Community Colleges would be closest with Chandler-Gilbert Community College and Mesa Community College simply because of their proximity to ASU East. Those relationships are good. What we didn't expect was the interest from Phoenix College, the Maricopa campus located in central Phoenix. Additionally, we have been working with the faculty of Yavapai College in Prescott, the community college in Yavapai County, who see our program as being a natural extension of their communication program. They also see the fact that ASU East is located on an old air force base with housing that is appropriate for families as being an important draw for their students.

Currently, we see almost an equal number of students interested in our undergraduate program and our post-baccalaureate certificate. The undergraduates are primarily former community college students or returning students. There are some who were taking classes at the ASU Tempe campus and, when discovering our program, decided to change majors. Most of these, however, are also older students. The post-baccalaureates tend to be working professionals. Some are already employed in technical communication positions. Some are interested in gaining a credential that will help them break into the field. Most would prefer to be enrolled in a master's program. We are aware of the interest and the need for graduate education in technical communication in the Phoenix metropolitan area. We will act as soon as we have sufficient full-time faculty to support both an undergraduate and master's program.

The second outside group we identified was the Phoenix Chapter of the STC. STC is not the only professional organization with whom we hope to work; however, it seemed to make sense to target it as the first. Marian had been an active member of the Phoenix chapter for years. Additionally, Barry had worked closely with the Arkansas chapter during his years in Little Rock. He had also worked with the International Association of Business Communicator (IABC) while in Little Rock and hopes, as the program matures, to connect to the Phoenix chapter. Barry has already made contact with the Arizona Chapter of the Society of Marketing Professional Services (SMPS). Still, STC members are more likely to be in jobs that are most like the ones the program's students seek and work for organizations that are most likely to employ the program's students. At this point and for the foreseeable future, STC remains the program's primary external partner. There is also a Southern Arizona chapter of the STC located in Tucson. We are also in touch with its leadership, have had them on campus, and consult with them as we do the Phoenix chapter.

BUILDING A CURRICULUM:
WHAT GOES WHERE?

Having written a sentence describing the program to its primary audiences, we were then able to start talking about real curricular issues. Barry asked Marian to brainstorm a list of topics that were crucial to the curriculum. He did the same. He then tried to combine Marian's brainstorming, his brainstorming, and the suggestions made by Shriver. The results are three yellow legal pages presently in a file folder in Barry's filing cabinet.

Barry's next job, even before beginning to think about creating individual classes, was to try to make some sense from his compiled notes. After several conversations with Marian, he made the decision not to offer separate courses in what he termed the *sensitivity-based* areas—cultural, ethical, and global economy issues. His decision was driven by his feeling that these issues are too important to play isolated roles in the curriculum. He was determined to integrate them into all of the program's courses. (Barry will privately admit there was a part of him that wanted to do the same with technology. However, with part of the program's name asserting that it is "multimedia," he ultimately gave up his own preferences.) After more discussion, we emerged with the following statement we can make to our students.

In the Multimedia Writing and Technical Communication program, students will learn the following:

- Oral and written communication skills to effectively communicate across audiences.
- Issues of ethics in technical communication.
- Awareness of the global nature of technical communication— both culturally and economically.
- Critical thinking skills to evaluate print, oral, and electronic sources.
- Technical genres and their appropriateness.
- Writing and editing skills.
- Effective visual and design elements to incorporate into written documents and oral presentations.
- Decision-making processes to identify appropriate media.

Finally, we had to make the most difficult decisions of all. We needed to decide what to require of our students. That meant naming and creating new courses. We were also working under a severe time constraint. Although it has changed its policy, at that point ABOR was only considering new programs twice a year. If we didn't get the proposal to ABOR in time for its June 30 meeting, we would have to wait another 6 months. That meant not only getting the proposal written but also getting all the new courses written and approved through the ASU East curricular process before that date.

College faculty who have tried to get one new course through a campus curricular process know how difficult and time consuming that can be. Our task was to propose a new program that included 13 new courses. We had to get everything approved on campus in 5 months in order to meet ABOR's deadline. In order to do that, we had to develop a curriculum that would be both theoretically sound as well as not raise any "red flags" in the process. For example, proposing a course that would require technology that we didn't have when the course was proposed would have been a real problem.

Eventually, we realized that the curricular possibilities that we were discussing really fell under one of four different rubrics: technical communication, visual communication, media/technology/digital, and technical editing. We were hoping to require four courses, one from each of these areas. We were also hoping to come up with parallel course titles. Parallel titles proved impossible. We settled on the following course titles: Principles of Technical Communication, Principles of Visual Communication, Principles of Writing with Technology, and Principles of Technical Editing. All four of these classes are offered as a senior-/graduate-level class. Additionally, we created a junior-level class, as an introduction to the program for our undergraduate majors. In this first course, our intent is to expose our students to the four cornerstones of the program.

In addition to the five required classes, the program also asks majors to take two genre courses. The first genre courses created were Proposal Writing, Manual and Instructional Writing, Computer Documentation, Technical and Scientific Reports, and Business Reports. We wanted to expose students to the idea of technical genre and to give them experience in multiple genres.

We also made a conscious decision to keep this first round of genre courses as "vanilla" as possible. Starting out with limited faculty resources, we did not want to lock into highly specialized courses that we might not be able to deliver regularly because only one person can teach the course and that person might have to teach some other required course. We did not want to promise something to students that we knew would be difficult, or impossible, to deliver. We were also aware that "plain vanilla" genre courses were less likely to be questioned by faculty in other disciplines sitting on the curriculum committee. For examples, courses mentioning specific topics such as web development would likely be looked at closely by faculty in ASU East's computer graphics program. Such a question was, indeed, raised about a Special Topics class Barry taught his first summer at ASU. The discussions between the two programs were good ones, and Barry taught the course. However, if those questions had been raised on the new courses, the program's approval would have been delayed for at least 6 months.

Additionally, the Multimedia Writing and Technical Communication program also realized it would be providing service courses to programs in technology, business, and life sciences. Creating genre courses that would be general enough to serve both program students and act as service courses was another important consideration.

Finally, the program asks its students to take a capstone class. In this class, students will be developing a professional portfolio as well as reflecting (in writing) on their experiences in the program. (The May 2003 graduating class made formal presentations of their electronic portfolios at the May meeting of the new ASU student chapter of STC. Invited guests at the meeting were interested students and faculty from Phoenix College.) The program strongly encourages an internship. Because the program is new, we felt it was imprudent to require internships before we had the means of offering them to all of our students.

We also had to deal with the program's commitment to interdisciplinarity. This proved to be, yet, another area where differing market forces competed. The reality of the situation in any academic institution is when a program requires a course in another academic area, it is at the mercy of the other area in terms of scheduling. Barry decided he needed to make a commitment to the Multimedia Writing and Technical Communication students of when they could expect classes to be offered so that they could plan for graduation. As a result, the only required courses in the program bear the Multimedia Writing and Technical Communication (TWC) prefix. However, the major is what ASU terms a "lean major"—requiring only 33 hours. That leaves students the opportunity for many electives. The program strongly recommends students, in conjunction with an advisor, develop a cohesive "related area" of at least 12 hours. Although we are aware that we are preparing our students as technical communicators and not subject matter experts, we want them to be aware that understanding the content of the area they work in is a crucial part of being an effective communicator. The areas most likely to be suggested (although there is no restriction) are those programs found on the East Campus that were originally Applied Psychology, Computer Graphics, or General Business. The recent addition of programs in the life sciences, Nutrition, Exercise and Wellness, and Applied Biological Science creates a new emphasis in biology and health-related fields that our students can pursue. The actual curriculum and the requirements for the program's degrees and certificates are listed in the Appendix.

DELIVERY OF COURSES

Finally, we are consciously addressing one other factor that touches on market issues. That is scheduling of courses. Because it is already becoming clear that many of the program's students work, the program has made a firm commitment that all degrees and certificates will be able to be completed, in a timely fashion, during times other than traditional daytime class hours. Initially, this means all required courses are offered in the evenings as well as during the day. The program is looking at the possibility of holding weekend classes. The program is also committed to offering classes online. Since we have been unable, for economic reasons, to hire tenure-track faculty, in Fall 2002 we started offering online classes using faculty who live all over the country. During the first year of online classes, we have had instructors from Tucson, Arizona, Houghton, Michigan, and Seattle, Washington. As of Fall 2003, the entire post-baccalaureate certificate was offered online. By Spring 2004 the entire undergraduate major was available online. What this means is that it will be possible for ASU students to major in multimedia writing and technical communication without ever stepping foot on the ASU East campus. For example, students who live in the far west valley, as much as 60 or 70 miles from ASU East, could take all their classes, except for their major, at ASU West. This was not part of the plan as originally conceived. However, it is a good example of how we have tried to remain sensitive to the needs of our student market and respond quickly to the need. Our online courses are becoming very attractive. We're discovering that although most of our students are nontraditional, night classes don't always work best. We have a good number of students who either work in the evening or have child-care problems in the evening. They prefer day or Internet classes. Eventually, we plan to have courses available day, night, and online. Until then, we'll continue to try to meet our students' needs given our limited resources. One other delivery option that we continue to explore is the possibility of using ASU's interactive television capability to offer classes across the greater Phoenix metropolitan area.

FINALLY, A NEW BEGINNING

By the end of April 2000, Barry had completed the Request for Implementation Authorization Proposal for the new programs in Multimedia Writing and Technical Communication. ABOR approved the proposal on June 30, 2000.

On July 1, 2000, Barry Maid posted the following e-mail on multiple listservs:

Subject: A new program blooms in the desert

Folks—

Please forgive the cross-postings, but this is good news. Yesterday, the Arizona Board of Regents approved a BS in Multimedia Writing and Technical Communication at Arizona State University East. It is the only technical communication program in Arizona. We'll start recruiting students instantly and begin to offer classes in Spring 2001.

I'll post the url for the program's website once it goes up on the ASU server, probably on Wed.

Barry Maid

Barry.Maid@asu.edu

In sending the proposal to ABOR, Barry Maid, Marian Stone, and David Schwalm had given the "fantasy" number that the program should have 25 enrolled students after the first year. In the Spring 2002 semester, there were already 35 combined majors and post-baccalaureate students. Given the limited resources, we have not been actively recruiting. However, there were 45 students in the program for the Fall 2003 semester. That's around as many as we can handle given the current faculty. The desert flowers are awesome.

APPENDIX

The new courses sent for approval to the ASU East Curriculum Committee in May 2000 were as follow:

> Multimedia Writing and Technical Communication Curriculum
> TWC 301 General Principles of Multimedia Writing
>> Introduction to writing in a variety of media, understanding the consequences of integrating media, and effective editing techniques.
> TWC 401 Principles of Technical Communication
>> Basic information design principles to produce effective written, oral and electronic technical communication.
>> Understanding of rhetorical and audience analysis.
> TWC 403 Writing for Professional Publication
>> Analysis of the market and examination of the publication process, including the roles of the author, editor, and reviewer.
> TWC 411 Principles of Visual Communication
>> Basic principles of visual communication in print and electron-

ic media. Understanding graphic and document design, including typography and color.

TWC 421 Principles of Writing with Technology
Understanding historical and social impact of technology on writing, with emphasis on multimedia design, computer-mediated communication, and hypertext.

TWC 431 Principles of Technical Editing
Basic principles of technical editing (for print and electronic media) including copyediting, reviews, standards, style, and project management.

TWC 443 Proposal Writing
Developing persuasive strategies and themes for researching and writing professional proposals.

TWC 444 Manual and Instructional Writing
Design and development of a user manual, writing instructions, improving graphics and page design, and usability testing.

TWC 445 Computer Documentation
Introduction to writing documentation for the computer industry.

TWC 446 Technical and Scientific Reports
Introduction to strategies, formats, and techniques of presenting information to technical and scientific audiences.

TWC 447 Business Reports
Introduction to strategies, formats, and techniques of presenting information to business and other workplace audiences.

TWC 484 Internship
Application of classroom work in a supervised workplace environment

TWC 490 Capstone
Development of a professional portfolio, creation of a "culminating document," and synthesis of undergraduate experience

Requirements for the BS degree in multimedia writing and technical communication are as follows:

TWC 301 General Principles of Multimedia
TWC 401 Principles of Technical Communication
TWC 411 Principles of Visual Communication
TWC 421 Principles of Writing with Technology
TWC 431 Principles of Technical Editing
TWC 490 Capstone

An Internship (TWC 484) or supervised work experience is
strongly recommended.

The remaining hours will be elective in the major (TWC) at least
6 of which need to be in such genre courses as TWC 443
Proposal Writing or TWC 447 Business reports.

Each student will be encouraged to present a "related area" consisting of 12 hours of study in one other discipline. At least 9
of these 12 hours must be upper level. Suggested disciplines
might be, but are not limited to, applied psychology, business
administration, or computer graphics. Students, with the help
of an advisor, may also develop a coherent interdisciplinary
related area.

Students must meet all other ASU graduation requirements.

As noted earlier, the initial charge from the dean was to create programs for
the BIS and the BAS as well as the BS degrees. The BIS and BAS programs
were created to meet the needs of specific student populations. The BIS is a
program where a student's interests may not lie within the traditional structure of university majors. The student is given the option to develop two
academic concentrations. In Multimedia Writing and Technical
Communication, the BIS option requires 18 hours to include TWC 301
General Principles of Multimedia Writing and TWC 401 Principles of
Technical Communication. One of the other core courses (TWC 411
Principles of Visual Communication, TWC 421 Principles of Writing with
Technology, or TWC 431 Principles of Technical Editing) must be taken.
    Students must also take three other 400-level TWC courses, at least two
of which must be genre courses, such as TWC 443 Proposal Writing or
TWC 447 Business Reports. In addition, students must take the BIS
Capstone course.
    The BAS degree is an option for students who transfer to ASU and hold
an associate of applied science degree from a regionally accredited postsec-
ondary institution. The BAS option requires 20 hours to include TWC 301
General Principles of Multimedia Writing, TWC 401 Principles of
Technical Communication, and TWC 490 Capstone. One of the other core
courses (TWC 411 Principles of Visual Communication, TWC 421
Principles of Writing with Technology, or TWC 431 Principles of
Technical Editing) must be taken.
    Students must also take three other 400-level TWC courses, at least two
of which must be genre courses, such as TWC 443 Proposal Writing or
TWC 447 Business Reports. In addition, an undergraduate certificate was

created, which requires 18 hours to include TWC 301 General Principles of Multimedia Writing and TWC 401 Principles of Technical Communication. One of the other core courses (TWC 411 Principles of Visual Communication, TWC 421 Principles of Writing with Technology, or TWC 431 Principles of Technical Editing) must be taken.

Students must take three other 400-level TWC courses, at least two (2) of which must be genre courses, such as TWC 443 Proposal Writing or TWC 447 Business Reports.

The post-baccalaureate certificate, the final new program that was created, requires 18 hours to include TWC 501 Principles of Technical Communication. Two of the other core courses (TWC 511 Principles of Visual Communication, TWC 521 Principles of Writing with Technology, or TWC 531 Principles of Technical Editing) must be taken.

Students must also take three other 500-level TWC courses, at least two of which must be genre courses, such as TWC 543 Proposal Writing or TWC 547 Business Reports.

REFERENCES

Barchilon, M. and J. Matson. "Technical Communication Programs for the Future." *Forum 1995.*
Schriver, K. *Dynamics in Document Design.* New York: John Wiley, 1997.
———. "Suggestions for the Arizona State University (East Campus) New Major in Multimedia Writing and Technical Communication." Unpublished consultant report, 1998.
Skelton, T., and S. Andersen. "Professionalism in Technical Communication." *Technical Communication.* 40 (1993): 202-07.

1⓪ *Marketing Rhetoric in the Market Economy*

Selling the Value of Rhetorical Knowledge to Business

Yvonne Merrill

University of Arizona

The University of Arizona's Graduate School of Management, one of the nation's most competitive MBA programs, wants its graduates to be good communicators. Since the late 1980s, it has employed six consecutive faculty members to teach business writing. Their status in the program and their business expertise decreased with each new hire. The program finally turned to credentialed "writing specialists" to teach their students "how to write." Yet, each writing teacher remained affiliated with the program for only 3 years, at the very longest. To remain in the program, each taught less and edited more. Sharing experience with the others who taught writing in the program has revealed to me the business faculty's perspective. Combined with my additional experience over the last 17 years teaching writing to engineers in and out of the academy, teaching writing in businesses and industries, coordinating writing across the curriculum at the university, and directing the business and technical writing program in the English Department—I find the reason for this phenomenon has to do primarily with disciplinary turf and whose disciplinary knowledge has greater perceived value. Because academic disciplines are defined by their theoretical frameworks, those disciplines perceived as creating more practical value and/or employing more complex theory are more highly esteemed.

Both the undergraduate and graduate programs in business colleges, as well as in most professional academic programs around the country, however, have recognized that communication skills—both written and oral—have to be addressed if students' theoretical training is to be effectively applied in any workplace. Yet, in my experience, business faculty and especially their students don't buy the rhetorical theory that one's ability to understand and apply concepts is directly related to the ability to articulate them to others. Our MBA program exercised enormous ingenuity developing different organizational structures for delivering the writing "instruction" it claims to want, and until 1999, we had no classes in the undergraduate program. Each graduate plan has eventually been discontinued when faculty complained that their students' writing failed to improve and students complained that writing instruction was irrelevant to their learning of business concepts. It is this disjunct in fundamental theoretical bases that I maintain creates the outcomes gulf between those trained in business and those trained in rhetoric. Business training elides the intervening process between stated purpose and response to the text. How to get from one to the other still mystifies many business writers, even those who have learned a very effective style through mimicry and endless practice with increasingly successful results in the same contexts.

In the recurring periods between formal writing programs, our business faculty handled writing in their own way. Their solution has typically been to disavow responsibility for *teaching* writing at all, it being "outside" their field, so they resorted to awarding split grades for writing projects. The majority of the grade went to the more valuable "content," whereas the "writing" grade was based on an impressionistic sense of the difficulty level in processing the text, their focus being strictly on effectiveness of organization and linguistic features. This very narrow definition of *writing* ignores the entire thinking process involved and allows writing to be perceived as merely a skill that is applied to, but subordinate to, the ideas and business concepts that can be completely developed first, before attention to language. Business-trained people don't buy the theoretical language that writing specialists are selling—that rhetorical effectiveness is developmental and an intellectual activity closely implicated in cognitive development. Bottom line: in order to deal with this attitude, I argue that the most effective approach is to persuade our faculty colleagues in the business and industry training programs that a rhetorical approach to teaching professional writing *is* both theory-based and practically effective in the workplace—that writing is a *process* necessarily different for different contexts.

The business communication versus writing skill stand-off is particularly ironic because both sides fail to recognize the nearly identical theoretical constructs underpinning rhetoric and marketing, and to find a common language in which to communicate their shared goals and values. It is not an ideological confrontation between anti-capitalistic, Marxist humanism and the free market economy. It is the unequal social value between one field claiming to purvey *knowledge* that is based on research and theory, and the other teaching a skill learned by practice and rote memorization of a generalizable set of conventions. This value differential is thus based on the latter's perception by the former as intellectually nondevelopmental and sterile, consisting of a finite body of "rules" that are drilled rather than cumulatively and cognitively developed according to theoretical principles. Such a perception is pervasive and translates into an inequality of authority whenever writing personnel first attempt collaborative relationships with faculty and practitioners in other disciplines. In order to develop effective partnerships with other academic disciplines, or even more pragmatic partnerships with people in the world of work, rhetoricians face a highly rhetorical job to emerge from their inferior position vis-à-vis other disciplines, most especially the academic business and industry programs that teach "practical knowledge."

Negotiating a common language that would reveal the mutual values shared by rhetoric and nonwriting fields would prove beneficial to the latter, as writing professionals have demonstrated in the successful writing-across-the-curriculum (WAC) programs across the country. These WAC programs emphasize writing to learn as the means of learning to write in various academic contexts. Each field is now too narrowly focused on its own disciplinary theoretical priorities and vocabulary, though they are not, however, incompatible. Rhetoricians, considering themselves specialists in the discipline of effective communication, are most focused on the *theory and process* of writing itself. But as professional communicators and as the marginalized community, we bear the primary responsibility for making the communicative effort. Because the market economy is the dominant culture, its terms are the social "god terms," and its only interests are in the *results* of effective writing. Writing theory is not a value to most who teach other theory-based knowledge.

Nonwriting academics and most practicing business people haven't a precise language for text components and contextual constraints to understand clearly what textual elements contribute to the results they wish to achieve in particular or conventional contexts. They haven't the linguistic resources for symbolizing, and thus internalizing, textual or contextual categories. Communicating our terminology to faculty and professionals outside of English would create the necessary "shared signs" that Sorenson, Kennedy, and Ramirez claim are essential for effective business communication (2). Without the language for our theoretical concepts, it is unreasonable to expect rhetoric outsiders to know that we *have* a theory. One approach to bridging the communication gulf creating this value differential would be to take a Burkean rhetorical approach that would help each field identify with the other's needs. A fruitful work for both might be Burke's chapter on "The Range of Rhetoric" from the *Rhetoric of Motives*. It concludes with this passage:

> The use of symbols, by one symbol-using entity to induce action in another (persuasion properly addressed) is in essence not magical but *realistic*. However, the resources of identification whereby a sense of consubstantiality is symbolically established between beings of unequal status may extend far into the realm of the *idealistic*. (46)

I would say *theoretical*. A major discussion in the *Rhetoric of Motives* is Burke's analysis of covert versus overt motives. I suspect that, in the case of people in disciplines interested primarily in communication to achieve other specific desired outcomes, they do not have covert motives so much as motives for which they have no vocabulary because these motives are unspoken and assumed. In fact, it is the unspoken agendas of both rhetoric and marketing, for example, that obscure the common goals of both.

These motives are so embedded in disciplinary discourse and contexts that they are often not raised to conscious awareness. But the essence of what all disciplines are about is *selling ideas in words*. When rhetoricians deal with the "other," this motive should be articulated, as well as those that are discipline-specific, for better understanding and communication between them. Reliance on context-specific language, as any linguistics scholar will tell us, makes mutually understandable communication extremely difficult.

A little more history of our school of management will help me develop the thesis I have just posed.

ANALYZING THE CASE STUDY

> Give a man a fish and you feed him for a day. Teach a man to fish and you feed him for a lifetime."
>
> (Chinese Proverb)

The first structure the MBA program created for teaching writing was a required three-credit course called "Managerial Communications," co-taught by an assistant professor of management and an associate professor from the communications department (in social sciences). The management professor had a very strong background in writing pedagogy, in addition to impressive credentials from Northwestern's graduate business school. She was also an effective writing teacher, despite having 150 students in the class. During the first two thirds of the course, she used the favored business pedagogy of working from actual case studies in real corporations to teach students all the necessary documents and genres of communication required to solve authentic business problems. Her curriculum was very rhetorical and very challenging. She made it possible for her students to assume authentic rhetorical roles in each case, and thus produce rhetorically effective written communications.

The students, however, rebelled because they felt there was too much writing, and it was too difficult and labor intensive. They maintained that the course's emphasis on understanding rhetorical strategies for effective texts was beside the point. In their student evaluations, they argued that merely solving the issues in the case was all that should be required, despite the fact that it took all the documents they wrote to solve a real business problem and that all their other core courses were also focused exclusively on solving business related problems using only business theory. They had missed the point that the entire goal of the course was to teach *effective communication skills* to solve corporate problems. They perceived the rhetorical concern for contextual constraints, genre conventions, linguistic accuracy, and matters of tone and style irrelevant.

When describing aspects of students' texts, such as content, organization, or style, the management professor regularly employed the phrase *effective for the reader* or the *purpose*, and reminded them the readers were actual people involved in a real case, with whom they needed to identify. She underlined that part of a business writer's ethos rested on his or her use of clear, accurate and effective language. It wasn't just an academic exercise, and she was using familiar business pedagogy—case studies—to teach business writing. Although a business specialist, she had consulted the rhetoric faculty when developing her course curriculum. She used *Style: Ten Lessons in Clarity and Grace* by Joseph M. Williams as one of the three texts she required students to read—the other two being a large notebook of previous student case documents and her own continually revised and business-focused writing text. She required that students understand rules for mechanics, appropriate tone and diction, persuasive organization, and principles of effective style for each of the particular contexts addressed. She required that students work collaboratively on each project, both in real and in cyberspace, very much in the spirit of actual workplace writing. Not only was she a credentialed business expert, but she employed conventional business pedagogy. She was a disciplinary native.

She had the combined ethos of being both a faculty member in the graduate business school and a theorist of rhetoric and its pedagogy. Yet she was let go because she taught the *wrong* theory; in fact, it was apparent to those of us who worked with her that students considered what she taught had *no* theory. They wanted an editor. They wanted someone to "fix" their writing and not require them to learn the principles and theory that would enable them to improve their writing. The wanted the fish, not the fishing lessons.

Thus, an effective business writing professor was not encouraged to pursue tenure because she emphasized writing theory and rhetorical principles, which the students apparently devalued primarily because their other business faculty shared their perceptions. When my successor in the MBA program and I later compared notes about our experiences, we discovered that the faculty there had been regularly devaluing our contributions to the students by admonishing them that it was the *business* faculty's expectations, and not ours, that the students were to meet—"readable" reports were the only raison d'être for the writing workshop. We were just English teachers, after all, with no qualifications to question their *ideas*, an attitude their professors were reinforcing overtly. As Robert Cason points out in the first chapter of his business writing text, "Written communication is probably the most overlooked aspect of the business world—at least from the perspective of those just entering the job market or from the perspective of those with scant knowledge of the business environment" [a category from which I would not necessarily exempt business faculty, many of whom have not actually worked in business outside the academy] (1).

Following the departure of the management writing professor, the class was eliminated to appease the students, who also resented being required to take a three-unit course that lowered their grade point averages. Instead, a series of adjunct writing instructors was hired to function only as editors and graders for the core course papers. That was when I was hired as a newly minted rhetoric and composition PhD, although a 25-year veteran writing teacher. I was to co-teach a workshop with the communications professor. I, too, made the mistake of teaching rhetorical principles, requiring drafts before finished assignments, and holding conferences to discuss issues of audience awareness, effective appeals, persuasive organization, the ethics of reifying human beings, and content selectivity in terms of specific reader needs. Although I was highly credentialed in writing and had experience teaching writing in real workplaces, I had little ethos at the business school because I was identified with the English Department. Those who followed me had the same credibility problem.

The business faculty mandated a hands-off policy on report content, justified by our being *writing* specialists not trained in business theory. My recommendation to the organizational management professor that student teams, who visited actual local businesses, be allowed to do in-depth analyses and provide their reports to the real executives was summarily dismissed as a potential embarrassment to the program because the "writing" was so bad, by which he meant the surface linguistic features only—exclusive of content, organization, tone, style, or format. Although, in my mind, writing to a real audience about an actual business scenario would have been even more effective case-study pedagogy, what they wanted was an editor who would teach their students "good grammar" and mechanics. To marshall ethos for a broader rhetorical focus, I convened an external writing advisory council of business and industry executives to affirm the principles and practices I was teaching.

The Karl Eller faculty could not make time from their "important work" to meet with these real-world informants. The one meeting I was able to schedule between writing emphasis teachers in some of their majors and the advisory council was double booked into a room with a class in session, and the associate dean for curriculum whom I'd asked to speak to the council about the business college's plans to improve writing was unable to provide any concrete details, even though he had just hired the new "expert" who was going to implement them. The council unanimously came away with the sense of being dismissed for having nothing valuable to contribute to the business college's plans.

Although this is a rather extreme illustration of the perception of writing and those who teach it, it is a fairly ubiquitous one outside of English departments, as I have learned being the coordinator for a writing-across-the-curriculum (WAC) program. The complete independence of "content" from expression, and text from context, are assumptions shared by almost anyone not trained in composition or rhetorical theory. I run into this theoretical wall in every conversation I have that is not with a writing colleague. It typifies the experience that writing personnel often encounter when attempting collaborations with other disciplinary faculty and practicing professionals in fields outside English. The scientists with whom I've worked, for instance, see almost no similarity between scientific reporting and "English writing" because they haven't the theoretical language to understand that there are adaptive rhetorical principles at work, which result in the apparent textual differences. Social scientists feel superior to writing specialists because they feel they have actual "ideas" to convey. Because social science students also, in fact, do a lot of writing, they quickly learn the conventional forms expected in their disciplines solely through imitation and internalization, or their writing washes them out of their majors. The College of Social and Behavioral Science was the first college to undertake a serious plan to assess and support the writing of their incoming majors and to deplore the writing of general education students.

Most recently this clear-window perception of writing was brought home to me when I had the opportunity to read the Educational Testing Service's (ETS) Tasks in Critical Thinking with an interdisciplinary group of faculty from the three general education curricular strands—social sciences, humanities, and sciences. We were piloting the test as a possible mid-career evaluation of our revised lower division general education curriculum. The 14 readers from general education and I could collectively speak to the required writing in general education. When members of all three other disciplines found serious theoretical errors in the tasks for their areas, they remonstrated vociferously because they did not want their students asked to apply erroneous theory. On the other hand, when I took issue with ETS' requiring two grades for the culminating essays—one a "core" score for content and one a "holistic" score to be used as a measure of students' communication skill—no one but me saw a theoretical problem.

I argued that the holistic score should, in fact, comprehend both content and expression and there was no justification for two separate—and different—rubrics. The writing rubric was the same for all texts in all the different disciplinary tasks because its criteria were strictly linguistic and structural. But the core score rubric was different for every step in every task because the criteria were based on the number and complexity of specific concepts treated. When I was the second reader on the essays, I found that the majority of the first readers, no matter which discipline they represented, consistently awarded different scores for "core" and "holistic" evaluations. My rhetorical question was "If you don't understand the language the student is using, how can you evaluate the ideas it attempts to articulate?" When I expressed my feeling that the theoretical error in this procedure was just as serious as those found by the other disciplinary specialists, I was silenced for holding up the reading by the other participants and the ETS trainers.

If writing people *are* enlisted to help teach students to write in other disciplines, it is usually for "remediation" of grammar and expression. What none of the nonrhetoric people understand is the heavy onus on the writer to "sell" his or her ideas, using rhetorical principles to achieve Burkean identification and effective Aristotelian appeals. Identification in this sense is nothing short of being accepted as a member of another community through a shared language and its embedded values. As Burke claims, "we are clearly in the region of rhetoric when considering the identifications whereby a specialized activity makes one a participant in some social or economic class. 'Belonging' in this sense is rhetorical" (Burke 27-8).

Only after extensive faculty development do most faculty and administrators begin to understand that the thinking/writing process is recursive and codependent on conceptual development for its growth. I have only begun to broach the subject of socially constructed reality through mutually negotiated language. Such theory goes far beyond the limits of interest to nonspecialists. Yet, through successful rhetorical approaches with key individuals and committees, I hear the writing vocabulary I purvey for these previously unarticulated rhetorical concepts being used by my frequent conversants. This indicates to me that I have successfully constructed some new realities about writing that these speakers had not had before. It becomes especially gratifying when that language is used in administrative policy, general education outcomes statements, funding allocations for faculty development, nonrhetoric graduate assistants' syllabi, and students' reflective writing on their mid-career (rising junior) writing assessment.

In 1999, as I mentioned earlier, the business college again hired a retired business professor to "revamp" the business writing program, both graduate and undergraduate. Not only was she to try yet another structure for the MBA students, she was to develop an undergraduate writing program, which had never really existed except for a token four writing emphasis courses in the six business majors — none of which required more than simple emulation of typical reports in economics, marketing, management and policy, and management information systems. Business majors are not required or even encouraged to take the upper division business writing course offered by the writing program. Of the typically eight sections offered every semester, we may enroll three or four business students who take it voluntarily.

In the business college, the only professor who ever taught a writing-intensive course in the accounting major left in disgust 8 years ago for lack of support, and he was never replaced. Of all the business faculty, he had been the only one willing to serve on the Intercollegiate Writing Committee, which was constituted to include *two* faculty members from each of our 11 colleges. The finance major has never offered a writing intensive course, despite a writing emphasis course having been a graduation requirement for all majors for the last 18 years.

As a business person, the newly hired writing director had the ethos to persuade the college to hire two English graduate students to grade all the papers for the MBA program, 75 reports apiece from each of three core courses, but she had little time and few resources to devote to the proposed undergraduate writing program. Because she dispensed knowledge, she did not actually read the graduate papers herself at all for issues of expression and effectiveness — just content — and there were no norming sessions to develop a common vocabulary and rubric for defining *rhetorically effective writing*. Our hierarchically inferior writing teachers merely graded skills, and students received double scores — a generic "writing" grade, and a class-specific "content" grade. But as Katherine Gottschalk argued in her 1994 CCCC paper, "we should not work with faculty members who want the writing program to supply the "writing segment," that is, to supply an unwanted addition to the "real" subject. Instead, the writing program's goal for faculty members is one they already have: to improve their teaching of their subject matter, through improved attention to language" (5).

By her second hiring year, our new business writing director was unsuccessful in recruiting any more English graduate assistants (read "graders") for the MBA program, to which she now had to commit all of her own time. She turned over the entire undergraduate "writing core" to post-graduates in English. As the WAC coordinator, I was unsuccessful in arranging a meeting with the director, who ostensibly supervised the English person, to find out the details of the undergraduate program. What I gleaned from the English recruit is that she "helps students write" for their required upper division business courses. She apparently functioned as a free-floating tutor, workshop leader, editor, and proofreader. I don't know because she herself was confused by her charge and invented her job as she went along—completely unassisted by any grounding in rhetorical theory and composition pedagogy. In the last four years this writing director has been able to hire three underemployed English graduates to teach a newly installed junior writing course—none of whom have business training or experience.

History lesson over. This is how I analyze it. Rhetoric and composition specialists have a big sales job to do in order to work with disciplinary faculty who teach "marketable" theory and content—and this isn't just business faculty—in order to persuade them that rhetorical knowledge (not the same as *skill*) has value for their students, value that can translate into professional and economic benefits. We can do that by communicating two well-understood theoretical concepts in our field to our nonrhetoric colleagues—creating identification and using effective rhetorical appeals—and by showing them how to teach these concepts.

CREATING IDENTIFICATION

First, we have to establish some mutual ground. We have to identify common concepts and values with those programs with whom we partner to prepare students for the marketplace. As Gottschalk says, we have to identify with something they already want—to improve their students' subject learning. Robert Jones and Joseph Comprone encourage the dialogue between writing teachers and other disciplinary faculty to aim "toward balancing humanistic methods of encouraging more active and collaborative learning in Writing across the Curriculum courses with reinforcing the ways of knowing and the writing conventions of different discourse communities"(61). What this means to me is that we start by identifying with their goals and then show them how rhetorical theory can help them achieve those goals.

When working with marketing students in my workshop, I saw immediately that the principles of marketing are exactly those of rhetoric. We just use different terms for what we do, but the values are the same. What people who have to market anything—a product, a service, themselves, a curriculum—do is *market analysis* in order to identify a *market niche*, or need, that can be filled. Even if the need doesn't exist, they can create one through *advertising*. Then they develop *products/services* to fit their market. Rhetoricians do exactly the same things. They do *audience analysis, assess the particular situation,* and *identify a rhetorical purpose.* They design appropriate *texts* using *persuasive language* to address the situation and appeal to the particular audience.

Outside the academy, business and industry people understand the critical importance of identifying their market and being thoroughly familiar with its needs and desires. They understand that whatever product or service they are selling has to meet those requirements or cut back development, lose their funding, or go out of business. They hold two wrong assumptions about rhetoric: (a) They don't recognize that rhetoric does the same thing as business, sell *ideas* and package them in language that the target market will entertain and "buy"; and (b) they behave as though they believe ideas exist independently of the words used to express them, considering them an add-on skill, which although valuable, has little to do with the ideas conveyed, as long as they get results. So the disjunct occurs because, for example, business relies exclusively on business theory to achieve a return on investment; whereas rhetoric teaches a theoretical process that can be applied to achieving any field's social goals. What we have to show is that investment in learning the latter will help achieve the former and produce a more marketable and effective professional.

How then do we create this identification between rhetoric and other disciplines? For one thing, we rhetoricians have to give *our* audience what it wants . . . instruction in editing and conventional genres. Then we have to persuade them that this *knowledge* alone does not provide the long-term benefits they want. They want a fish; we want to teach them fishing. We need to collaborate with our nonwriting colleagues to accomplish both objectives. We need to articulate the long-term benefits that instruction in rhetorical theory can provide any professional person. We need to do and share our research . . . how much writing and in how many genres does the average practitioner of X field write, what's at stake when she does, how does effective writing promote professional success, increase business? For example, we could quote the facts by textbook writers such as Locker, and Bovee and Thill, who *have* done their homework: the average company produces 18,000 pages of paper for each white-collar employee, with 4000 pages added each year (Bovee and Thill 23); nonbusiness entities such as the air force produce 500 million pages per year (Locker 6); and overall, the United States generates about 30 billion documents a year (Bovee and Thill 23). Writing is, in fact, how jobs get accomplished everywhere.

We need to have this kind of information and answers ready to hand. Bringing in successful practicing informants, particularly those who have risen to executive positions or those charged with training employees to improve their performance, increases the ethos of our theory enormously. Most of these authorities, as do those on Arizona's Writing Advisory

Council, will tell academic faculty and students just how much their own success has relied on effective writing, or how difficult it was to accomplish goals when their written communications were ineffective or lost credibility for linguistic problems, or they relied too heavily on oral transmission of messages. Kitty Locker claims that "'[a]lmost all businesses require their accountants, salespeople, and managers to write their own documents'" (Cason 1), and Bruce, Hirst, and Keene state that "'[t]he higher you go in management, the more time you will spend reading reports—and writing them'" (Cason 1).

After 4 years of earning a marginal living as an independent writing consultant and trainer, I found I still had little credibility in the workplace because I was an *English* academic. The successful trainers were business people, people who offered quick, easy, and expensive one-day writing workshops, in which they dispensed formulaic approaches to typical business scenarios, lists of effective and ineffective organization patterns and diction choices, recipes for conventional genres, and the "seven worst grammar errors to avoid." Corporations are willing to spend $43 billion a year trying to improve the effectiveness of their employees, much of which goes into such writing workshops because 65% of human resources executives state that their employees' writing needs improvement ((Boone and Kurtz 27). Rhetoricians can certainly provide this education *and* give their business associates "added value" by sharing the rhetorical principles behind these effective techniques. But rhetoricians have to do what non-writing people want first, drill the skills, in order to create opportunities to explain the theory and its potential benefits.

As the course director for the business and technical writing courses offered by the Writing Program in the English Department, I found that people teaching and practicing technological fields who send us their students understand better than business faculty and businesses that they are actually selling *ideas* to a wide range of possible audiences. My advisory council includes several practicing engineers, engineering patent attorneys, and research and development supervisors, who have made the necessity of rhetorical analysis clear to university faculty on numerous occasions. They have readily picked up rhetorical jargon by seeing its similarity to language they themselves invented to describe their writing/thinking processes. I myself enjoyed a very positive collaboration with two engineering professors to co-teach the required senior design course in electrical and computer engineering. Our teaching together helped students see how important writing was in the research and development stages of engineering practice—not to mention in the manual writing and marketing stages.

These engineers and their students were far more receptive to rhetorical theory because they saw its applicability to writing proposals for real consumers, persuading their teammates how to implement their projects, showing timely progress toward completion of projects, and remembering who the eventual users of the technology would be and how little this audience would know about it. Again their writing is goal driven, but understanding the enormous diversity of readers they had to address just to pursue one project, and how critical it was to persuade each reader, made them grasp rhetorical theory quickly. They could apply it immediately in real and varied contexts that could not be assumed unproblematically.

What probably accounts for the differences in their receptivity to our theory and that of business people is that, even though most are in the "business" of developing and marketing new technology, the long road toward those goals includes much more "selling" of their ideas. Ideas are hard commodities to market—especially new ideas. For engineers, it's not just a matter of inventing and selling a better mousetrap. It's a matter of finding out if anyone still *needs* a mousetrap; whether a mousetrap is the solution to a new problem; what it takes to persuade supervisors, intellectual property lawyers, the patent office, and potential customers that what they've invented is not just another mousetrap after all, but a whole new thing that does something significantly different and better than anything else currently available! In other words, engineers may find it easier to identify with the value of rhetorical fishing lessons.

Yet rhetoricians like Cindy Berrie are making important overtures to business fields. In her 1996 Rhetoric Society of America Conference paper "Prospects for Rhetoric across Disciplines and Workplaces," she actually uses the word *rhetoric* in conjunction with accounting. Citing the American Accounting Association's claim that despite an overwhelming emphasis on writing skills, accounting firms still claim accounting graduates do not have adequate communication skills and "therefore, are not meeting the needs of others." She consequently argues that "rhetoric must take on a larger and more obvious role in business communications, particularly in the accounting industry, and not confine itself to English classes." (Berrie)

Both the business representatives and the engineers on our Advisory Council provided my colleagues across the curriculum with detailed charts showing their writing/thinking process at each stage of a particular workplace document. These were clearly rhetorical analyses that helped the writers plan all aspects of their communication. In 2001, the electrical and computing engineering department actually began using a portfolio of student writing to assess the effectiveness of the program itself. The judging committee includes both faculty and industry people . . . the common assumption now being that if engineers can't effectively articulate what they know to multiple, specific audiences, they won't be very effective engineers.

In the English Department, our technical writing students learn writing theory and process much faster than do the business students, who were ironically locked out of their business majors if they failed our universally required mid-career writing assessment. When attempting to appeal their score, they claimed the analytic writing sample had "nothing to do with business." The engineering programs, on the other hand, offer support services to those who failed and/or sent them to take a 5-week refresher workshop with us. Although the reverse situation could also occur at another institution, the difference lies in how clearly each discipline recognizes the need to use such theoretical approaches as contextual and textual analyses and "usability testing" with real readers in the processes of creating written texts that achieve their desired results.

Unless written field knowledge is forced to stand the market test, most academics simply require students to emulate the scholarly texts valued by the academy. Preprofessional programs, on the other hand, are held accountable, not only by outside employers, but by accrediting associations and funding agencies. When these pressures are applied to academic programs, rhetorical awareness rises significantly. We have seen this happen at Arizona with the new Accreditation Board for Engineering and Technology (ABET) requirements, which were the driving force behind the portfolio assessment of the engineering program. ABET says engineering has to teach students to write effectively about engineering concepts. If our graduate business school were to experience a drop in the employment rate of its MBAs, it would surely respond by attempting a more sincere effort to address writing—in theory. It has already experienced a drop in qualified applicants. But the solution was to hire a new dean and associate dean, neither of whom sees a theoretical approach to teaching writing as developmental and integral to teaching the concepts in their curriculum.

It appears to me, therefore, that it is primarily the business school with whom rhetoric faculty at Arizona have to establish some common ground and mutual language. On rhetoric's part, we have to do a cost/profit analysis to learn how much it will cost us to identify with our business colleagues' value system and what we get out of it. How much will we have to invest in the necessary outreach and dialogues, how much research time can we afford to devote to their field's needs and practices in order to effect a meeting of the minds? How much rhetorical theory and pedagogy are we willing to translate and/or postpone until we establish a working relationship? If we create this new market for our theory, can we meet the demand? These are questions each institution and each faculty must consider, and the only justification for doing so at all is to give our own taxpayers value for their money. Every institution serves a particular constituency—*context* in our vocabulary—and each needs to do its own market analysis. But given the recent public calls for general reform of undergraduate education across the country, such as the Boyer Commission Report, by getting back to foundational knowledge and fundamental concepts, writing, like math, has received more attention from politicians and press than it has for a couple of decades.

What we have to gain, then, is insurance of public support for writing instruction—a very big benefit, given the current state of public funding and confidence level in our programs. As the *Chronicle of Higher Education* pointed out when discussing why states were raising admissions standards, "Lawmakers . . . put little emphasis on basic research, especially when it isn't tied to state priorities or teaching" ("Massachusetts" A29). Most of our state legislators are business people, most boards of regents are business people, most of the employers who hire our graduates are in business. We can't continue to alienate ourselves from the market and workplace, even if only through neglect to remember the perspectives of our own multiple audiences. We entice them with the fish— to create identification—and then sell them fishing lessons. For the very survival of our writing programs, we have to raise the profile and value of what we teach because as Gottschalk said, "A writing program that occupies an adversarial or 'janitorial' position is unlikely to succeed" (6).

According to trainers at Arizona's University Teaching Center, only about 15% of the general population are introverts, but nearly 70% of academics are. Thus, we're easily stereotyped as hiding in our ivory tower developing our theories and unwilling to communicate what we do and why it's important to the population at large. Scientists have been brought to this realization abruptly, when public funding for their research has suddenly been cut and the media began questioning the value of "pure science" or theoretical research. Consequently, there has been a resurgence of interest in public rhetoric on the part of many scientists. From Aristotle to Kenneth Burke, theories about the effective means for accomplishing rhetorical ends are being revisited. Translating disciplinary jargon into "plain English" for the benefit of nonspecialists has become a priority in many specialized fields—for very real economic reasons. It needs to become a priority in ours as well.

We thus cannot achieve a framework for identification with our rhetorical audiences until we find a common language for shared goals and values. In giving advice to business writers, Barbara Krasner-Khait recommends thinking "like the suits," and her advice is highly rhetorical: (a) understand the client's business, (b) know your target audience, (c) become a turnaround artist (she gives average times it should take an effective writer to produce such texts as presentations, brochures, technical documents, and marketing letters), (d) broaden your skills by getting experience in copywriting, reporting, technical documentation, web content, and presentation development; and (e) price your services right (31-2). In other words, she also says we create value for our work by placing an appropriate value on it. Rhetoricians should learn to "think like the suits," too.

As in most cases of intercultural communication, bilingualism is an asset, code switching for different cultures a necessity. I use the term *code switching* from a social constructionist perspective. By that I mean, through the acquisition of new linguistic labels for concepts, we can actually understand the concepts and learn to think in the same way that the native speakers of the other code do. By doing so, we develop a deeper identification through linguistic negotiation in order to achieve shared working realities. Business faculty teach students that successful practitioners have to use the language of their target market to attract customers, and so do rhetoricians in order to sell our ideas. It's identification; it's ethos. But business faculty and students, who speak our dominant cultural language, are not motivated to learn rhetorical language, just as in the world arena dominant English speakers are not motivated to learn foreign languages. Yet business writing teachers Sorenson, Kennedy and Ramirez introduce their business writing text with the following assertions about the effects of symbolic representation in language:

> Symbols are shared signs which stand for something else. . . .
>
> Although it is only through the use of symbols that we can represent our meaning to others, because of individual limitations and difficulties in the communication process itself, words and actions may both fail. To increase the chance that we will succeed, we can use simple words that mean the same thing to most people, we can repeat ourselves by saying the same thing in different ways to ensure understanding, and we can explain and define our words and actions whenever a listener seems to need help. . . .
>
> A major quality of symbols is that they are frequently interpreted or understood differently. Our interactions depend upon our previous experiences and habits of interpretation. (2)

Thus, without using our specialized vocabulary, it's up to us to persuade nonspecialists that understanding rhetorical principles will benefit them. We have to code-switch to create a dialogue. We have to talk about "targeting our communication market," "selling ideas" (marketing routinely uses the phrase "selling a concept"), "returning value on investment," and "cost–benefit" ratio.

How then do we establish this common language that doesn't end with superficial code switching, but achieves an interdisciplinary culture that shares the same understanding and value on rhetorical principles? As foreign language teachers know, we are also acculturated by acquiring a new tongue, the realization behind the English-only controversy. When in Rome, speak like the Romans—but remember the *particular* audience, purpose, and situation. Language is too nuanced, value laden, and context specific, even within cultures, simply to legislate a dominant lexicon. It's our individual conversations that will negotiate and effect our rhetorical goals, not a global assault on an entire culture. It is our personal ethos that will prevail.

USING EFFECTIVE APPEALS

The first means of establishing a shared reality and our ethical and pathetic appeals in a market culture is, therefore, talking like the natives. The next thing, of course, is discovering what motivates each individual we speak to, an essential heuristic for invention, and locating the "available means of persuasion" for our logical appeal. From Aristotle's comprehensive taxonomy (*On Rhetoric*, 2.2-17) to Kenneth Burke's covert motives (*Rhetoric of Motives*) and Robert Hochheiser's pragmatic list (*Don't State It . . . Communicate It!*), appealing to the audience is a rhetorical necessity. I've observed many 1-day workshops in which business writing consultants effectively convey strategies for identifying readers' motives and choosing appropriate appeals. The problem is that the participants never understand, in these short exposures, the *why* that makes them work, which limits their ability to use them consistently and effectively under the diverse conditions of real-world communications.

Rhetorical theory can benefit practitioners of any field. If an academic discipline only teaches the conventions of a limited number of field genres, mostly those associated with disciplinary research, students of those disciplines cannot anticipate or cope with the proliferation of contexts, genres, and conventions they will face when they actually practice in their fields. For example, Smith, Nelson, and Moncada list among their 16 most frequent types of accounting communications such genres unfamiliar to college students as working papers, systems documentation, electronic messages, review reports, tax research reports, audit programs, and performance reviews (44). Just as economics and accounting graduates have to understand the *theories* behind the conventional strategies and principles to practice those fields, they also need the principles for successfully meeting the communications requirements presented by the new problems they will face in their professional careers. WAC advocates who teach writing-intensive courses in accounting and economics have also realized the benefits of writing to the learning of those field's theoretical concepts (Hansen, Cohen and Spencer, and Smith, Nelson, and Moncada).

What rhetoricians must be able to convey is that learning to fish gives more return on investment than buying the fish. In terms of rhetorical *topoi*, it's a question of the *quality* of possible benefits. Market-wise appeals have to begin with the logical appeal. How can the audience benefit from understanding rhetoric? What will make our "pitches" credible to our market in the other academic disciplines. As I said, we have to speak their language authoritatively, so we can state the benefits in terms they recognize. That means we really have to understand how business is conducted, how business enterprises succeed, and exactly how writing accomplishes those things. We should try to acquire some field expertise through research and encourage our students to pursue real-world projects and shadow business people writing in the line of their work. We can collect actual business documents through advisory groups or our individual contacts, and bring these "native informants" into classes and faculty workshops. Whenever we teach professional workplace writing or attempt to implement disciplinary writing programs, we need to enlist the cooperation, not only of faculty, but also of administrators, who must value and support them.

That means we have to do what all enterprises have to do—advertise. We have to devise market-specific advertising campaigns to sell rhetorical principles. Isolated academic introverts have a hard time doing this because it requires going out and "selling" ourselves, as well as our "product"—the principles of rhetorical theory. In my own institution, for example, I need to practice the appeals identified by Jib Fowles, whose article "Advertising's Fifteen Basic Appeals" is required reading for our first-year composition students. He begins by quoting Marshall McLuhan, "'The continuous pressure is to create ads more and more in the image of audience motives and desires'"—classic pathetic appeal. Fowles lists several emotional appeals that rhetoricians could use to advantage: the needs for affiliation, achievement, aggressiveness, dominance, prominence, attention, and autonomy, for instance (Alvarado and Cully 3, 4).

In addition to doing our homework in actual business practice and advertising what we do, we should probably model our rhetoric for business schools, students, and graduates on the current popular business publications, which are a booming industry. The forum section of the third issue of 2001 *Management Communication Quarterly* argues that academic scholars of business rhetoric cannot afford to ignore the genres and styles of popular business writing. Australian academician Mike Pratt crossed over into the world of popular managerial writing and claims, after analyzing the best seller *Peak Performance*, "I don't think it will be possible for me to return to the formal approach of academic journals with any degree of enthusiasm. The knowledge of the limited audience for one's scholarly endeavors through this medium further minimizes motivation" (481).

In other words, we also have to adopt the business ethos—which means becoming not only business knowledgeable and fluent, but being extroverted, competitive, aggressive, and capable of taking the initiative to promote and advertise what we do. For example, we have to do top-down persuasion—sell what we have first to executives and administrators and observe the stated and unstated rules of corporate behavior for creating value, looking for opportunity, providing effective management, and commanding equal respect and pay for what we do. In the market mentality, if you give away what you have, it must not have real value. We lose ethos by it in the academy because few will identify with low-value service providers, as Gottschalk has argued. When I taught 2-week writing workshops in businesses, I could charge $40 to $60 an hour (which had to build in the necessary unseen preparation time). But at the business school, I was only paid one third of a humanities faculty salary—hardly comparable to that of the business professors I worked with. We lose credibility if we are rhetorically unable to create value for ourselves and our work. Thus, we need to practice our appeals on those with power and influence from whom we need support to do our business.

Thanks to my worksite experience, I was able to sell myself with an ethical appeal that enhanced my pathos and logos. I took the opportunity to interview managers, human resource people, tellers, and department heads. I collected samples of what they wrote, and I used them to teach rhetorical analysis, not forms. I listened to what they wanted and gave it to them, but used the opportunity to focus on context awareness for choosing appropriate content and effective text design, diction, style, and tone. I didn't sell them a fish—a standard form or formula- but taught them how to use the right equipment for the precise fish they hoped to land. Though many of us may not have such field research opportunities, we can certainly do similar kinds of interviewing and research among our academic colleagues and encourage our students to do this research in the line of pursuing real-world projects that help them apply their disciplinary knowledge through writing.

Yet, as I said, even in the workplace, I still had the taint of the writing specialist—the *English* teacher. What's in a name? Everything! Names put labels on realities and construct them in particular ways. Rhetoricians have two terms to deal with that have socially negative connotations and hinder our ethos when working with people in other fields: *rhetoric* and *English*. In the popular mind, rhetoric is without either logical or ethical appeals. It's understood as being preceded by the word *empty*—an indefensible, opinionated rant. *English* identifies us with a discipline that is literary and humanistic, whose leanings *are* sometimes antithetical to the pragmatic needs of practical business—more interactional than transactional. But as Kennedy, Sorenson, and Ramirez claim, all communication is fundamentally transactional (4). If rhetoricians could jettison those terms or reconstruct the realities they imply, we would have an easier time of it. Many of our potential audiences would "buy" *communication specialist*, but coming mostly from English departments, we would risk stepping on the toes of our faculty colleagues in speech and media arts. Again, we create our individual ethos, pathos, and logos in the particular dialogues we participate in. We can't assume that, as a discipline, we deserve the right to be heard, and like all other professionals, we have to be language sensitive. Just as other academics, we still have to establish our own credentials and prove our worth.

Whichever approach we choose, we have to rely on creating a strong personal pathetic appeal to counter our discipline's poor ethos and logos.

Once we achieve our audiences' sympathetic attention, we will have the opportunities to validate our argument—to warrant the claim that understanding rhetorical principles will benefit them. Naturally, identifying with the audience is a good way to begin our pathetic appeal. But just as classical rhetoricians did, contemporary business people understand the need to appeal to an audience's (client's, customer's, consumer's) higher and lower emotions.

The higher emotional appeals, particularly to other academics, administrators, and CEOs are preferable. What can we say that will persuade them to change their minds or behaviors because the decision is right, honorable, loyal, beneficial, enlightening, or altruistic. Allowing our conversants to act upon positive overt motives is the most successful pathetic appeal to people who see themselves as intelligent, effective, and valuable leaders. In order to do so, we can talk in terms of helping our students become more "marketable," helping managers acquire better communication skills, enabling positive teamwork, creating healthy work environments, facilitating learning in both the academy and the workplace, and sustaining professional, social and business relationships. These are qualitatively *good* motives, and people want to be credited for having them. They would be doing the right thing!

Naturally, however, we can't forget appeals to the covert motives as well. Hochheiser has supplied an almost exhaustive list appropriate to this endeavor. For example, he lists the following appeals among others: offering opportunities for fun, power, pride, fame, financial success, revenge, status, and praise, or opportunities to avoid failure, loss, pain, risk, rejection, and embarrassment (11-2). Thus we have to talk about raising institutional rank and reputation, increasing student full-time equivalency, raising entrance and exit standards, attracting better students or more "customers," acquiring more money, growing, dominating the competitors, or avoiding loss of public support, customers, money, and value. In other words, we emphasize potential success for achieving whatever particular goal drives our specific audiences. We can't generalize. If our MBA program wants to stay among the top ten graduate business schools and attract only the highest caliber of student, I have to talk about improving the marketability of their students by citing big people in successful businesses and tracking our students' recruitment by status of employers. How many of our students land jobs in Fortune 500 corporations? How many run their own successful businesses? What do *these* people tell us about the importance of writing to their careers?

All of this research is just good business practice, and in the academy it needs to count as theoretical research in our field. It is. How can we know if our current state of knowledge is accurate unless we continue to test it? (Note how many rhetorical questions I've relied on here. This, too, is one of the ways business people "hook" their audiences and engage them to think about what they're selling.)

CONCLUSION

Thus, we have to create shared working realities through dialogue with other disciplinary specialists and workplace professionals to achieve identification and make effective appeals. We have to "learn the language" because communication transacts constructed reality. To do so, we have to get out of our disciplinary box and do our ethnographical research. We must, therefore, grapple with Clifford Geertz's anthropological problem of researcher objectivity ("From the Natives's Point of View: On the Nature of Anthropological Understanding," *Interpretive Social Science*, 1979), which compromises our ethos. In order to construct new realities through language with our market conversants, we have to be open to reconstruction of our own. Dialogic exchanges involve the transformation of both parties by the linguistic negotiation at work.

An encouraging sign that other professional writing specialists are thinking along the same lines is the recently published and auspiciously titled *Competitive Communication: A **Rhetoric** for Modern Business* [boldface is mine] by Barry Eckhouse (Oxford, 1999). Eckhouse organizes the entire text around effective rhetorical appeals using business language to identify with traditional business writing goals. His first chapter is called "Rhetoric and Competitive Advantage," in which he connects "discovering the client" with "discovering the audience." Chapter 3 is titled "Classical Argument and Modern Business," in which a discussion of the form of claims follows that on the "principle of exchange." He proffers the desired fish by giving actual fishing lessons in diction, syntax, punctuation, and grammar in chapters 8-12, but as each chapter title says, for the purpose of "Managing Ethos." Eckhouse's advocacy of business cultural immersion, along with similar recommendations by Berrie and Krasner-Khait mentioned above show how we can "boldly go" into the marketplace to sell our theoretical wares.

REFERENCES

Alvarado, Beth, and Barbara Cully, eds. *Entry Points*. New York: Longman, 1999.
Aristotle. *On Rhetoric: A Theory of Civil Discourse*. (Trans. and Intro. George A Kennedy). New York: Oxford, 1991.
Berrie, Cindy. "Prospect for Rhetoric Across Disciplines and Workplaces." Rhetoric Society of American Conference. Tucson, AZ, 1996.

Boone, Louis, E., and David L. Kurtz. *Contemporary Business Communication.* Englewood Cliffs, NJ: Prentice Hall, 1994.

Bovee, Courtland L., and John Thill. *Business Communication Today.* 4th ed. New York: McGraw-Hill, 1995.

Bruce, Harry J., Russel K. Hirst, and Michael L. Keene. *A Short Guide to Business Writing.* Englewood Cliffs, NJ: Prentice Hall, 1995.

Burke, Kenneth. *A Rhetoric of Motives.* Berkeley: U of California P, 1950.

Cason, Robert E. *Writing for the Business World.* Upper Saddle River, NJ: Prentice Hall, 1997.

Cohen, Avi J. and John Spencer. "Using Writing Across the Curriculum in Economics: Is Taking the Plunge Worth It?" *Journal of Economic Education* 24.3 (1993): 219-30.

Eckhouse, Barry. *Competitive Communication: A Rhetoric for Modern Business.* New York: Oxford, 1999.

Geertz, Clifford. "From the Native's Point of View: On the Nature of Anthropological Understanding." *Interpretive Social Science.* Eds. P. Rabinow and W. M. Sullivan. Berkeley: U. of California P, 1979, 225-41.

Gottschalk, Katherine K. "The Writing Program at the University." *ADE Bulletin* 112 (Winter 1995): 1-6.

Hansen, W. Lee. "Teaching a Writing Intensive Course in Economics." *Journal of Economic Education.* 24.3 (1998): 213-18.

Hochheiser, Robert M. *Don't State It . . . Communicate It!* Woodbury, NY: Barron's, 1985.

Jones, Robert, and Joseph J. Comprone. "Where Do We Go Next in Writing Across the Curriculum?" *College Composition and Communication* 44 (1993): 59-68.

Krasner-Khait, Barbara. "Five Keys to Corporate Writing. To Write Successfully for Big business—Think Like the Suits." *The Writer's Digest* 80.9 (2000): 31-32, 54.

Locker, Kitty O. *Business and Administrative Communication.* 3rd ed. Boston: Irwin, 1995.

"Massachusetts Raises Standards for Admission to Public Colleges." *The Chronicle of Higher Education.* January 12, 1996, A28.

Pratt, Michael J. "A Story of Peak Performance." *Management Communications Quarterly* 14 (2001): 476-83.

Smith, Douglas C., Sandra J. Nelson, and Susan M. Moncada. "What Writing Skills Should Accounting Students Be Taught." *Business Education Forum* 52.4 (1998): 43-4.

Sorenson, Ritch, Grace Kennedy, and Ida Ramirez. *Business and Management Communication: A Guide Book.* Upper Saddle River, NJ: Allyn & Bacon, 2000.

Williams, Joseph M. *Style: Ten Lessons in Clarity and Grace.* New York: Longman, 2000.

11 Consuming Composition

Understanding and Changing the Marketplace of College Writing

Kristine Hansen

Brigham Young University

Those of us who teach in or administer writing programs at the college level face a rapidly changing educational marketplace. In the 1970s, our only "competitors" were other colleges and universities, whose courses we might be asked to accept for transfer credit, and the advanced placement (AP) program, which was relatively small and apparently justified in its claim to offer college-level education to well-prepared high school seniors seeking a challenge for which their agemates were not ready. But these were friendly competitors, each filling a niche in the market, yet really doing similar jobs. Now, however, more nontraditional competitors have entered the market: private entrepreneurial colleges staffed almost exclusively by adjunct faculty who have other day jobs; online universities without proper campuses; dual-credit or concurrent enrollment programs that aim to provide high school *and* college education in the same course; and a rapidly expanding AP program that is being aggressively promoted to nontraditional and younger students and is now starting to establish "pre-AP" programs in the public schools.

As if the diversification of "suppliers" were not enough, the "customers" for writing courses are changing as well. Education is increasingly viewed as tantamount to a product to be purchased, rather than as a long-term process that promotes the development of individuals' intellectual, social, and personal abilities, preparing them for the demands of participation in a democratic society. Many students, as well as their parents, and—increasingly—politicians seem to view education as a set of goods to be purchased from the vendor who offers the best price or the quickest and most efficient way to acquire the product. Just as many of today's children are attempting to grow up faster than ever—dressing in fashion clothing at 8 years old, dieting at 9, dating at 10, coping with depression and stress at 11, and drinking, smoking, and doing drugs at 12—in many cases they are also seeking and being offered a microwave version of education. They want to be *done* faster than ever in acquiring the diplomas and degrees that have become synonymous with credentials for participation in professions. There are increasing opportunities and pressures for them to enter college with enough credit hours already earned that they can graduate sooner and start seeking the economic rewards that generally follow from having those credentials.

What has brought us to the point that the values, the vocabulary, and the practices of the economic marketplace have so insinuated themselves into the institution of education? What, if anything, should college writing programs do in response to this bewildering brave new world we find our-selves in? This chapter attempts to give some answers. First, I explore what Lyotard and others have called the commodification of education, showing how converging forces in contemporary consumer culture have changed traditional notions of education. Then I discuss how the lack of careful articulation and alignment between the secondary schools and institutions of higher education has created a vacuum allowing competitors of tradition-al first-year writing courses to flourish, particularly dual-credit and AP pro-grams. Finally, I propose ways that we who work in college writing pro-grams at nonprofit institutions can attempt to redefine education in terms of outcomes rather than in terms of credit hours accumulated. I argue that we must think creatively and work cooperatively with teachers and administra-tors at other levels of education in order to educate students who are not only economically viable but also well prepared for meaningful civic and personal lives. Because the institutions in which we work exist in an exceed-ingly complex educational market, we must consider carefully what we offer that is unique and how we can persuade students to see the value of investing their time and efforts in acquiring a genuine education in writing rather than consuming and amassing credit hours offered as its surrogates.

THE COMMODIFICATION OF EDUCATION

When economists use the term *commodity*, they mean undifferentiated products, such as wheat and beef or T-shirts and tube socks, the purveyors of which are called "price-takers" because they have to accept the price the market is willing to offer. If they ask for more, the demand for the com-modity falls to nothing, and the commodity doesn't sell. So savvy mar-keters try not to be purveyors of a mere commodity; they want to be price-setters rather than price-takers. They look for a way to differentiate their product, in the way, for example, that Starbucks markets coffee. It's really just coffee, but it is marketed in such a way that consumers believe some value has been added to the product, and they are willing to pay a higher price for it.

Although this sense of commodity is part of what I aim to get at here and later in this chapter, I want to invoke Lyotard's notion of *commodification*, raised in his discussion of how the nature of knowledge has been changed by the emergence of computers. Lyotard proposes that "the proliferation of information-processing machines" has transformed the "circulation of knowledge," just as improved transportation systems transformed the circulation of humans, and just as the media were transformed by advancements in the circulation of visual images and sounds. The effect of increasing computerization is to change the very nature of knowledge because knowledge "can fit into the new channels and become operational only if learning is translated into quantities of information" (4). In fact, Lyotard predicts that any kind of knowledge that is not susceptible to this kind of translation will be abandoned. He continues,

> We may thus expect a thorough exteriorisation of knowledge with respect to the "knower," at whatever point he or she may occupy the knowledge process. The old principle that the acquisition of knowledge is indissociable from the training (*Bildung*) of minds, or even of individuals, is becoming obsolete and will become ever more so. The relationship of the suppliers and users of knowledge to the knowledge they supply and use is now tending, and will increasingly tend, to assume the form already taken by the relationship of commodity producers and consumers to the commodities they produce and consume—that is, the form of value. Knowledge is and will be produced in order to be sold, it is and will be consumed in order to be valorized in a new production: in both cases, the goal is exchange. Knowledge ceases to be an end in itself, it loses its "use-value." (4-5)

Knowledge and the processes of learning and teaching are commodified, then, when they are viewed as mere objects in an exchange, valuable not in themselves but only for the material advantages they will procure for the individual. Lyotard adds that "it is not hard to visualize learning circulating along the same lines as money, instead of for its 'educational' value or political (administrative, diplomatic, military) importance" (6). He thus suggests that the traditional purpose of applying knowledge to improve society will also be a casualty of the commodification of knowledge.

Lyotard's prediction is an ominous one, in my opinion, foretelling a future in which a college transcript will be more significant than the processes by which it was acquired. Yet several observers of the educational scene in Canada, New Zealand, and England believe that Lyotard's predictions have come to pass. Writing about higher education in New Zealand, Peter Roberts states that the increasing privatization of educational processes has transformed the public sphere to the point that the old ideals of "welfare, community, and a sense of obligation toward others" have been replaced by the ideals of the market. He presents multiple indicators that education has become a commodity—"something to be produced, packaged, sold, traded, outsourced, franchised, and consumed." Canadians Mike Sosteric, Mike Gismondi, and Gina Ratkovic similarly argue that universities have been "colonized" by the discourses of consumerism, enterprise, efficiency, accountability, and market discipline to the point that traditional ideals of social betterment, public debate, teaching, and research are endangered. They argue that as Canadian universities become less dependent on public funding and more on "private sources of revenue that come with strings attached," the universities will become "Fordist-style degree mills." In these mills, the intellectual labor of professors will be Taylorized to the point that they lose the freedom to create curriculum, use the pedagogical techniques they deem best for the subject and the students, and choose books and other materials because these will be created and "canned" elsewhere. The result will be that students are forced to pay more and herded into larger classes where they will prepare to take their places in the corporations that have colonized the universities. Sosteric et al. cite Norman Fairclough's definition of commodification:

> Commodification is the process whereby social domains and institutions, whose concern is not producing commodities in the narrower economic sense of goods for sale, come nevertheless to be organized and conceptualized in terms of commodity production, distribution, and consumption.

Following this process, universities are construed as sites of production, professors as laborers, courses as products, and students as consumers of those products.

Taking a somewhat different tack in his analysis of current funding methods of public universities in England, Hugh Wilmott shows how and why faculty research has become a commodity. Universities are generally public-sector organizations funded by surplus revenues generated in the private sector and then appropriated by the state in the form of taxes. State control of universities has increased because politicians and civil servants retain their jobs by safeguarding the "accumulation process" (i.e., the ability of the private sector to earn money, some of which it will then pay in taxes). So the university is expected to legitimate the capitalist state "by extending to (a larger elite of) citizens the opportunity to study subjects that have little or no apparent relevance for this task but, nonetheless, provide graduates with access to the most lucrative labor markets" (999). Wilmott claims there has been "a rapid intensification and commodification of the work undertaken by academics" as governments have tried to reduce public expenditures by stimulating the accumulation process (1000). Academic work is not yet fully commodified because the providers of higher education do not directly exchange their research with individual purchasers. However, as universities are increasingly required to be accountable for the tax monies that fund them, they are seen less as "traditional liberal institutions comparatively unbowed by commercial demands or political ideology," and more as "modern dynamic organizations that are more responsive to their 'customers'—students, research councils, and employers" (Peters, cited in Wilmott 994). The commodification of academic work thus "occurs as its *use* value, in the form of its contribution to the development of the student as a person, as a citizen or at least as a depository and carrier of culturally valued knowledge, becomes displaced by a preoccupation with doing those things which will increase its *exchange* value" (1001-2). In other words, as professors start to see their work in terms of the resources that will flow directly or indirectly to them and their institutions from high evaluations of their research output (and, to some extent, teaching skill), they will become more concerned with those evaluations because they can be "exchanged" for more resources. They will start to see themselves more as laborers in a system of exchange, in which the object is to get more return for their efforts, rather than to do research for its own sake.

Although Wilmott believes that academics would find the idea incompatible with their professional self-image, they, like other employees, must "sell their labor" in order to support themselves and their dependents (995). The usefulness of their labor, in terms of what it does for individual students, thus becomes secondary because resources seldom flow back to them directly from the students, only from the evaluations of their research productivity. Wilmott continues:

> As the work of academics has been represented in terms of its exchange value, rather than in terms of its use value, students have been explicitly constituted as "customers," a development that further reinforces the idea that a degree is a commodity (or "meal ticket") that (hopefully) can be exchanged for a job rather than as a liberal education that prepares students for life, citizenship, or the continuation and enrichment of a cultural heritage. Students are increasingly enjoined to understand themselves as consumers of educational services. (1002)

The analyses of Wilmott and others may overemphasize the materialistic nature of research and education, but they are corroborated to some extent by the observations of Theodore Mitchell, who notes pressures on American universities from governors, boards of trustees, and regents to function more like businesses and to use business processes such as Total Quality Management and re-engineering to make themselves more efficient. Mitchell also notes the increased pressures to make research as utilitarian and commercially profitable as possible and to make undergraduate curricula more responsive to job markets. Although there are still significant ways that universities are not like businesses or mere training operations for employers, it is not difficult to see that economic incentives drive and define a good deal of what happens on campuses today.[1]

This fact is perhaps inevitable, if James Livingston is right. He asserts that Americans now live in consumer culture, in which "under the auspices of corporate management, the commodity form penetrates and reshapes dimensions of social life hitherto exempt from its logic—to the point where *subjectivity itself seemingly becomes a commodity* to be bought and sold in the market" (416, italics added). In this culture, one can fashion a self by consuming products marketed so that they seem to be able to make one attractive, powerful, intelligent, and so on. Livingston cites Georg Lukacs, who described how the bureaucratic rationality of corporate culture reifies even the consciousness, the qualities, and the abilities of a human being so that "they are no longer an organic part of his personality, [but instead] they are things which he can 'own' and 'dispose of' like the various objects of the external world" (cited in Livingston 417). In consumer culture it becomes plausible that one can buy an education and therefore possess the qualities that earlier generations thought one had to inculcate into oneself through a laborious process of maturing and developing under the guidance of mentors. Now it as if one can "have" those qualities in the same way one can "have" a sports utility vehicle, a DVD player, or clothing of the latest fashion.

Evidence for this consumer approach to education comes from a 5-year study of U.S. undergraduate attitudes and expectations conducted from 1992 to 1997 by Arthur Levine. He found that today's students want their experience with college to be similar to the relationships they already have

---

[1]Winston notes that nonprofit colleges and universities (and by extension primary and secondary schools) differ from for-profit businesses in several important ways. Four of these are the following: (a) colleges and universities don't distribute profits, even when they make profits, because they don't have owners; (b) their managers are motivated by more idealistic goals than the managers of for-profit businesses; (c) they offer something that students largely have to trust will be beneficial, worth their time and money, just as cancer patients have to trust that a proffered treatment will heal them; (d) they depend to a great extent on "customer-input technology" (i.e., the fact that a good deal of the value gained from college comes from peers).

with "their bank, their gas company, and their supermarket" (6). In other words, they want the college to be "nearby and open during the hours most useful to them—preferably, around the clock. They want easy, accessible parking, . . . no lines, and a polite, helpful, efficient staff. They want high quality education at a low cost" (7). In short, Levine concluded, students

> are bringing to higher education exactly the same consumer expecta-
> tions they have for every other commercial enterprise with which they
> deal. Their focus is on convenience, quality, service, and cost. They
> believe that since they are paying for their education, faculty should
> give them the education they want, and they make larger demands on
> faculty than students in the past ever have. (7)

The students Levine studied seek the best value in higher education, the best return for the money and time they have available to spend.

The consumer attitude of today's college students is further described by James Twitchell, who blithely claims that consumption is "the central meaning-making act" in our postmodern world (14). Arguing that we cre-ate and change ourselves through the things we buy, Twitchell views col-lege as just one more of those things: "[Many] students think of themselves as buyers of a degree. They can even tell you how much a credit hour costs. . . . A diploma is valued for how much it improves your starting wage" (24). But students are not the only ones to view higher education as a commer-cial transaction. The colleges themselves know that they have to cater to the consumer-student, as Twitchell describes:

> Just look at the admissions process, complete with competitions for
> financial assistance. Schools live and die by what *US News and World
> Report* or *Money* magazine says about them. You make a deal with one
> school. You show the deal to other schools. They make counteroffers.
> It's just like car shopping. (24)

Twitchell even believes that grade inflation is soaring in the nation's universities because "an unhappy student/consumer is as bad as a defective product" and bad word of mouth means fewer customers (25).

Although many institutions of higher education would not accept Twitchell's assessment, some are perfectly happy to describe themselves as vendors of a product. Here, for example, are the words of Darris Howe, president of five satellite campuses of the University of Phoenix (UOP), a for-profit university that caters to working adults. When asked whether labels such as "diploma mill" or "McEducation" bother him, he replied "No" and added, "Look at McDonald's. You've got a consistent quality product. . . . We too deliver a consistent, quality product." Howe referred to the fact that the UOP creates a scripted curriculum for every course it offers, and teachers of a given course follow the same curriculum, regardless of which of the 85 campuses they teach at. The concept appears to be working, as the year 2001 marked the 25th anniversary of the UOP, which also celebrated the enrollment of 95,000 students in 70 cities across the United States (Stewart B-1). The UOP and institutions like it indicate, according to Mitchell, that "a social demand for teaching and training" is not being met by traditional universities. He cites a major securities firm that told investors, "Education is the largest market opportunity for private (for-profit) sector involvement since health care in the 1970s" (288-9). It will not be surprising to see the emergence of more institutions such as the UOP, as entrepreneurs and investors notice this opportunity and aim to meet the student-consumer demand.

At this point, we need to remember the usual economic meaning of *commodity*. As an undifferentiated product, a commodity commands the price that consumers are willing to pay. In order to be a price-setter rather than a price-taker, the purveyors of a product have to differentiate it from the generic or most common product. If education is a product, then the demand for it is currently satisfied, Martin Trow argues, by three kinds of higher education distinguished by their cost, aims, characteristics. The first form of higher education Trow calls universal access education. Offered largely by extension services, it is sought by people who "study all sorts of things for all sorts of reasons that escape categorization" and who do not necessarily want certificates or credit toward degrees (295). Increasingly, universal access education emphasizes "anytime, anywhere"; thus, it has become a leader in the development of distance and online learning. Trow's second kind, mass higher education, is oriented toward conferring diplomas that indicate the student possesses "useful skills and knowledge" or at least "the capacity to learn at certain levels of difficulty." Mass higher education centers on the transmission of knowledge. High student–teacher ratios tend to make this transmission relatively impersonal and not too intense, factors that also serve to make mass education compatible with other activities, such as part-time work and childrearing (295). As examples of these two kinds—universal access and mass education—one can think of institutions that offer only moderately differentiated products, a cut above a genuine commodity, perhaps, but possessing little in the way of added value that would command high prices.

Trow's third kind, elite higher education, offered in the best private liberal arts colleges and in the undergraduate divisions of leading private research universities, does offer the added value that commands higher prices. As a result, it is fairly rare. Elite higher education aims at something like the 19th-century goal of character development, focusing on the "shaping of mind, character, and sensibility" or what Trow calls "adult socialization" (294). It is achieved through intense, prolonged contact between teachers, who are plentiful and ostensibly stimulating, and students, who are unencumbered by family, job, and other responsibilities. Unlike the "anytime, anywhere" of universal access education, elite education emphasizes the here and now: Students go to a particular place to receive it, and it unfolds on a defined schedule. A costly form of education, it nevertheless survives because it prepares students for entrance into powerful and prestigious career networks and into the best graduate and professional schools (294-5). This kind of educational product is definitely not a generic commodity. It is brand-name education, adding value such that consumers are willing to pay more than for the first two kinds.

Trow points out that all three kinds of education can be found in different proportions at nearly all institutions of higher education, yet most institutions and most students at them are engaged mainly in mass higher education, such as the UOP provides. Although the UOP is not inexpensive (tuition is about $6,000 a year), it holds costs down by hiring part-time teachers, maintaining low overhead costs, putting its library online, and not offering the amenities and extracurricular activities typical of nonprofit institutions. It is probably safe to say that any institution offering mass higher education cuts a few corners in its service to customer-students looking for a decent Ford Taurus type of education. Ultimately, for most students, as for most consumers in any market, convenient access and an acceptable price for the quality of the goods are deciding factors.

But it is not just goods themselves that give our lives meanings, Twitchell argues. Powerful meanings are added to goods through marketing techniques—advertising, packaging, branding, and fashion. In that sense, even the elite institutions are implicated in the movement to commercialize education. Harvard and Yale, Berkeley and Bryn Mawr have brand-name status. They package and advertise themselves so that they attract students who want their education to be more like a Lexus than a Taurus. Twitchell asks, "Why go to a prestigious school?" And he answers, "Because the school name improves the relative worth of the line on the vita, the certificate. The assumption is, you pay your money, you get your degree" (25).

But Twitchell doesn't have that last line quite right. Earning a degree from a brand name institution means that you actually get much, much more than you pay for. Recent studies of the economics of higher education by Gordon Winston and associates show that students who choose top-drawer institutions receive a much higher subsidy than those who choose institutions lower on the ladder of prestige. Winston ranked 3,300 nonprofit institutions of higher education by how much each subsidized students' education from donated resources. All students at all institutions receive some subsidy, Winston shows, with the average subsidy in 1995 at $8,800. However, students in the top decile of institutions got an average subsidy of $24,112 because the average cost of 1 year of education at those institutions was $29,894, yet the average price was only $5,782. In effect, students in the top 10% of institutions paid $0.20 on the dollar for 1 year's instruction. In contrast, students in the bottom decile paid $0.70 on the dollar, or an average of $5,799 for 1 year of education that actually cost $8,419, a subsidy of only $2,620 (reported in Palattella 71).

Winston's findings mean that, where higher education is concerned, "a BMW . . . will cost you less than a used Geo" (5). The reasons for this odd economic fact: A large subsidy means a better bargain in the form of more resources: better faculty, better facilities, and smaller classes. A better bargain means higher demand. Higher demand means the institution offering the large subsidy can be more selective. Higher selectivity means a higher concentration of bright, well-prepared students who demonstrably help to educate each other, thus magnifying the school's initial investment even more. High student quality improves the school's reputation and its ranking in magazine surveys. Graduates of these leading schools earn more and donate more as alumni. The school grows wealthier and can subsidize future students even more, thus creating increased demand, as the cycle continues. The converse of this pattern is that low subsidies lead to lower student demand, which leads to low selectivity and thus to lower educational quality and therefore to greater scarcity of resources. Higher education is thus the prime example of a winner-take-all market (Winston 6-7). Even though mass education is the most affordable, elite education promises the greatest return for the investment.

The foregoing lengthy analysis of the commodification of higher education has, I believe, much to do with the commodification of first-year composition, the subject I turn to shortly. However, as a prelude to an analysis of the competitors in the marketplace of first-year writing, I must first discuss public and private goods in education and their interaction with our changing society and economy.

EDUCATION AS A PUBLIC AND A PRIVATE GOOD

Taxpayer-supported public education has long been a democratic ideal in the United States. At the elementary level, public education comes close to being a pure public good. Economists define public goods as those that would be either under-supplied or not supplied at all by competitive markets; therefore, these goods are supplied at no charge by governments, which finance them through taxes. True public goods are defined by two characteristics: (1) nonrival consumption (i.e., one person's consumption of the good does not reduce its consumption by others); and (2) nonexclusion (i.e., no one can be prevented from using the good because the cost of creating barriers would simply be too high). National defense is a common example of a public good; everyone benefits from it equally and no one is excluded from it, including those who pay little or nothing in taxes, or free riders. It would be cost-prohibitive to devise a system of national defense that excluded free riders, so the good is extended to all, regardless of the amount they pay to the public coffers that support it (Ruffin and Gregory 384-85).

Public elementary education is generally characterized by nonrival consumption: One child's presence in the school does not prevent another child from attending. However, it is starting to become difficult to characterize elementary education as nonexclusive. It still is nonexclusive in the sense that every child can go to an elementary school—although not necessarily the best ones. Some exclusiveness is almost certainly now the result of parental demands for school choice privileges that allow them to place their child in any school they choose, as long as they are willing to transport the child there. Exclusiveness will also be the result of proposed voucher programs that will permit wealthier parents to use their tax assessment to afford private schools. By and large, however, the United States extends taxpayer-supported elementary education to all—including to free riders. Apparently, taxpayers still acknowledge the cost in wasted human potential that society would later pay by excluding children from elementary education.

As for secondary education, compulsory attendance laws would seem to indicate that the people of this nation consider it also to be a public good; yet, as one gazes up the public education ladder, it is clear that the higher the level, the less it bears the defining marks of a public good. Secondary education is still largely characterized by nonrival consumption, yet there are exclusionary costs associated with some of the educational activities offered at the secondary level—fees charged for books, lockers, special equipment or clothing, labs, field trips, and so on, which may exclude some students from certain educational benefits. (To be sure, many schools waive most or all of the fees in some instances, but the availability of waivers is not always publicized, so the effect is often exclusion nonetheless. Free riding is possible but not encouraged.) Moreover, some students are excluded at the secondary level by their inability to pay for private goods and services (e.g., sports training, music lessons, dance lessons, fashion clothing, etc.) outside of school that would enable them to take advantage of certain curricular and extracurricular educational activities enjoyed by more prosperous classmates. So the public secondary school appears to be a mixed good—largely public with some private elements. In spite of this, the public secondary school is still a highly democratic U.S. institution in that it attempts to provide to all an equitable opportunity for the kind of basic education that will allow one to be a self-supporting and contributing member of society.

Higher education is largely a private good. Although it is true that open admissions institutions are founded on the ideal of nonexclusion so far as academic aptitude is concerned, there are generally financial barriers, however modest. And although open admissions colleges also appear to value nonrival consumption, because there are, ultimately, physical and financial limits to the number of students who can be admitted to them, more students consuming the same pie means each one gets a little less. Moreover, Winston's analysis of the economics of higher education shows that low selectivity in an institution virtually guarantees that admitted students will in effect be competing for thinly spread resources (and paying more per dollar for the opportunity than students in selective institutions).

Open admissions aside, in selective institutions higher education is clearly a private good, even at state-supported colleges, because it excludes those who lack the ability to perform academically and to pay tuition and fees. Higher education is also rivalrous wherever limits on enrollment mean that one student's admission results in another student's rejection—even if the rejected student has the ability to pay. For those who can't pay but who merit entrance because they can perform, scholarships and other forms of financial aid are available. So the generally private good of higher education is offered most abundantly to those who have made the most of their opportunities in secondary schools in order to demonstrate that they merit the chance to pursue this private good.

The last sentence seems to state the obvious. But what is worth noting about it, perhaps, is that the demonstration of merit in high school has become more important than ever. As recently as 1973, reports the National Commission on the High School Senior Year, "education and employment were only loosely related" as students with high school diplomas—or even without them—could still land fairly high-paying manufacturing jobs. Just 40 years ago, the same commission states, high school dropouts held more than one third of those jobs (2). Statistics collected since the 1980s, however, repeatedly show that those with only a high school education lag significantly behind college graduates in annual and lifetime earning power. Data from the U.S. Census Bureau show that in 1998, the median income of a high school graduate was $34,373, whereas the median income of those holding a bachelor's degree was $66,474 (Statistical Abstract 467). The National Commission on the High School Senior Year notes that in the high-tech service economy of the information age, the proportion of skilled jobs has nearly tripled compared to 1950, when only about 20% of jobs required skills gained in either high school or college. Skilled jobs and their financial rewards now go to those who can think abstractly, do advanced math, tolerate ambiguity, and function self-confidently in an increasingly global and multicultural world. In most cases, postsecondary education is required for such jobs (National Commission 2-3)

Currently, however, the secondary schools are widely perceived as failing to produce students who are ready for the increased level of education required to succeed in today's world. What's more, this perception may be quite accurate. The National Commission on the High School Senior Year estimates that from one third to one half of secondary students are graduating unprepared for either jobs or higher education. The perception of the public schools' failure is surely one reason why virtually all state governments have begun to implement standards and assessments for students in elementary and secondary education in order to measure achievement and readiness for higher education. Falling test scores, slackened standards for graduation, and teacher ineptitude are all cited as reasons why the states need to define standards and create tests that will make students, teachers, and administrators more accountable for their time and for the public funds spent in schools. Of course, the accountability rhetoric obscures many other plausible reasons for the poor results coming from many public secondary schools—reasons that include increased numbers of impoverished and single-parent families, large class sizes, poor facilities, low pay for teachers, lack of needed books and supplies, increased numbers of students whose first language is not English, requirements that students with various disabilities be mainstreamed, and a general weakening of societal mores that once made schools more civil and orderly places. It could also be argued that curricular changes in high schools are not keeping up with the pace of societal change, so that even under the best of conditions, many students would be leaving school ill-prepared to step into skilled jobs or succeed in a college curriculum that is more responsive to the new global economy.

Whatever the causes, when the private good of selective higher education bumps up against the quasi-public good of nearly universal secondary education, the latter is seen as outdated, inefficient, and weak. Once again, this perception appears to be quite accurate. The National Commission on the High School Senior Year found that remediation in reading, writing, and high school math "takes place in all community colleges, in four out of five public four-year universities, and in more than six out of ten private four-year institutions" (4). The irony of these statistics is overwhelming when one realizes that this extensive remediation is occurring in a time when the senior year of high school is largely wasted. It is now the case that students are accepted into colleges and universities largely on the basis of grades and test scores earned in the junior year of high school. The authors of "The Lost Opportunity of Senior Year" write:

> For a variety of reasons, student motivation drops in the senior year. Short of a miserable failure in the senior year, practically every college-bound student knows that what they have accomplished through Grade 11 will largely determine whether or not they attend college, and if so, which college. As a result, serious preparation for college ends at Grade 11. Some students who have already been accepted to college routinely ignore the high school's academic standards. The same is true for students entering the world of work directly after high school graduation. Bored and unable to see what work in the classroom has to do with work after high school, they view academics as pointless and spend their time daydreaming. (National Commission 6)

In the economy of education, where "economy" is understood as the organization or structure of an ordered system, secondary education is arguably the weakest link in the system. In the final stage of secondary education, it seems that students must cool their heels while they wait for the opportunity to begin earning a living or earning the credentials that will qualify them for a career.

In a consumer culture that values education mainly (if not solely) for its commercial value, the perceived lack of good service or a good product in the secondary segment of the system leads, I argue, to competitors moving in to meet the demand for something better. I now discuss two of these competitors: one is concurrent enrollment or dual-credit courses; the other is the AP program. Both of these compete with the standard high school curriculum by offering a private good—one for which students must pay—within the context of the mainly public good of secondary education. The aim of either program is not only to give students a better experience in high school but also to prepare them to take advantage after high school of the private good of higher education by ostensibly helping them acquire the knowledge they would otherwise have to wait to get once they are enrolled in college. Both of these programs offer credit hours—and, in the case of AP, the promise of more credit hours at college. These credit hours function as tokens that students can use in an exchange with the colleges they choose to attend. Students use them to demonstrate to institutions that they are serious about higher education and deserve to be admitted, but they also use them to avoid taking courses at college. To students, these credit hours mean that they already *have* what they would get in college. They have paid their money and believe they have thus consumed the knowledge and experiences these programs are surrogates for. Both dual credit and AP courses are offered in many subjects, but I focus on English composition, describing the possible pluses and minuses of these competitors as compared to the traditional first-year writing course taken on a college campus.

CONCURRENT ENROLLMENT COURSES

Concurrent enrollment courses, also called dual-credit courses, are courses in which students earn credit for both high school English and first-year composition at the same time. The motivations behind such courses, which have operated in some parts of the country since the 1970s, are to prevent duplication of instruction in high school and college, to provide opportunities for capable and highly motivated students to avoid unstimulating high school courses by beginning college work, and to shorten the time to graduation once those students are in college (Fincher-Ford 2-5). Dual-credit courses take many forms, running the gamut from those that are rigorous and of unassailable value to those that are unchallenging and of dubious educational quality. Space does not permit an exhaustive treatment of dual-credit programs, so for purposes of illustration, I describe programs at each end of this spectrum.

In one version of the respectable dual-credit course, students from a nearby high school go to a university or college and take a first-year writing course from a teacher employed by the institution of higher education. Students pay tuition for the course, and they earn both college and high school credit. In another version of sound dual-credit courses, a university brings high school teachers to its campus for training in how to teach the first-year writing course. These teachers then return to their schools where, using the texts, curriculum, and methods of the university course, they teach well-prepared high school seniors the same course those students would get if they were at the university. The university sends a faculty member or administrator periodically to visit the sites where these courses are offered, both to consult with the teachers about concerns and to verify that the course is proceeding as planned. In well-supervised programs, students who are struggling with the curriculum are counseled out of the course so that high standards are maintained and the institution of higher education is not put in the embarrassing position of giving credit for a sub-par performance. Students pay tuition for the course, which goes to the university with some of the money being paid to the high school teacher. Upon successful completion, students get credit that counts for both the university first-year writing course and for graduation requirements from high school. This kind of "double-dipping" may be justified as long as the dual-credit program is well-conceived and well-supervised and as long as it serves students who are genuinely ready for college-level work.

In more dubious incarnations of dual-credit courses, a university or college enlists high school teachers to teach what is ostensibly a first-year writing course, but little or no training is given to the teacher; curriculum and materials are not aligned with those at used at the college nor are they carefully monitored; little or no onsite supervision is provided; and courses are open to all high school seniors (and sometimes juniors) who want to enroll, regardless of maturity or level of preparation. In some cases, the high school makes no distinction between its own course and the college course; that is, some of the students in a particular class will be taking it for dual credit and others only for the high school credit, prompting questions of whether the course really qualifies as college level. In such versions of dual-credit courses, it appears suspiciously that the institution offering the college credit is more concerned about the tuition to be earned from the high school students than about the equivalence of the high school course to a first-year writing course taught on the college campus.

Some universities that would not offer a dual-credit course of the dubious kind just described may nevertheless find themselves in the awkward position of accepting credit for just such course. Suppose a student takes a poor quality dual-credit course offered by College X, which sponsors such courses mainly for the revenue they provide. The student then presents the credit at University Y, which has an articulation agreement with College X, which, in effect, sold the credit to the student. University Y has no choice but to accept the credit, even if there is a legitimate question about the student's ability to actually perform as a college-level writer. In one populous midwestern state, the hypothetical situation just described actually occurs. A private institution is the largest purveyor of dual-credit English courses in that state. Because of statewide articulation agreements, all the public institutions of higher education in the state must accept the credit students earn in these dual-credit courses—yet, astonishingly, the private institution does not accept its own dual credit from students who enroll at that institution. This example powerfully suggests that some institutions see the offering of dual-credit as a money-making venture, rather than an educational program which they guarantee the quality of.

Whether dual-credit courses are good, bad, or in-between, they are evidence that high school students who take them (and their parents) believe two things: First, that the standard high school curriculum is somehow lacking, and, second, that completing what is represented as college-level work in high school is a smart economic move. The student gets two courses for the price of one and the promise of graduating from college even faster. It must be granted that this is rational economic behavior on the part of people who are already inclined to see education in economic terms. One fundamental principle of economics is that people economize by choosing the alternative which seems best because it involves the least cost and greatest benefit. The cost of a dual-credit course is usually relatively low, and if it buys two-for-one, then it seems to bring the greatest benefit. Another basic economic principle is that the opportunity cost of something is the second best choice people give up when they make their best choice. In this case, the second best choice is the standard high school course; foregoing that is not a problem because in a dual-credit course it really isn't foregone. Finally, this option is rational economic behavior because students are responding to an economic incentive—the promise of a lower college tuition bill, one that does not include the cost of the typical first-year writing course. But when parents and students make such decisions purely from an economic standpoint, they provide more evidence for the claim that education is being commodified because they don't seem to question whether the learning the students have done has actually prepared them well to succeed in other college courses. They take the credit hours the student has earned as a token of preparation, rather than asking for other evidence of the student's readiness to write successfully in college.

ADVANCED PLACEMENT COURSES

Like dual-credit programs, the AP program in English was originally premised on the belief that some students are bored in unchallenging high school courses and ready for college work. Sponsored by the College Board, AP has been a part of high school curricula since the 1960s. The first AP courses grew out of the desire of faculty at elite colleges to "channel the best of the increasing number of college-bound students into their schools" (Foster 3). These faculty theorized that they could get the best students from highly visible prep schools if an exam could be devised that would indicate that a particular student was ready for advanced placement once at college. Foster believes that the ultimate goal was to lessen the student load in introductory courses and increase enrollments in upper division courses, which most college faculty enjoy teaching more than introductory ones. The key to the success of this stratagem, however, was first devising a preparatory course that would prepare students for the advanced placement test. "Through the back door, as it were," Foster asserts, "the cagey pioneers of Advanced Placement gained entry into high school curricula" (4). The course they helped create was entirely constrained by the nature of the test. In other words, the testing tail wagged the curriculum dog because, normally, tests are created to assess what courses teach, but in this case the course was created to prepare for what the test would ask. Foster notes that the planners of the test from its inception up to now have given extensive material to high school teachers to help them teach the course, (e.g., sample course outlines, assignments, and test questions). Although they are free to teach an AP course as they see fit, only "by incorporating many of the test-oriented strategies can AP teachers give their students the best possible preparation for the exam. Indeed the limits of this standardized final exam, over which teachers have no control, constrain the entire AP learning experience" (Foster 6).

There are currently two versions of the AP English exam: one is called Literature and Composition; the other is called Language and Composition. According to the College Board's pamphlet, *Access to Excellence: A Guide to the Advanced Placement Program*, both exams consist of "60 minutes of multiple-choice questions and 120 minutes of free-response questions." The multiple-choice questions on the Literature and Composition exam test the student's ability to analyze passages of poetry and prose; on the Language and Composition exam, they test the student's "skill in analyzing reasoning and the expression of ideas in prose passages" (15). The free response questions in either exam are based on the reading of three fairly complex passages chosen from the writings of significant authors, living and dead. Writing prompts that follow each passage require the test-taker to write three essays, each one in only 40 minutes. On this multipart exam students can earn an overall score between 1 and 5. To earn a 3 — the grade that the College Board insists is indicative that the student is "qualified" to earn college credit — the test-taker need answer only "about 50 percent of the multiple-choice questions correctly and do acceptable work on the free-response section" (46). I have not found "acceptable work" defined anywhere in the College Board literature, but from having participated in the scoring of AP essays in 2000 and 2001, I would say that it means the rough draft of an essay that would likely be graded C- or lower in college. In other words, a less-than-mediocre performance on the AP exam will net a student an overall score that is likely to qualify him or her to earn college credit and/or be exempt from a first-year writing course.

Given a test of the kind described, it would be fair to assume that high school teachers preparing students for the AP exam would spend considerable time rehearsing students in the writing of timed essays and in choosing the right answer in a multiple-choice test of reading. My own (unpublished) research based on interviews with students who took AP English courses in high schools all across the country bears this assumption out. Some reported that, in an entire school year, they did not write a single paper that took longer than 40 minutes. They did no pre-drafting, drafting, revising, or editing, except that which could be accomplished in the space of 40 minutes. When asked if they wrote a library research paper in their AP course, many acted surprised, saying, "No, I did that in tenth grade." And here it must be noted that many students are now taking one AP English course and test as a junior and sometimes taking the other as a senior as a way of hedging their bet for college credit one way or another.

When one compares a high school course of the kind described to the typical first-year writing course in college, the mismatch is clear. Most college writing courses are not focused on the reading of literature, as about two-thirds of high school AP courses are. College writing courses typically do not dwell on the reading and analyzing of prose or poetry; they have few or no multiple-choice tests and probably few timed essays. Most college writing courses *do*, however, focus heavily on the processes of writing, requiring students to do multiple drafts of an individual paper over a period of days or weeks. They teach students how to do research in a college library, how to select and synthesize source material to build an argument, how to organize the argument, and how to document it. If a course is a commodity, then it is clear that the AP course that students purchase in lieu of the college course is in the same general category, but it is not exactly the same kind. It is as if the high school students have bought a typewriter, when what colleges are offering students these days is a personal computer.

Yet so successful is the marketing of the AP program that 273,591 students took the two AP English exams in 1999. Of those, 36% took the Language and Composition exam, and 64% took the Literature and Composition exam (*Advanced Placement Program Course Description* 69). On the 1999 Language and Composition exam, 62% scored 3 or better; on the Literature and Composition exam, 68% scored 3 or higher. Each student taking a test was charged $76. The schools those students attended received a $7 rebate for each exam, so the College Board took in approximately $18.8 million (*Access to Excellence* 39) on the two English exams in 1999. The College Board hires ETS to conduct the scoring of the exams—a massive operation that entails flying hundreds of high school and college teachers from all over the country to a central site, where they are housed and fed for 1 week while they score thousands of essays per day. Both the College Board and Educational Testing Services are nonprofit organizations, but clearly they must make enough from the testing to pay overhead and salaries for a well-educated staff to keep the programs going and growing. Robert Schaeffer, director of public education for FairTest, an organization that promotes awareness of the impacts of testing on students, notes that the people who write and promote AP exams "make very good livings," even though the organization they work for is not for profit (cited in Ganeshananthan A46).

Probably no students or parents begrudge the College Board or ETS employees their salaries, because they are likely see $76 as a small price to pay for a shot at 3 or more hours of college credit. As with dual-credit courses, students who take AP courses are likely motivated by sound economic reasoning. The second best choice they are giving up is the standard high school course, which would not be as impressive to a college admissions committee as an AP course that ostensibly demonstrates that the student is capable of succeeding in the competition for the private good of higher education. Students and their parents are choosing the alternative that seems best because it involves the least cost and greatest benefit. They are thinking about the future, as economics theory says we all do; it is only the future that we can influence through our choices now. But they might think twice about spending the money to take the test and indirectly buy the credit if they thought there was a good chance they wouldn't get the credit—a distinct likelihood, according to William Lichten.

Lichten, a critic of AP marketing, believes that in 1998-1999, the College Board may have earned more than $20 million from students who took one of the 31 AP tests now offered in 19 different subjects in the belief that they stood a very good chance of getting college credit for the results. Lichten analyzed the widely promoted College Board claim that about two thirds of students taking an AP test will succeed in scoring a 3 on the test and earning college credit by determining the number of institutions who actually granted credit for scores of 3. His results showed that, although most colleges will grant credit for scores of 4 and 5, only 55% accept 3s. Moreover, Lichten found that the biggest discrepancy between what the College Board promised and what colleges actually granted was in the English Literature and Composition exam. In selective colleges, a score of 4 was usually required for credit; in some colleges not even a 5 was accepted.

The College Board disputes Lichten's claims, of course (see Camara et al.). Bad word of mouth about their product could spoil their plans for expansion and thus their future revenues, for if a commodity does not find consumers its production must cease. Nevertheless, the old warning *caveat emptor* comes to mind. In this case, student customers are being encouraged to take a high school course and pay for a test that is marketed by a middle man, the College Board, as a college course; yet there is no guarantee that the college they want to attend has authorized this middle man to sell the promise of credit for the college. One has to wonder how the College Board has so successfully insinuated itself into high schools that it has, in effect, been able to dictate the curriculum of so many courses. Even now it is aggressively promoting "pre-AP" programs in middle schools and even elementary schools on the premise that the way to "attain academic equity and excellence" is to "promote access to AP for all students" by building "rigorous curricula" founded on the "skills, concepts, and assessment methods" that "prepare students for success when they take AP and other challenging courses" (*Pre-AP* brochure). One has to wonder how the College Board has for years successfully gotten so many colleges to acquiesce in its promise that the colleges would grant students credit hours for tests the colleges did not help construct and have no control over. One has to suspect that in the overall economy of education, there is something of a vacuum at the nexus of high school and college, and that enterprising organizations, such as the College Board and purveyors of dual-credit courses, have seen a way to fill that vacuum by exploiting the lack of coordination between high schools and colleges, which so far have failed to define how their objectives, curricula, and assessments should or could mesh. How this lack of definition might be rectified is the problem I turn to next.

TOWARD A NEW ECONOMY OF EDUCATION IN WRITING

The word *toward* in the above heading is meant to alert the reader that I don't have a comprehensive solution to the problems adduced above but rather a few suggestions that I hope will generate further discussion. And the word *economy* is intended to be read in the sense of the orderly distribution and interplay of parts in a structure or system. Despite the many signs that the educational system is increasingly becoming a marketplace in which the usual economic factors of supply, demand, and costs determine just about everything else, I want to state my unequivocal belief that we educators must resist viewing our work as only an exchange in which we sell what we know to buyers who receive credit hours and credentials as a token of having paid their money and/or their time. We must certainly be aware of the economic value of education and acknowledge that we help to prepare students for participation in economic life. But to ensure that we also provide students with other values besides the ability to earn money, we must have a grander view of education, one that includes the more intangible effects we want it to have in students' lives, both individually and collectively. In order to do this, we must view the educational system as a whole, rather than simply focusing on the level—primary, secondary, or postsecondary—and the field of education we find ourselves engaged in.

In focusing on the educational system as a whole, we would do well to consider the suggestions of Robert Shoenberg, senior fellow at the Association of American Colleges and Universities. Shoenberg notes that in an age of high student mobility, the early 20th-century invention of the credit hour as "the standard unit of academic currency" has greatly facilitated students' transferring from one institution to another because it is relatively easy to calculate the "exchange rate" of this currency as students cross borders between institutions. Nevertheless, Shoenberg argues, "the convenience of the credit hour as common currency has driven out the better but far less fungible currency of intellectual purpose and curricular coherence" (2). As student transfer has increased since World War II, and colleges have entered into articulation agreements, they have often done so without sufficient consideration of how those agreements would affect the curricular coherence of the education a student receives. Indeed, they have paid little attention in these agreements to the overall purpose and nature of the baccalaureate degree. The result of facilitating transfer among institutions, Shoenberg argues, is "a lowest-common-denominator general education program, based invariably on loose distribution requirements. And since unique courses of study only serve to make transfer difficult for students, schools have an incentive not to make their own general education offerings too adventurous or challenging" (4). For an institution of higher education, choosing increased efficiency in transfer usually means sacrificing integrity in its curriculum and overall purpose, thereby decreasing the institution's ability to be accountable for the quality of education students receive. The solution, Shoenberg believes, is "to stop treating this as a problem for the *individual* institution" (4). Noting that most students start and complete their higher education within a single system, he continues:

> The only way to reconcile the demands for efficiency and accountability is to come to inter-institutional or, better yet, system-wide agreement about the intended outcomes of the general education program, and then to link those outcomes closely to the transfer agreement. Accountable to a clear, coherent, and common set of purposes, individual schools might then invest in local curriculum reforms without having to worry about ease of transfer. (4)

Shoenberg is fully aware that his proposal to define purposes, rather than just match up semi-equivalent courses, would require dialog among all the institutions within a system to agree on the nature of curriculum requirements and on the student outcomes that would demonstrate mastery of those requirements. He is further aware that this dialogue will entail the development of new outcome-based assessments credible enough to break the "credit hour addiction" (7). But this shift to outcome-based learning, rather than simply accumulation of credit hours, would do much to ensure that students are actually acquiring an education worthy of the name. Shoenberg notes that professional accrediting associations, regional accreditors, and state legislatures are already demanding that students demonstrate they have achieved the outcomes specified in requirements, and he is optimistic that "cross-institutional and cross-disciplinary groups of faculty, assembled at the state level, can fairly readily arrive at a mutually agreeable statement of the general intentions that implicitly underlie basic skills and distribution requirements" (7). He cites the examples of Georgia and Utah, which have undertaken state-wide discussions of general education programs in their institutions of higher learning in order to facilitate transfer within these systems without sacrificing curricular coherence.

The final report of the National Commission on the High School Senior Year, "Raising Our Sights," makes a recommendation similar to that of Shoenberg, but instead of involving just institutions of higher education in a statewide dialog, the Commission recommends that states create "seamless" systems of education extending from pre-school to four years of post-secondary learning (not necessarily at a university). The Commission claims that 18 states are currently engaged in such efforts (making particular mention of efforts underway in Maryland, Georgia, and Oregon), and it recommends that every state in the nation "create a P-16 Council and charge it with increasing student access to (and success in) postsecondary education" (23). The three main goals of these P-16 councils would be to improve alignment of standards, curriculum, and assessment between P-12 and postsecondary institutions; raise achievement at all levels; and provide more alternatives and more rigorous alternatives for students in the last 2 years of high school to prepare them to make the transition to college or work (21-2). The first of these goals, alignment, is particularly critical because high schools too often prepare students for admission to college but not for success in college, as evidenced by high dropout rates, slow time to graduation, and widespread remediation in the first 2 years of college. The Commission notes the paradox that "K-12 and postsecondary institutions frequently find themselves doing each other's job" (32) and states that the move "away from seat time to student competence as a measure of readiness to progress" (31) will help make the final year of high school more meaningful. Recommendations include "creating multiple new structures for the last two years of high school"— including such possibilities as marrying coursework with community service, employment, and internships (31); and beginning postsecondary study at age 16 or 17, if students are ready for it then (32).

Although some of the Commission's suggestions of what to change in secondary education may be debatable, the creation of state P-16 Councils to align various levels of education and the transitions between them would, I think, be a fruitful first step toward remaking the economy of education. Representatives from college writing programs and other postsecondary institutions should surely be among those participating in the deliberations of such councils, working carefully with teachers from the K-12 institutions to plan comprehensive curricula that promote student development in writing over the presumed 16 years of education. Brandenburger and Nalebuff's 1996 book *Co-opetition* proposes a way we might think about dialogs in these councils from an economic standpoint. They state that in business or any other enterprise with multiple players, such as education, "you have to compete and cooperate at the same time"—cooperating "when it comes to creating a pie," and competing "when it comes to dividing it up" (4). Teachers at all levels of the educational system need to be interested in the whole writing "pie." We want students to be the most proficient communicators they can be at the end of 16 years of schooling. Therefore, we need to cooperate to define and describe the entire set of writing knowledge, skills, achievements, experiences, and genres that, optimally, would best prepare students to succeed in life. As for division, it seems to me that we want to divide not the pie, but the process of making it, so that at each level of education we are measuring and mixing the right ingredients to ensure that students (who, after all, will help bake this pie) get full benefit from it.

To divide the pie, we need a better understanding of the developmental needs and readiness of students at various ages and ability levels, so that they don't, for example, attempt something they are not ready for or languish when they are prepared to move ahead. This objective will require research into the cognitive development of students, but also into their social development, including the ways that social and educational environments influence the kinds of writing experiences and assignments students will have and the skills they will need to negotiate those. For example, we need rigorous studies of how actually attending a postsecondary institution changes students' understanding of academic writing and their ability to produce it as compared to students who are not yet in that milieu.

Likewise, we will need to develop sophisticated assessment tools to measure readiness for certain kinds of writing instruction and to measure achievement of the outcomes defined for each level of education. At the college level, we already have the Writing Program Administrators' (WPA) Outcomes Statement for First-Year Composition; we need similar statements of the outcomes we expect from writing instruction in elementary, middle, and high schools in order to create this new economy of education in writing. One of the assessments we need to undertake is measuring whether students who take dual credit and advanced placement courses in high school are actually capable of demonstrating the abilities described in the WPA Outcomes Statement. If students are, then we college educators would have to acknowledge that these competing courses are, in fact, equivalent to the ones we offer at college. If students are not, we would have reason to call into question the value of these courses and the ideology of consumption that supports them. Perhaps many 17-year-olds and some 16-year-olds are ready to demonstrate college first-year writing outcomes, but we may need to devise different courses they can take in high school to prepare to do so. And we would need to rigorously assess their ability to transfer college writing skills learned in high school to other college courses when they begin college.

Brandenburger and Nalebuff propose that education can be described as a game with many players who relate to each other in what can be depicted as a "value net" (17). At the center of this net we can put an elementary school, a high school, a trade school, or a university, depending on the perspective we want to take. The value net assumes a diamond shape surrounding the center, and the four corners are labeled "customers," "competitors," "suppliers," and "complementors." The first three of these terms are easily understood, but the fourth may not be. A complementor is the provider of a product or service that makes another product or service successful. For example, the computer software industry is a complementor to the hardware industry, and vice versa. As one builds a better product, it gives the other a reason to do so as well, and both benefit. "Thinking complements is a different way of thinking about business. It's about finding ways to make the pie bigger rather than fighting with competitors over a fixed pie" (14). Up to now, I believe many different players in the value net—teachers, students, parents, and the purveyors of dual credit and AP programs—have been thinking of college writing as a pie of a fixed size. Some of them been thinking if students can consume the pie before coming to college, they shouldn't have to eat it again. Others, like me, have been thinking that many students with dual credit and AP credit have eaten an inferior pie that competes with the real thing. But if college and high school teachers were jointly to research, rethink, and redesign dual credit and AP programs in such a way that they were complementors to college writing courses rather than competitors, we could then ask what they provide that postsecondary institutions can build on.

It doesn't take long to realize that most institutions of higher education need a more diversified and stronger writing curriculum (i.e., a bigger pie). There are typically very few undergraduate courses in writing (sometimes as few as one), and they usually meet general education requirements. The relatively small numbers of PhDs in composition studies at a university typically teach graduate students and oversee those students and adjunct faculty in their teaching of multiple sections of the few required courses. It is time to think bigger and more broadly to conceive of a series of undergraduate courses, both general education and elective. We ought also to be planning for minors and majors in writing, and working to create departments of writing staffed by PhDs who represent a range of specialties. Communicating in various media, particularly electronic media, is one of the most important cultural practices of our age. This and other kinds of writing should be studied more and taught better than they are. We would not need to worry so much about pre-college students taking writing courses that might be inadequate competitors if we had in place a varied and well-defined curriculum at the college level. With more diverse offerings and better articulated purposes and outcomes for writing instruction, it would be easy to persuade (or require) students to get more education in writing at college regardless of the kind of instruction they had in high school or how good it was. The value such courses would add to students' education would be so apparent they would demand these courses.

None of this will happen, however, without more dialog at the nexus of high school and college about students' developmental and academic needs and each institution's role in meeting those needs. Each institution should want the other to be as strong as possible in doing what it does best; such strength in both partners would allow each one to demand the most of students and produce the most growth. The dialogue I am proposing would also help us reclaim at all levels some of the traditional territory associated with education, asserting its use value rather than merely its exchange value. Education is now inextricably linked with economic goals, both at the individual and the national levels. But economic success by itself is hollow, for either individuals or nations, if the intellectual, personal, and social values long associated with education are not cultivated as well. Education can prepare young people for the marketplace, but it can also teach them how a market economy should sustain a higher economy of social relationships, ideas, and ideals that elevate life above mere consumption. Education should foster and advance the ideals the nation was founded on: liberty, justice, unity, peace, and progress. The role of writing and other communication arts in promoting these ideals must continue to be taught. We who are the inheritors of the long rhetorical tradition that has always aimed to produce good citizens and good societies may actually be in the best position to rekindle an understanding of the intangible value, not just the economic value, that flows from a comprehensive and well-designed curriculum in the language arts, particularly writing.

REFERENCES

Brandenburger, Adam and Barry Nalebuff. *Co-opetition.* New York: Doubleday, 1996.

Camara, Wayne, Neil J. Dorans, Rick Morgan, Carol Myford. "Advanced Placement: Access Not Exclusion." *Education Policy Analysis Archives* 8 (August 1, 2000). 29 June 2003. <http://epaa.asu.edu/epaa/v8n40.html>.

College Board. *Advanced Placement Program Description: English.* New York: CEEB and ETS, 2000.

_____. *Pre-AP: Achieving Equity, Emphasizing Excellence.* n.p.: n.d.

_____. *AP, Access to Excellence: A Guide to the Advanced Placement Program.* New York: CEEB and ETS, 1999.

Fincher-Ford, Margaret. *High School Students Earning College Credit: A Guide to Creating Dual-Credit Programs.* Thousand Oaks, CA: Corwin Press, 1997.

Foster, David. "The Theory of AP English: A Critique." In *Advanced Placement English: Theory, Politics, and Pedagogy.* Eds. Gary Olson, Elizabeth Metzger, and Evelyn Ashton-Jones. Portsmouth, NH: Boynton/Cook, 1989. pp. 3-24.

Ganeshananthan, Vasugi. "AP Program Faces New Criticism Over Its Testing Standards." *Chronicle of Higher Education* (14 July 2000): A45-46.

Levine, Arthur. "How the Academic Profession is Changing." *Daedalus* (1997): 1-20.

Lichten, William. "Whither Advanced Placement?" *Education Policy Analysis Archives* 8 (June 24, 2000). 29 June 2003. <http://epaa.asu.edu/epaa/v8n29.html>.

Livingston, James. "Modern Subjectivity and Consumer Culture." *Getting and Spending: European and American Consumer Societies in the Twentieth Century.* Eds. Susan Strasser, Charles McGovern, and Matthias Judt. Cambridge: Cambridge UP, 1998, 413-29.

Lyotard, Jean-François. *The Postmodern Condition: A Report on Knowledge.* Trans. Geoff Bennington and Brian Massumi. Minneapolis: U of Minnesota P, 1984.

Mitchell, Theodore R. "Border Crossings: Organizational Boundaries and Challenges to the American Professoriate." *Daedalus* (1997): 265-92.

National Commission on the High School Senior Year. *The Lost Opportunity of the Senior Year: Finding a Better Way.* 14 June 2003. <http://www.woodrow.org/CommissionOnTheSeniorYear>.

_____. *Raising Our Sights: No High School Senior Left Behind.* 29 June 2003. <http://www.woodrow.org/CommissionOnTheSeniorYear.org/Report/report.html>

Palattella, John. "Ivory Towers in the Marketplace." *Dissent* (Summer 2001): 70-3.

Roberts, Peter. "Rereading Lyotard: Knowledge, Commodification and Higher Education." *Electronic Journal of Sociology* 3.3 (1998). 29 June 2003. <http://www.sociology.org/content/vol003.003/roberts.html>.

Ruffin, Roy J. and Paul R. Gregory. *Principles of Economics.* 6th ed. Reading, MA: Addison-Wesley, 1997.

Shoenberg, Robert. "Why Do I Have to Take This Course? Credit Hours, Transfer, and Curricular Coherence." *General Education in an Age of Student Mobility: An Invitation to Discuss Systemic Curricular Planning.* Washington, DC: AAC&U, 2000.

Sosteric, Mike, Mike Gismondi, and Gina Ratkovic. "The University, Accountability, and Market Discipline in the late 1990s." *Electronic Journal of Sociology* 3.3 (1998). 29 June 2003. <http://www.sociology.org/content/vol003.003/sosteric.html>.

Stewart, Kristen. "Learn While You Earn: Nation's Largest Private University is Flourishing in Utah." *Salt Lake Tribune* (27 August 2001): B1-B2.

Trow, Martin. "The Development of Information Technology in American Higher Education." *Daedalus* (1997): 293-314.

Twitchell, James B. *Lead Us Into Temptation: The Triumph of American Materialism.* New York: Columbia University Press, 1999.

U.S. Census Bureau. *Statistical Abstract of the United States: 2000.* 29 June 2003. <http://www.census.gov/prod/2001pubs/statab/sec14.pdf>

Wilmott, Hugh. "Managing the Academics: Commodification and Control in the Development of University Education in the U.K." *Human Relations* 48 (September 1995): 993-1027.

Winston, Gordon C. "Why Can't a College Be More Like a Firm?" *New Thinking on Higher Education: Creating a Context for Change.* Ed. Joel Myerson. Vol. I in *Forum for the Future of Higher Education.* Bolton, MA: Anker Publishing, 1998.

"WPA Outcomes Statement for First-Year Composition." *Writing Program Administration* 23 (Fall/Winter 1999): 59-63.

Author/Subject Index

Printed in the United States
26957LVS00004B/202-219

9 781572 735750